Everyday Sexism

in the Third Millennium

Everyday Sexism

in the Third Millennium

edited by

Carol Rambo Ronai

Barbara A. Zsembik

Joe R. Feagin

ROUTLEDGE

New York   London

Published in 1997 by

Routledge
29 West 35th Street
New York, NY 10001

Published in Great Britain in 1997 by

Routledge
11 New Fetter Lane
London EC4P 4EE

Copyright © 1997 by Routledge

Printed in the United States of America
Design: Jack Donner

Library of Congress Cataloging-in-Publication Data

Ronai, Carol Rambo
    Everyday sexism in the third millennium / edited by
Carol Rambo Ronai, Barbara A. Zsembik, Joe R. Feagin.
        p.   cm.
    Includes bibliographical references and index.
    0–415–91550–3 (hb). — ISBN 0–415–91551–1 (pb).
1. Sexism—United States.   2. Sexual harassment of women—United States.
3. Heterosexism—United States.   4. Sex role—United States.
I. Zsembik, Barbara A. II. Feagin, Joe R. III. Title.
HQ1237.5.U5R65 1997
304.42'0973—dc 20   96–34631

Contents

Introduction

Living with Everyday Sexism
in the Third Millennium

CAROL RAMBO RONAI, BARBARA A. ZSEMBIK, AND JOE R. FEAGIN

I think the overall goal of the "feminist" movement has been to promote homosexual power—not women's equality.

You must be willing to work for the rights that other people have earned through hard work instead of whining for them . . . so just shut the hell up about it.

Modern feminism should not deny or overlook the fact that a substantial segment of our society is changing for the better; in other words, don't let a few narrow minded, ignorant few dampen the significant progress which has been achieved over the years.

—Student responses to an informal survey on feminism, conducted by
the Memphis Woman's Action Coalition,
a campus student organization.

The editors of this volume have had common experiences in the classroom and workplace that were the genesis of this collection. Each of us has been issued the following challenge by our students and colleagues: "Sexism is a thing of the past, so why spend so much time on it in the classroom?" Other remarks, such as "Things are better now than they used to be, women should quit whining and get over it," and "With everyone walking around on eggshells about sexism, it makes it seem like more of a problem than it really is," have revealed to us an atmosphere where students and colleagues seemed to be angry, uncomfortable, or fearful about discussing sexism.

Additionally, students and colleagues over the years have voiced doubts and fears about feminist theory, finding it alienating and irrelevant to their everyday lives. Women confessed to us that they agree with the basic tenets of feminism, but they do not want to be thought of as overbearing or unfeminine, or to be ascribed the dreaded status of "lesbian." Men have voiced fears about not knowing how to act towards women, losing power over their lives to women and seeming unmanly (that is, homosexual) for embracing a feminist perspective.

As we stand on the threshold of the twenty-first century, we believe that now, more than ever, it is time to take stock of current experiences with and perceptions of sexism. We are living at a particularly crucial historical moment for examining the problem of sexism. Many popular observers and authors have recently argued that sexism is exaggerated if not on the decline in the United States. The current climate in the classroom and workplace reflects this conservative rhetoric about the decline of sexism, yet the content of this volume strongly suggests otherwise.

From debates like this, we determined that there is much confusion about what sexism and feminist thinking are, and have decided that it would be useful to address the following questions in an edited collection: Is there still sexism in the late twentieth century? And if so, how does it manifest in our everyday lives?

The social and political climate as it is reflected in the classroom and in the contemporary mass media suggests that sexism has been in the nation's collective consciousness and in our collective discourse. In the last few years, the mass media have given increased emphasis, if not intelligent analysis, to sexism in everyday life. If we accept the news as a reflection of the issues we deal with in our everyday lives, then we must concede that sexism is a topic that concerns us all. One has only to read accounts of events like the 1995 O.J. Simpson trial in Los Angeles to hear discussions about domestic violence (Should the police and the judicial system have responded differently to Nicole Brown Simpson's 911 calls for help?) or about gender discrimination in the workplace (Should Marcia Clark, the prosecuting attorney, have lost her children to her ex-husband for spending too much time working on the Simpson case?). Similarly, the early 1990s congressional hearings on Clarence Thomas's nomination to the Supreme Court served, in light of the accusations of sexual harassment from his subordinate Anita Hill, to heighten the national debate about sexual harassment.

This edited collection features new and original research from the 1990s on the range of sexism still faced by girls and women in this society. In an examination of the chapters, the reader will encounter diverse and innovative research materials that overwhelmingly contradict the commonplace sentiment that the existence of sexism is exaggerated in U.S. society. These new empirical materials document gendered oppression as it is endured by women of various age, racial, ethnic, class, and sexual orientation groups. In this book we add greater depth to our knowledge of the daily lives and experiences of women in a wide range of interactive settings, including the home, the workplace, unions, educational institutions, and the Internet.

Gender and the Matrix of Domination

Most social scientists accept the view that gender is a critical component in understanding social experiences. Increasingly, many social scientists also recognize the importance of examining the effects of gender in their own research, offering a useful corrective to a predominantly male-dominated social science. Nonetheless, in much research there is still a tendency to think of gender only as a "variable" or as an individual trait (Stacey and Thorne 1985). From our perspective, gender should be viewed as an aspect of social organization, not a variable or trait. Sexism is a far more complicated process than men oppressing women at every turn. It is part of a larger system of social organization, which includes, among other things, the actions and consciousness of women themselves, who can in their turn reinforce or resist sexism. In addition, gender is only one of several overlapping social hierarchies that organize human relationships within a society like the United States.

Feminist scholars such as Patricia Hill Collins (1990), Marilyn Frye (1983), Audre Lorde (1984), and Dorothy Smith (1979) have observed that boys and girls, men and women, are situated within several different but related systems of domination and oppression. We have sought out researchers who can enlighten us on the interrelationships among these systems. In the articles in this collection, the reader will find domination and oppression located at the intersection of gender and racial groups in eight of the articles; of gender and class in two of the articles; of gender, ethnicity, and class in one; and of gender, class, and sexual orientation in one.

Within these intersections we discover that women are simultaneously oppressed and capable of oppressing others by perpetuating the practices and discourses of sexism, racism, classism, and/or homophobia. For example, Christine Michele Robinson's chapter on African-American and interracial lesbian relationships illustrates this. To heterosexual African-Americans, black lesbians are often considered race traitors. By refusing to be in a heterosexual relationship, some black Americans argue, black lesbians fail to support black men, and thereby engage in a type of group genocide by failing to produce traditional male-female families. While African-Americans, both homosexual and heterosexual, have experienced racial discrimination, heterosexual black Americans use heterosexist practices and discourses (for example, sexist assumptions about the "proper" role of women in society) to isolate and harm black lesbians.

All the articles examine the sexist discourses—the ways in which men and women think about, talk about, and "do" gender in our everyday lives. Sexist discourses become institutionalized as public knowledge and are disseminated throughout society so effectively that they assume a "given" quality. The sexist discourses lying behind antifemale discrimination encompass many "sincere fictions" about both women and men. Sincere fictions are personal mythologies that reproduce societal mythologies at the individual level (see Feagin and Vera 1995). These myths and misconceptions are linked to how people in particular settings articulate their perceptions of gender and "do" discrimination.

As we will see in the chapters that follow, our authors have various ways of conceptualizing these fictions: controlling images, discursive constraint, stereotypes, and family idealizations. These sincere fictions trigger and rationalize behavior ranging from sexual harassment and workplace exclusion to domestic violence. Everyday discrimination triggers sexist discourse in the form of sincere fictions, which in turn feeds more gendered discrimination.

Gendered Spaces: Towards a Dialectical Theory of Domination

Initially, the editors of this volume planned to feature the idea that gender existed within a complex web of hierarchies that intersected to create a matrix of domination. After reviewing the research submitted for inclusion in this volume, we came to the conclusion that this approach was inadequate. For women and men, the matrix of social ties and relations extends out in all directions in space, both in physical spaces and in socially constructed spaces. Women's everyday lives have many facets; the matrix approach allows us to examine the surface of only a few facets at one time. The chapters in this collection, taken as a whole, reveal multiple levels of sexism that are linked together and layered in a reflexive, interactive manner. This reality suggests the need to move away from a static matrix model and expand the conception of gendered oppression to include a major dialectical dimension.

This book's chapters and its overall organization underscore our view of sexism as dialectical processes and interactive complexities. We fuse the concepts "gendered space" and "dialectical relationships" together to expand the matrix of domination into a "dialectic of domination." By this latter term we mean that sexual domination is not a static "thing" found at one point in time or at one place, but rather it has a history and is webbed across many places in time and space. Gendered domination of a particular sort, or at a specific place, inevitably has external connections with other types of gendered domination, as well as with other types of domination. In our view, gendered oppression at one place is part of a process that contains both the history of gendered domination and possible futures, including futures of resistance.

A dialectical approach emphasizes that the "parts" of sexism, eloquently described in our chapters, are but segments of a larger whole that includes the present, past, and future of gendered domination not only for the "subjects" being researched but also, as several of the articles make very clear, for the researchers and the research process. "The perspectival element—recognizing that things appear very different depending on who is looking at them—plays a very important role in dialectical thought" (Ollman 1993).

Dialectics of Gendered Spaces

Persuaded by this dialectical approach, we have arranged our chapters into sections organized around three sensitizing concepts: identities as gendered spaces, bodies as gendered spaces, and economic/political arenas as gendered spaces. We do not argue that these are the only types of gendered spaces possible, but rather that these are the three interrelated dimensions that recur in the chapters of this collection.

The women presented in these chapters have often lost control of the definition of personal and social situations, because these spaces are highly gendered. "Gendered spaces" are social arenas in which a person's gender shapes the roles, statuses, and interpersonal dynamics and generates differential political and economic outcomes and interaction expectations and practices (Elshtain 1981; Oakley 1979; Siltanen and Stanworth 1982; Zsembik 1995). "Social relations are physically structured in material space, and human beings often view space expressively and symbolically. In most societies those with the greater power and resources ordinarily control the use and meaning of important spaces in a society" (Feagin, Vera, and Imani 1996, p. 49). Gendered spaces are those where the sexist biases of the most powerful generally define their character as social arenas, with the consequent feelings of control or lack of control over them. Spaces are gendered substantially because sets of sincere fictions delimit the boundaries of these spaces and the practices that occur there.

Gendered spaces mean that sexism is pervasive in women's histories and experiences, although sexism manifests itself differently across the several, often overlapping spaces discussed in this volume. As we noted above, gendered space entails more than a physical place, for it usually involves recurring social interactions and complex, constructed meanings. For instance, sexual harassment on the Internet, as discussed by Kimberly J. Cook and Phoebe M. Stambaugh (Chapter 5), is a clear example of a place where interactions occur that do not occupy a physical space as such. In that space the sexist discourses engaged in by some male participants posting on-line messages to the sexual harassment discussion group were shaped by a number of sincere fictions about how men and women are supposed to "do gender" in U.S. culture.

Some groups or individuals deliberately engage in sexist discourse for the purpose of controlling girls and women. Many times, the face of this oppressor is a boy or a man, but sometimes it is a woman. Often sexist discourse and practice takes place in public settings, such as in the workplace or on the Internet, while at other times it is perpetrated in the most private areas of our lives, in our homes, and even our bedrooms. In most cases presented in this volume, the inequalities perpetuated by gendered spaces are sexualized. Sometimes, too, the boundaries of gendered spaces are crosscut or reinforced by the languages of class, racial grouping, ethnicity, and sexual orientation.

Dialectics of Resistance

Whether the gendered space in question is identity, the body, or political/economic arenas, it becomes for women a space where they find themselves emotionally, physically, or financially impacted in negative ways. Each gendered space or dimension is dialectically related to another, which is to say that one affects how the others will manifest themselves. A woman's identity affects her physical well-being and her political and economic status. Moreover, physical or sexual abuse of a woman's body impacts both her identity and her ability to function in the political and economic arenas. Likewise, blocking women from fair access to the political or economic processes because of gender discrimination makes her vulnerable to psychological or bodily harm.

This is not to say that the women discussed here do not find ways to resist discrimination and contest control over the definition of social situations. Sometimes they resist actively through strategies such as verbal protestation, physical resistance, or court action. At other times they withdraw, resisting passively so they can be around to fight another day.

Each chapter of this book can be viewed as an overt act of resistance on behalf of women. Certainly, the subjects of the chapters do resist. Many women resist gendered oppression by refusing to accept the negative identities offered them. Through autoethnography, Andreana Clay, tammy ko Robinson, and Carol Rambo Ronai engage in resistance by publicly telling about experiences that mainstream America does not want to face or discuss. The activists whom Barbara Ellen Smith interviewed went so far as to request that their identities not be disguised. They interpret their participation in the project as a political act, deliberately designed to promote discussion about potentially divisive issues.

Yanick St. Jean and Joe R. Feagin report that African-American women often fight back and challenge discrimination. These African-Americans want to consolidate black efforts, seeking to work together for racial equality rather than allowing gender to be a discourse that fragments camps of black women and black men. The lesbians in

Christine Michele Robinson's chapter find support for their relationships, avoid hostile environments, and take self-defense courses, all forms of resistance. In their chapters Barbara Zsembik and Barbara Ellen Smith show us how women, through political activity, resist the gendered spaces of both the economy and ethnoracial and class identities. Barbara Ellen Smith's subjects found it necessary either to separate from their community of origin or turn to their community for affirmation, depending on their racial group.

For Kimberly J. Cook and Phoebe M. Stambaugh, women's resistance had serious consequences on the Internet. At the individual level, if someone posted an objection to being sexually harassed, she risked being flamed. Ultimately debate was banned in the discussion group to stop sexual harassment, an ironic result given that the discussion group's original purpose was to be a forum to fight sexual harassment.

Often, exiting the situation is the best form of resistance. At other times ignoring abuse or, as with Melissa J. Monson's video store clerks, interpreting and categorizing oppressive behaviors as another form of everyday rudeness serves as a more passive resistance strategy. Solidarity with similarly situated individuals is discussed in many of the research articles. Resistance at the level of identity, of the body, or of politics or the economy often has a cascade effect on society because of the interrelated, dialectical nature of gendered spaces.

Methods: Modes of Feminist Interpretation

In addition to their substantive and theoretical contributions, the chapters of this book present an introduction to several of the research methodologies used by researchers to examine gendered oppression in U.S. society. The chapters in this book reveal diverse methodological and theoretical orientations that reflect the state of active feminist theory and research as we approach the third millennium. Still, they have common threads that unite them into one, more or less cohesive whole. All address gender in particular places and times, and suggest that gendered oppression is dialectical and recombinant in nature, rather than categorical and static as in a matrix model.

Four chapters draw on secondary data sources, making use of previously published materials and secondary survey analysis. In-depth interviews are employed in four of the chapters in order to examine patterns of discrimination and the underlying ideologies and discourses that reproduce sexism in various social situations. Two other chapters make use of participant observation to view firsthand the effects of sexual harassment in the workplace and on the Internet. In addition, three chapters are autoethnographies or layered accounts (Ronai 1992; 1995; 1996), a provocative new methodology that makes the author one of the subjects of analysis. Each methodology marks a position on a continuum of storytelling formats or modes of feminist interpretation. They delineate a spectrum that moves from a very public macrolevel of analysis to a very private microlevel of exploration.

These modes of feminist interpretation reflect not only various methodological stances but also the fractured quality of feminist theory as we approach the end of the twentieth century (Stacey and Thorne 1985). As we move towards the next millennium, we observe a core of feminist thinkers eschewing global theories of sexism in favor of a feminist point of view that incorporates multiple perspectives. Some of these perspectives use the language of gender roles, biological differences, social psychology, psychoanalytic theory, Marxism, and socialism to explain sexism (see Lengermann and Niebrugge 1996).

Like other analysts, we consider this diversity of perspectives a strength rather than a weakness in analyzing the conditions and experiences of men and women in contemporary societies. In the past, many have criticized the mainstream feminist perspective for being dominated by white women who falsely universalized the category "white middle-class woman" and ignored or distorted the experiences of other subordinated groups such as "Blacks, Chicana/os, Native Americans, Asian Americans, homosexuals, working class people, the peoples of the third world—half of whom are women" (Stacey and Thorne 1985, p. 315). By allowing for differences in methodological and theoretical orientation, we enable more voices to be heard regarding how sexism manifests itself in the nooks and crannies of modern societies. The overall goal of incorporating multiple perspectives is not to attempt to find "one truth" about sexism, but to find the many truths of lived experiences and to generate public discussions about sexism that are inclusive rather than exclusive of various perspectives and viewpoints.

Gendered Oppression in the Late Twentieth Century

The gendered spaces of identity, the body, and the economy and polity involve a dialectic of domination. Clearly, sex discrimination is rooted in everyday social life. It is not merely a matter of an idiosyncratic incident for a woman who happens to be unlucky or in the path of the isolated bigot. Gendered spaces are part of every woman's and man's daily life.

Though most of the chapters in this volume address more than one gendered space at a time, each of the three sections features chapters highlighting one particular gendered space over the other two. In the section introductions we make dialectical linkages between identity as gendered space, the body as gendered space, and political/economic arenas as gendered space. Each introduction makes explicit how the dialectics of domination are articulated in the chapters to follow.

In our view this book is directly relevant to the lives of undergraduate and graduate students, scholars, and other citizens interested in matters of gender images, ideologies, roles, and practices. This book is appropriate for a wide variety of college courses in such fields as sociology, economics, anthropology, political science, education, women's studies, and racial-ethnic studies. Because of the issues raised about the economy and about politics, it is also appropriate for an array of courses in schools of public administration and public policy and in business schools.

With its broad range of methodological approaches, its multiple perspectives, and its focus on how discourse reflects and codifies everyday experiences with sexism in gendered spaces, this book suggests many reasons why sexism is still pervasive in everyday life. If we can come to a clear understanding of how sexism manifests itself and why it is perpetuated in contemporary society, we may have a chance to find solutions to the destructive system that is sexism as we move into the twenty-first century. If we start to change the way men and women talk about and do gender, we will reduce the oppressiveness of sexism in the everyday lives of women and men.

References

Collins, Patricia Hill. 1990. *Black Feminist Thought: Knowledge, Consciousness and Empowerment*. Boston: Unwin Hyman.

Elshtain, J.B. 1981. *Public Man, Private Women: Women in Social and Political Thought.* Princeton, NJ: Princeton University Press.

Feagin, Joe R. and Hernan Vera. 1995. *White Racism: The Basics.* New York: Routledge.

Feagin, Joe R., Hernan Vera, and Nikitah Imani. 1996. *The Agony of Education: Black Students at White Colleges and Universities.* New York: Routledge.

Frye, Marilyn. 1983. *The Politics of Reality: Essays in Feminist Theory.* Trumansburg, NY: Crossings Press.

Lengermann, Patricia Madoo and Jill Niebrugge. 1996. "Contemporary Feminist Theory," in *Sociological Theory*, ed. George Ritzer. New York: McGraw-Hill.

Lorde, Audre. 1984. *Sister Outsider: Essays and Speeches.* Trumansburg, NY: Crossings Press.

Oakley, A. 1979. Review essay: "Feminism and Sociology—Some Recent Perspectives." *American Journal of Sociology* 84: 1259–1265.

Ollman, Bertell. 1993. *Dialectical Investigations.* New York: Routledge.

Ronai, Carol Rambo. 1992. "A Night in the Life of an Erotic Dancer/Researcher: A Layered Account," in *Investigating Subjectivity: Research on Lived Experience*, eds. Carolyn Ellis and Michael Flaherty. Newbury Park, CA: Sage.

Ronai, Carol Rambo. 1995. "Multiple Reflections of Child Sex Abuse: An Argument for a Layered Account." *Journal of Contemporary Ethnography* 23: 395–426.

Ronai, Carol Rambo. 1996. "My Mother is Mentally Retarded," in *Composing Ethnography*, eds. Carolyn Ellis and Art Bochner. Newbury Park, CA: Altimira Press.

Siltanen, J. and M. Stanworth. 1982. *Women and the Public Sphere: Critique of Sociology and Politics.* New York: St. Martin's Press.

Smith, Dorothy. 1979. "A Sociology for Women," in *The Prism of Sex: Essays in the Sociology of Knowledge*, eds. J.A. Sherman and E.T. Beck. Madison: University of Wisconsin Press.

Stacey, Judith and Barrie Thorne. 1985. "The Missing Feminist Revolution in Sociology." *Social Problems* 32: 301–316.

Zsembik, B.A. 1995. "Racial and Ethnic Conflict: Perspectives from Women." *Annual Review of Conflict Knowledge and Conflict Resolution* 4.

PART I

Identity

as a Gendered Space

Dialectical Linkages

The chapters in Part I generally emphasize identity as a gendered space. Through sexist discourse, identity becomes appropriated by others seeking to control the targeted person or persons. The dialectical character of identity as a gendered space serves to gender the spaces of the body and the economic/political arena. We offer the following chapter descriptions to sensitize the reader to some of the dialectical aspects of identity as a gendered space. The linkages discussed here are a few among many possibilities.

In Chapter 2, "Growing Up In/Between the Lines," Andreana Clay shares with us a processual and emotional account of her experiences of being raised biracial. Through autoethnography and the use of a dialectical format called a "layered account," Clay treats her experience as a primary data source, weaving in black feminist theory and other texts as interpretive resources that invite readers to relate their experiences with her experience. The gendered space of identity dialec-

tically transformed her body into a gendered space through the medium of race. Her hair, her skin tone, her freckles, her shape—all were problematic for her identity because she did not fit into the existing categories or sincere fictions about white and black womanhood. She is neither black nor white, but both, and thus she is never an "appropriate" woman.

In Chapter 3, "Everyday [Hetero]sexism: Strategies of Resistance and Lesbian Couples," black and interracial lesbian couples face gendered oppression that is racist, classist, and heterosexist in nature. Through in-depth interviews, Christine Michele Robinson explores how mainstream society, through the use of controlling images, attempts to dictate the lives and identities of her subjects. While other commentators have suggested that coping strategies such as passing and staying quiet are counterproductive, Robinson suggests that silence, at times, is a legitimate act of resistance. Identity as a gendered space converges dialectically on both lesbian bodies and their economic situations. Through the medium of identity, the body becomes a gendered space where heterosexuals attempt to control the sexual behavior of lesbians. Additionally, if it is known that a woman is a lesbian, she frequently becomes the target of threats, physical and sexual harassment, even rape. Similarly, the economic arena becomes a gendered space when a lesbian's identity could threaten her job.

In Chapter 4, "Sexual Harassment from the Perspective of Asian-American Women," Edith Wen-Chu Chen determined, through the use of questionnaires, that Asian-American women are targets of a distinctive type of sexual harassment and violence that is different from that experienced by other women. Stereotypes such as "geisha," "prostitute," and "docile" are identities that are gendered and racial in character. As in the Clay chapter, we again see identity become a gendered space through the discourse of race. Likewise, as in the Robinson chapter, bodies become gendered spaces, threatened and appropriated, in this case, by and for the exclusive use of men. Chen suggests that future studies dealing with gender inequality must actively deal with crosscutting racial and ethnic inequalities.

In Chapter 5, "Tuna Memos and Pissing Contests: Doing Gender and Male Dominance on the Internet," Kimberly J. Cook and Phoebe M. Stambaugh examine, through a participant observation study, how some men and women "do" gender, and thus their identity, on the Internet. Cook and Stambaugh's electronic bulletin board was a space designed to be a safe forum for discussions by women and sympathetic men concerning sexual harassment. It became an oppressive space where the female and male participants were sexually harassed on-line. Virtual assaults on various participants' gender identities transformed the space into a bulletin board where debate was forbidden. As a result of this form of gendered identity discrimination, the economic/political arena emerged dialectically with the body as gendered space. Women concerned about sexual harassment issues were prevented from having interactions that could have assisted them on the job. Besides being a potential hindrance to upward economic mobility, lack of access to information could be physically harmful to women (such as the Wendy Breen case described in Chapter 14), thus dialectically ensnaring their bodies.

In each of these chapters, identity becomes a tool with which to create the gendered space of the body, the economic/political arena, or both. Subjects inevitably appealed to history as a way of explaining and/or resisting gendered spaces when they manifested. By focusing on the identity as a gendered space in this section, we explore how the discourses of gender, race, class, and sexuality overlap through time and define women's bodies and their political/economic opportunities.

2

Growing Up In/Between the Lines

ANDREANA CLAY

"I know now that I once longed to be white.
How? you ask.
Let me tell you the ways."

—Wong 1981: 7

"You have a lovely daughter," the tall, well-dressed woman said to my mother as she ran her fingers through my hair. Although I hated it when strangers touched me, I loved their compliments.

"Thank you," my mother said, not paying much attention. Today was our bimonthly visit to the mall. Mom and her friend Carla had decided that every other Saturday they would load up their daughters for a day of window shopping. Right now we were in our usual meeting place. Carla and Tiffany were late, and my mother was annoyed. The woman continued to compliment me. I didn't mind; Mom always told me what a pretty girl I was.

"How old is she?" the woman inquired.

"Six," my mother answered, looking over her shoulder.

"How did she get such a beautiful tan at six?" the woman asked, waiting, as if my mother was going to provide a long list of tanning tips.

My mother turned, looked her straight in the eye, smirked, and said, "She doesn't have a tan!"

The woman's face abruptly changed from admiration to horror as she stepped back, put both hands on her face, and said, "Wait a minute, is she . . . Is she . . . *Black*?"[1]

I am one of many children conceived out of the interracial marriage boom of the late 1960s/early 1970s (Gibbs 1989; Jones 1995; Root 1992). My mother is white, my father is black. They fell in love during high school on the heels of desegregation and married shortly thereafter.

Having failed to prevent the marriage, friends, relatives, and sometimes complete strangers pleaded with my parents to abstain from procreating. In spite of these warnings (and outright objections), three years later I was born. Contrary to popular belief, I was neither spotted nor striped, but, due to the jaundice I was born with, for one day I was blue-eyed and white. Over the next few weeks, the jaundice went away and my "milk and coffee" tone started to glow.

The social constructions of both race and gender pose problems for many individuals in this society. Various writers (Creef 1990; Jones 1995; Root 1992; Zook 1990) have written about these problems as they relate to biracial identity. Anzaldúa (1987) and Moraga (1981) have also addressed the intersection of race and gender as it relates to both biracial and lesbian identity. In this paper, I follow their lead and attempt to illustrate how the intersection of race and gender affected me as a biracial woman. I write about the complexities of these phenomena by communicating the personal as political (Lorde 1981). By this I mean that I acknowledge that my personal experience as a biracial woman influences my research.

I use my experiences to illustrate the various problems faced by biracial women with the social constructions of both race and gender (Krieger 1991). As illustrated in the opening vignette, race and gender issues are typically thought of as two separate issues. However, the white woman's astonishment over my race, in essence, meant that I could no longer be beautiful.

I use the writing format of a layered account so that I serve as both subject and object, researcher and researchee. A layered account is a postmodern ethnographic reporting format, which enables the researcher to draw on as many resources as necessary to convey the experience to the reader; these include journals, dreams, theories, and so on (Ronai 1992). By using this format, I am writing "from relational and emotional experience" and allowing the reader to immerse herself within the different layers (Ellis 1995, p. 314). I politicize my experience by situating my personal narrative within this particular format.

As I walked home, I felt the warm glow of sunlight surrounding me like a spotlight following the lead performer on stage, shining bright yellow and white streaks down from the sky right onto my white ruffled dress. Grandma had allowed me to wear the matching white socks she bought me at Woolworth's the other day, *and* I got to wear my favorite black tap shoes.

I was the star at school that day. Everyone threw compliments my way, in praise of my showstopping beauty. Mrs. Crump, my first grade teacher, said I looked like one of God's angels, and Mr. White said that I was his little princess. I knew that it was only a matter of time before everyone came around and realized that I was beautiful even though I was black.

I strained my ears as I walked, almost certain to hear the applause, whistles, and bravos from the audience. Perhaps that is why I wasn't prepared when Jeff Schneider and his brothers, Terry and Troy, called out to me from behind the green hedges in Mrs. Porter's front yard. I assumed they were simply showing their gratitude for having me grace the same street they walked on.

The eggs soared past me, but I could still feel shame clinging to my skin, as if replacing the yolk that was supposed to be there. I was stunned, but I kept the same pace and thrust my chin forward. Mr. Simon's German Shepherds ran up to the fence, barking wildly. I wasn't sure if they were joining in on my torture or coming to my rescue. All I could hear was "dirty nigger, ugly nigger" and the hiss of eggs crashing on the sidewalk around me.

How could this be happening, I thought, as fear began to envelope me. I was a beauty queen, a princess, an angel. Why me? I did everything right that day, and every other day. I never picked on anyone, I always smiled and said please and thank you. And why did they have to call me nigger, calling attention to my blackness? Why that day?

My shoulders sank, and my chin slowly but naturally made its way back to my chest as I turned the corner onto Kansas Street and made my way home. The years of shame of being born black forced my head downward. I thought that the many compliments I had received at school meant that I could walk with a new posture: chin up, head held high. The brothers Schneider reminded me that I was wrong.

My grandmother's blue and white polyester suit signaled my safety as she waved to me from the front porch. With a quick turn of my head, I made sure that the egg throwers were nowhere in sight, I couldn't let her see them. I didn't want her to know. She was one of the few who reminded me of my beauty and worth, I couldn't let her see that others didn't agree with her and that their beliefs were influencing mine.

Feeling safer and safer with every step, I focused on her big, black, horn-rimmed glasses and wavy gray hair. Simultaneously I waved and checked myself over for traces of yellow slime. Amazed to find nothing (laughing at their bad aim), I began to run, as if to escape the nausea that engulfed me.

I ran as fast I could up to the porch and plunged into her white, pillowy arms, pushing my face into her stomach as I held back my tears. I held onto her as she greeted me with kisses and cheek tugs. I was home. Then I left her to climb the big oak in our front yard as she watched. Among the leaves and branches, I hid from Grandma's smile and approval and replayed the events that had just taken place, until the words of the brothers Schneider finally rang true.

I internalized the words and actions of those boys for most of my childhood and adolescence. During these years I truly believed that I was a dirty, ugly nigger. I never shared this incident with anyone in my family and, until recently, I told very few others. I didn't want anyone to know how much I hated myself. I felt I could not grieve or complain about my feelings because they were a reflection of societal racism, and I could do little to change that.

I felt like my father's blackness was like some disease he had infested me with. It was similar to herpes or AIDS, something for which there was no cure. Sure, there were times when I could control it (as a light-skinned African-American, assimilation was somewhat easier), but I felt for sure that being black was something that I would always be plagued by and eventually die of.

Like a terminal disease, my blackness determined everything that I could do or be. The fact that I was a girl made it even worse. Not only was my intelligence being judged (black people in this society often have to prove our intelligence), but so was my potential beauty. My beauty, the only thing I could depend upon for self-worth as a female, was being questioned.

Internalized oppression has plagued African-American women (as well as other women of color) throughout history. Women of color have been represented as inferior in this society through a number of different mediums, including the media, the entertainment industry, and advertising (hooks 1994). Regardless of where we turn, we are continually bombarded with images that tell us that we are ugly, dirty, stupid, and absent of worth. Whenever we try to contradict or resist these images, we are stopped with full force.

"Ha!Ha!Ha!" the little girl laughed to herself, watching the other children step over themselves, trying to figure out who she was. She had fooled them all. She knew that if she had brought any other baby picture of herself (this one was taken the day of her birth, when her skin was pale and her eyes were blue) in for Mrs. Roper's annual "Guess Who This Baby Is Picture Challenge," she would have been identified first, being the only black girl in the class. She took pleasure in witnessing the confusion that she had created, eyes peering into the picture trying to distinguish her features from the others. Unfortunately her pleasure was cut short. A frustrated Robbie Gryder ended the suspense by lifting up her picture (which was strictly against the rules!) and finding her name on the back.

"Oh, that's Andreana!" he exclaimed, with a sigh of relief. He threw his hands in the air, shook his head, and said "Well no wonder we couldn't figure out where she was, she looks white in this picture!"

"What a fool!" she thought. Not Robbie, but herself. She struggled to hold back her tears. How could she be so stupid? To think that these people could understand her? How could they possibly understand the dreams she had to eventually become white again?

Previous research (Gibbs 1989) has shown that biracial children are particularly vulnerable to social rejection by their peers. Children of mixed heritage, particularly Afro-European ancestry, must struggle with identifying with a dominant culture that frequently rejects them and a "minority" culture that has been continually degraded throughout American history (Gibbs 1989). Other research (Russell, Wilson, and Hall 1992) also concludes that many children of color believe that they will one day become white. This is a common phenomenon, similar to boys thinking that they will one day grow up to be mommies.

I grew up in an environment that was supposedly "color-blind" (see Frankenberg 1993; Omi and Winant 1994). The white people in my family, at school, and in my neighborhood did their best to actively participate in color evasion, or not "seeing" race. (Frankenberg 1993). When I was growing up, my color "didn't matter." My race was unimportant, I was "just like everybody else."

In reality, my race was all that mattered and was the focus of everything. Being black meant that I was different from everyone else, because everyone else was white. I perceived this difference (with the help of the dominant culture's standards) to mean that I was unattractive, unintelligent, and, overall, unlikeable. I have few memories of thinking otherwise.

"Hey, aren't you the racially mixed girl I interviewed the other day?" the reporter said, waving an imaginary microphone in the air. *Oh my God!* I thought. Why is she doing this to me now? Please not here, not at Nancy's party (Nancy's dad was the weather man for a local TV station and was having another party downstairs). Please, not in front of these people. But it was already happening. I could feel, one by one, half a dozen heads turning, their eyes on me piercing my skin as they tried to figure out what she meant.

I had to shut her up, but how? If I said yes, I knew she would ask me what it was like, just like she did the other day when she was interviewing the *five* African-American students at my school about Martin Luther King's birthday. There, as she praised my beautiful skin tone and "cute little freckles," I flashed back to the probing mallgoer.

I knew that the four other black students hated me then more than ever. I could feel their discontent as they sucked their teeth and rolled their eyes in my direction. It was bad enough that I was "mixed," but to have someone (especially a "famous" white reporter) fawn over me was too much. The legacy of light-skinned blacks being more accepted by the white community still lingered in the late 1980s. By ignoring them, this reporter helped push me farther and farther into the margins.

Days later, on that particular night, I was simply trying to have fun with my friends at a party. It was my first time out with them. I had admired their beatnik clothing and hippie attitudes. I knew that they were free from preconceived notions, which included knowledge of my past or who I was. I could escape my hand-me-down house close to the highway with my mixed-blood family, and sink into the safety of their tree-lined and cobblestoned streets near the university.

I was a new person there, I felt comfortable. But then, I was in the midst of a crisis. A number of replies flashed through my mind as I tried to balance myself and stop the room from spinning. Finally, I opened my mouth, unsure of what to say, and mustered up an "Um—"

"Wow," she interrupted with a look of mysterious (albeit intoxicated) intrigue on her face. "It must be really hard being mixed, tell me what it's like again," she slurred.

She was drunk. Drunk and stupid and completely unaware of the crime she had just committed. I already felt ashamed of my mixed heritage, but then I just felt gross, as if everyone could see the swirls of vanilla and chocolate that made up my being. Now I had to call attention to myself amongst all these white people and explain my heritage. I hated this. I wished I could file a report to make her pay for what she'd done. I had been totally violated and, though there were many witnesses, no one saw a thing.

To this day, it is hard for me to sit in a room full of people (white or black) without feeling like I am going to be exposed. Similar to the experience of gays, lesbians, and bisexuals, I find myself "outing" my racial identity when I get to know people (Weston 1991). I feel I must tell people of my mixed heritage, or who I "really am," so I know whether or not they can accept me.

Although the theory of color evasion contributes to my understanding of racial experience, it fails to address adequately the effect of gender. By being told that my race was not an issue, that it didn't make me different, I was also led to believe that I had the same ability as white women to be beautiful.

Throughout history, societal standards of beauty have defined women. Women are told what we should look like by the media, the fashion industry, and the billion-dollar-a-year cosmetics industry (Faludi 1991; Wolf 1991). We are bombarded daily with messages of what an attractive woman is supposed to look like. These messages tell us that a beautiful woman is tall, thin, with long hair, and, in all but few cases, white. Obviously, the majority of women cannot fit into these guidelines, hence the increase in eating disorders and the overconsumption of hair relaxers, skin bleach, and plastic surgery (Faludi 1991; Russell, Wilson, and Hall 1992; Wolf 1991).

I soon realized that I was one of many who do not fit into the beauty myth. In spite of this realization, I became one of the "countless Black girls in the United States [who] share[d] the fantasy of being White" (Russell, Wilson, and Hall 1992, p. 41).

"Andreana, what are you doing with that towel on your head?" It was dinner time and, as usual, my mom was making trouble for me. I didn't have a towel on my head and she knew it. How could she mistake my long, shiny blond hair for a towel? I called her on it.

"This is not a towel, mother, it's my beautiful blond hair," I said as I flipped it behind my shoulders. She should be jumping for joy! I know she's always wanted a pretty little girl with long, manageable hair, not some nappy-headed black girl who had to sit between her legs everyday with a big ol' pink comb and a bucket full of hair grease.

"Oh, I thought that's what it was," my grandma chimed in, running her fingers through my hair. "It looks very pretty, maybe we can put it in a ponytail later on." I could do nothing but smile. I'm sure it would look really good in a ponytail, but it was really thick and we couldn't always fit it into the rubber band.

I had won. Grandma was on my side, and that made it two against one. I stroked my blond locks, reflecting on my victory.

I would like to say that the hair issue was just a childhood phase. Unfortunately, this is not the case. Like many other African-American women, I found that hair was an issue that would come up many times throughout my life, especially during my teenage years. It was then that I realized that hair was a sign of beauty for women.

Mia is so much prettier than I am. I spent the night with her once and when we were going to bed she put her long, beautiful, brown hair in these big, pink rollers. As soon as I saw it, I quickly tried to crack jokes in order to dislodge the boulder in my throat. My hair was full of activator and moisturizer, as is common with jheri curls. Mia's hair was straight, just like white girls'. As if that wasn't bad enough, she was thin, with long legs and pale skin. You wouldn't even know that she was a half-breed unless you saw her with her dad, who was black. I hated her. It was hard for me to look at her without feeling jilted by God for giving her those gifts.

I sat smoldering as she finally went over to turn out the lights. As I lay there in the darkness, one last hope flashed through my mind. I jumped out of bed, groped my way to the bathroom, and squeezed some of the juice out of my head so I could be just like her. As I washed my hands like a surgeon, anxious to remove any sign of "hair aid" products, I looked in the mirror and was pleased with what I saw. I was a real mixed girl with real mixed hair (wavy and manageable), free from morning pillow stains and greasy forehead. I was almost white.

Although this incident with Mia happened over ten years ago, I still get a twinge of jealousy when I think about it. I am embarrassed to admit that I sometimes fume over my not being blessed with my mother's straight hair instead of her freckles.

Some days I find myself wishing for the waiflike figure of the Winona Ryders and Kate Mosses. I yearn for the well-defined cheekbones, silicone pouty lips, and long, straight hair of the Cindy Crawfords and Nikki Taylors. Regardless of my years of feminist consciousness, at times I am unable to walk by my reflection without criticizing my shape and searching for the white girl that I once dreamed about being.

Shawn and I sat together in Speech class everyday. We would usually make fun of the other people in class as they took their turns portraying different characters from Neil Simon's *Barefoot in the Park*. Today was no different from any other. We were giggling to each other as David Kruger took a stab at one of the male character's monologues. I was trying to catch my breath—watching David try to communicate what he thought a newly married New York lawyer would say was almost more than I could handle.

I began to settle myself back into a sitting position when I was struck with the seriousness of Shawn's face. His straight-faced stare was usually a sign that Mrs. Dickinson was giving us the evil eye. But today his look was tender and soft. I focused on his face, trying to position my smile back into a straight line, when he said, "You sure are pretty for a black girl."

I almost burst out laughing again, but instead I just sat there, burning hot. I was so embarrassed. Shawn Nelson, one of the most popular boys in junior high, just told me I was pretty. (What did he mean, "for a black girl"?) I focused my eyes on the wood table as I struggled for something grateful to say.

"Uh, th-th-thank you!" I stammered, as I locked my arms tight around my stomach so that the knots wouldn't twist their way out. It was hard to believe that this monumental event was happening within the sterile, white walls of my junior high, and that no one else noticed.

I figured I should tell him how cute he was (but I didn't want to lie); maybe I could get a date to the eighth grade dance out of this. I knew I was ruining the moment by not saying anything, but I couldn't help it. It was my duty to smile, say thank you, and say something nice, but I couldn't speak. I couldn't think.

Fortunately, he took the initiative and said something that was out of this world, "Actually, you look kind of like Sheila E., that drummer for Prince. I didn't even know that she was black!" he said.

Sheila E.! Sheila E.! He thinks I look like her?!? I couldn't help but giggle. *Sheila E.!*, with her long, blond-streaked mane of brown hair, soft, Anglo features, and centerfold body. I had watched her video for "The Glamorous Life" so many times that I had all of her moves down pat. This was too much!

For a white boy to think that I was pretty was simply unheard of (except one time in the second grade), but to say that I looked like someone who didn't even look black was out of this world! How could I even think about snapping my fingers, swinging my neck around, and putting him in his place for not recognizing my beauty regardless of race? I looked "nonblack." My day was made. I was beautiful.

This boy's statements were such a boost to my ego. It was around this time that I was going through puberty. I was becoming a "woman." But what kind of woman was I? There were only a few socially defined images of biracial women, one being the tragic mulatto. This character is often portrayed in movies and literature as a "vessel of desire and pity, martyr, or [the] redeemed heroine" (Jones 1995, p. 50). She is desired because of her beauty, pitied because of her mixed blood, martyred for the same reason, and she is a redeemed heroine because she brings the races together (for instance, Alex Haley's *Queen*).

Not wanting blatantly to assume any of these roles, instead I believed that I had a choice. I could either fulfill the sassy, finger-snapping jezebel image delegated to black women (Collins 1991; Jewell 1993) or the trophied, docile image placed upon white women (Giddings 1984; hooks 1981). Some choice. At times, I found myself playing both of these roles, which both ultimately define the tragic mulatto.

"I hate this part of the application because I never know what to check!" Damon and I were sitting in his brand new Blazer while I was looking over some of my college applications.

"What do you mean?" he said. Uh-oh, what have I done, I thought. He obviously doesn't know what I am talking about. I felt stupid but still, I said, "Well, I never know whether or not I should check 'other' for race, since there is no box for me."

He tilted his head toward me, twisted his entire face up into a question mark and said, "Whatchu' mean there ain't no box for you? You look black, don't you?"

I knew he was mad. He always got mad when we talked about this subject. His voice would start to rise and his sentences got louder and louder the closer they got to the end, but I had to continue.

"Well, yeah but . . . "

I couldn't finish because he moved over and put his face right up to mine, close enough so I could smell the cinnamon-flavored gum rolling off his tongue and said, "But nothing girl, you better check black and get over it. You look black so that means you are black!" He laughed as he moved back over to his side of the seat, but I knew he was mad. I shouldn't have even brought it up. What was I thinking?

I wasn't doing anything right. This was just another reminder for him that he was dating a "mixed" girl. He didn't want to recognize that he had feelings for me. Oh, it was okay to fuck me, but he told me himself he could never marry a girl who wasn't "fully black." I was pretty enough to have on his arm to show all the other dudes that he was fucking me, but I never met his mom. His girlfriend (who was black) knew his parents, but we had to leave through the kitchen when his mom got home from work. And when it was my turn to get an abortion, he met me at the front door with less than half the money.

Still, I was lucky to have him and we both knew it. Everybody wanted to be with Damon, with his chocolate-coated skin, soft black eyes, and full, soft, pink lips. I got chills whenever I caught a glimpse of him when he wasn't looking. And as a bonus, he had this nice truck, a booming stereo system, and all the latest clothes. He was a major step up from the old, rusty Pontiacs and no-name jeans that I was used to. Even though he had a girlfriend, I knew it was only a matter of time, if I did everything right, that he would be all mine.

The sounds of Pink Floyd spilled out of the speakers as Bart stumbled his way through the maze of beer cans, searching for a place next to me on the tacky plaid sofa. He ran one hand through his short black hair and used the other to stroke my right leg, sending chills through my body.

Looking into his dark blue eyes, I was reminded of the many times I had watched him whenever he came into the pizza parlor where I worked. I caught him watching me too, when I rang up his order. He knew my friend Debbie, who also worked there, and one day he told her how pretty I was. When she told me, I was amazed to find that he didn't add the disclaimer "for a black girl."

From that day on, I wanted him. Something about him turned me on. I don't know if it was the casual way he dressed or the way he put his head down timidly when handing me his money. Or it may have simply been the fact that I was attracted to him and I wanted to try a new experience. There were only about 2,000 black folks in my hometown of 200,000, and I had dated most of the cute boys. It was definitely time for something new.

And that is why I was sitting in his room at the fraternity house.

Patty and I were tired of driving around that night, so I decided to take him up on an earlier invitation.

I wasn't sure what to say to him, I could have let him stroke my leg forever. He looked at me, somewhat confused, perhaps unsure how to phrase what he was about to say. He laughed a little, and said "You know, I've never dated a black chick before!"

My face turned red with burning rage. What an asshole, I thought. What did that have to do with anything? I had never dated a white guy either but you didn't hear me explaining. And besides, we were *not* dating—I went there to get laid! I wanted to tell him that going to bed with him was the only thing on my agenda that evening, but as soon as I opened my mouth I found myself explaining, "Well actually my mom's white."

What is going on here? Why in the hell did I say that, I thought. I don't have to explain myself to this schmuck. Dammit! I thought this was going to be something different, I just wanted to get laid. Why did I feel I had to tell him my life history before we got into bed together? But, nonetheless, I went there for a purpose, a new experience, and I was going to get it regardless of him and his stupid comments.

"Whatever," he said, kissing me. "You're still beautiful."

Damn right, I'm beautiful. And exotic too! If he wanted to play this little jungle fever game, I was ready. I was going to show him a night that he would never forget. I wasn't going to be like all those silly white girls he was used to. I was going to take him places he'd never been before, until he was begging for more.

Halloween, 1995. I went to a party dressed as Biracial Girl, superhero of the nineties. My outfit was fully equipped with a superhero cape, an oversized B on my chest, black clothing, and black and white paint on my face, exaggerating society's image of biracial people. To stretch the stereotypes even further, Biracial Girl's job was to save those individuals who were confused about the social definitions of race (a little sociological humor gone awry).

As I was standing around the hors d'oeuvres table trying to come to a decision, a white woman, dressed as a drag queen, approached me to comment about what I was wearing.

"I really like that costume!" she said, beaming.

"Thank you, I made it myself," I said, happy that someone other than my sociology friends understood my humor.

"You know, I was going to dress up like that, but I was going to be O.J. Simpson's daughter, you know, and show how confused she was about being half and half, but a friend of mine said that that would be offensive!" she said laughing.

"Oh," I said and quickly turned to fix myself a plate. I couldn't believe it. There I was, a graduate student, aged 24, at a party with my friends, and it was happening all over again. I was faced with the same ignorance that I had grown up with. What surprised me the most was that this comment was coming from someone who was equally as marginalized in this society; this woman was a lesbian.

I made a choice not to say anything to her, but left her to wallow in her stupidity. I didn't have to live out the superhero that I was portraying. It wasn't my duty to save her.

Over the years, with the help of counseling and feminism, I have realized that it is my duty to save myself. I refuse to adhere to both societal definitions and expectations of race and gender. Like many others, I have struggled with internalized race and gender oppression, and I am continually discovering other ways of knowing. I was told to choose between both black and white, and black and female, but in reality, I am all of these. My life experiences transgress the boundaries between race and gender, making the space that I embody simultaneously black, white, and female.

This is the reality for all of us in this society. As people of color, white women, and white men, we are forced to conform to societal expectations. These expectations have been set up to benefit a small minority. In order to foster that minority and keep it in power, a norm has been established that the majority of us do not reflect. As women we are expected to fulfill certain definitions that are often uncharacteristic of who we really are. As people of color we must fulfill similar definitions that also contrast us to the "norm." We internalize these stereotypes and myths about our race and gender that cater to our oppression.

Either/or dichotomous thinking does not adequately reflect individuals in this society. For this reason, we must make an effort to dismantle these dichotomies and construct new realities for ourselves. We can refuse to live within confining definitions of race and gender (as well as class, sexual orientation, and so on) by creating alternative definitions to live by—definitions that will help end our oppression. As bell hooks (1994) states, "those wounds will not heal if left unattended."

Acknowledgments

I would like to thank the editors of this collection for squeezing me in, with special thanks to Carol Ronai for giving me this opportunity. I would also like to thank Becky Reitzes, Rick Napier, Ellen O'Donnell, Hokulani Aikau, and Rabecca Cross for their many readings of this paper, helpful comments, and endless encouragement. I am currently pursuing a master's degree at the University of Memphis.

References

Anzaldúa, Gloria. 1987. *Borderlands/La Frontera: The New Mestiza*. San Francisco: Spinters/Aunt Lute Books.

Creef, Elena Tajima. 1990. "Notes from a Fragmented Daughter," in *Making Face, Making Soul*, ed. Gloria Anzaldúa. San Francisco: Aunt Lute Books.

Collins, Patricia Hill. 1991. *Black Feminist Thought*. New York: Routledge.

Ellis, Carolyn. 1995. *Final Negotiations: A Story of Love, Loss, and Chronic Illness*. Philadelphia: Temple University Press.

Faludi, Susan. 1991. *Backlash: The Undeclared War Against American Women*. New York: Crown.

Frankenberg, Ruth. 1993. *The Social Construction of Whiteness: White Women, Race Matters*. Minneapolis: University of Minnesota Press.

Gibbs, Jewelle Taylor. 1989. "Biracial Adolescents," in *Children of Color*, eds. Jewelle Taylor Gibbs, Larke Nahme Huang, and Associates. San Francisco: Jossey Bass Publishers, pp. 322–350.

Giddings, Paula. 1984. *When and Where I Enter: The Impact of Black Women on Race and Sex in America*. New York: Bantam Books.

hooks, bell. 1981. *Ain't I a Woman: Black Women and Feminism*. Boston: South End Press.

———. 1994. *Outlaw Culture: Resisting Representations*. New York: Routledge.

Jewell, K. Sue. 1993. *From Mammy to Miss America and Beyond*. London: Routledge.

Jones, Lisa. 1995. *Bulletproof Diva: Tales of Race, Sex, and Hair.* New York: Doubleday.

Krieger, Susan. 1991. *Social Science and the Self: Personal Essays on an Art Form.* New Brunswick: Rutgers University Press.

Lorde, Audre. 1981. "The Master's Tools Will Never Dismantle the Master's House," in *This Bridge Called My Back,* eds. Gloria Anzaldúa and Cherrié Moraga. New York: Kitchen Table Women of Color Press.

Moraga, Cherrié. 1981. "La Guera," in *This Bridge Called My Back,* eds. Gloria Anzaldúa and Cherrié Moraga. New York: Kitchen Table Women of Color Press.

Omi, Michael and Howard Winant. 1994. *Racial Formation in the United States: From the 1960s to the 1990s.* New York: Routledge and Kegan Paul.

Ronai, Carol Rambo. 1992. "The Reflexive Self Through Narrative: A Night in the Life of an Erotic Dancer/Researcher," in *Investigating Subjectivity: Research on Lived Experience,* eds. Carolyn Ellis and Michael Flaherty. Newbury Park, CA: Sage, pp. 102–124.

Root, Maria P.P. 1992. "Within, Between, and Beyond Race" in *Racially Mixed People in America,* ed. Maria P.P. Root. Newbury Park, CA: Sage.

Russell, Kathy, Midge Wilson, and Ronald Hall. 1992. *The Color Complex: The Politics of Skin Color Among African Americans.* New York: Harcourt Brace Jovanovich.

Weston, Kath. 1991. *Families We Choose: Lesbians, Gays, Kinship.* New York: Columbia University Press.

Wolf, Naomi. 1991. *The Beauty Myth.* New York: Anchor Books.

Wong, Nellie. 1981. "When I Was Growing Up," in *This Bridge Called My Back,* eds. Gloria Anzaldúa and Cherrié Moraga. New York: Kitchen Table Women of Color Press, pp. 7–8.

Zook, Kristal Brent. 1990. "Light Skinned-ded Naps" in *Making Face, Making Soul,* ed. Gloria Anzaldúa. San Francisco: Aunt Lute Books, pp. 85–96.

3

Everyday [Hetero]sexism

Strategies of Resistance and Lesbian Couples

CHRISTINE MICHELE ROBINSON

Introduction

This paper examines a particular kind of gender oppression—hetero-sexism—and the ways in which African-American and interracial les-bian couples resist heterosexism in everyday life. Heterosexism is the unconscious or explicit belief in the inherent superiority of heterosex-uality—that heterosexuality is the only "normal" mode of sexual and social relations. Heterosexism is an essentialist notion of sex differ-ences; that is, biological differences between women and men result in correspondingly different feelings and behaviors, including those regarding sexuality. Heterosexuality is thus constructed as normal and natural, while any other form of sexuality is deviant and in need of explanation. According to Marilyn Frye:

> As most people see it, being heterosexual is just being. It is not *interpreted*. It is not understood as a consequence of anything. It is not viewed as possi-bly a solution to some problem, or as a way of acting and feeling which one worked out or was pushed to by circumstances. On this sort of view, all women *are* heterosexual, and some women somehow come to *act* otherwise. No one *is*, in the same sense, a lesbian. (Frye 1983, p. 159)

Studies of lesbian relationships offer little empirical research on the relationships of Black and interracial working- and middle-class les-bian couples (Mays et al. 1993). This study of lesbian relationships articulates the need for a multidimensional approach to the study of sexism. I will focus this inquiry primarily on the obstacles that inter-racial and African-American working- and middle-class lesbian couples face and the strategies of resistance they employ to counter heterosexism.

Patriarchal gender socialization and heterosexism have been consistently documented to be the main factors affecting white, middle-class, lesbian couples (Krestan and Bepko 1980; Schneider 1986). Because of the different gender-role socialization of Black and/or working-class women as compared to white and/or middle-class women, because heterosexism manifests differently in Black and white communities (Lorde 1984), and because many Black and interracial couples face race- and class-based oppression, heterosexism is a more complex phenomenon than has been articulated in the research literature on lesbian relationships.

Sample, Procedure, and Methodology

This study used semistructured in-depth interviews with three African-American and three interracial lesbian couples from the mid-South. All of the women in the sample self-identify as "lesbian" or "gay," and were interviewed individually. Fear of being identified as lesbian prevented some couples from participating in this project, and those who did were more likely to be "out" than those who chose not to volunteer. Each couple has at least one self-identified African-American woman in the relationship. Nine respondents identified as African American, two women identified as white, and one woman identified herself as biracial. Most had at least some college education. Four of six couples were cohabiting at the time of the interviews. Four couples had children; six of the Black women and one of the white women had children. All of the children were born of previous heterosexual relationships. The length of time the couples had been in the relationship ranged from eleven months to seven years. Six of the women have working-class backgrounds and six have middle-class backgrounds. The respondents ranged in age from nineteen to forty-four years old.

The format of the interview guide for this project is semistandardized. According to Berg (1989), a semistandardized interview involves a schedule of open-ended questions followed by probing questions, allowing the interviewer to ask general questions and to draw out more specific information from the participants. Open-ended questions also allowed the participant to stress what was most meaningful to her in defining and expressing her life experiences. Besides demographic information, I asked each partner in the couple a series of questions about her experiences with racism, classism, and heterosexism; strategies of resisting oppression; risks of being in a lesbian relationship; and perceptions of and involvement in various communities. Finally, this study excludes white lesbian couples. I purposely avoided making comparisons of Black and interracial lesbian relationships to white lesbian relationships so as not to construct white couples as the norm and Black and interracial couples as "other," as deviant by comparison.

Additionally, I took explicit measures to minimize the impact of my researcher privileges by sending each person a copy of the transcript or taped interview to edit before analysis. I stood in a power relationship to the respondents because of my white and middle-class, privileged statuses. As a lesbian researcher, I could not assume that my lesbian identity (*qua* woman and "gay") automatically established rapport with or overcame difference from African-American, biracial, or raised working-class white or Black lesbians.

Findings and Analysis
Cultural Framework for Strategies of Resistance

Tracy Robinson's and Janie Victoria Ward's research on cultivating resistance among African-American female adolescents provides a useful framework to articulate the strategies of resistance employed by the respondents in this study. Robinson and Ward (1991) posit that not all forms of resistance are in the best interest of women. They distinguish between strategies of resistance for survival and strategies of resistance for liberation. Strategies of resistance for survival are potentially destructive choices that are not conducive to the liberation of African-American women. According to Robinson and Ward strategies of survival include:

> self-denigration due to the internalization of negative self images, excessive autonomy and individualism at the expense of connectedness to the collec-

tive, and "quick fixes" such as early and unplanned pregnancies, substance abuse ... and food addictions. (1991, p. 89)

Strategies of liberation occur when women, in this case Black and interracial lesbian couples, acknowledge the problems of and demand change in an environment that oppresses them. This approach supports African-American, biracial, and white women's transformations into "self-conscious agents engaged in battle on their own behalf" (p. 89).

I would like to suggest that this model be revised to be less dichotomous. Survival strategies are often temporary and necessary for sustaining the lives of those who use them. For example, while passing for heterosexual can be destructive to self-esteem, it is not necessarily indicative of internalized homophobia and may be necessary to keep a job or avoid harassment. By precluding survival in liberation strategies, we risk blaming women for contributing to their own oppression, and often wrongly assume that healthy, alternative choices are available to them. I extend Robinson's and Ward's model by suggesting that while some strategies of resistance for survival are potentially destructive, many strategies of resistance for survival are necessary for liberation, because survival itself is a precondition for liberation. The women in this study made choices that were necessary for them to cope with the social, political, and economic consequences of living their lives. They identified heterosexism as impacting them on (at least) three levels: (1) within themselves, (2) from families of origin, and (3) in their communities; they also exhibited a wide range of strategies to resist oppression.

Self-Authorization and Claiming Identity

Heterosexism is shaped by race, class, and gender. In African-American communities, being lesbian is often viewed as antithetical to being either Black or female. Darryl Loiacano (1989) maintains that "[l]esbianism is considered incompatible with the role expectations of women in African-American communities." Black lesbians, as women who choose not to partner with Black men, are often seen as contributing to their common racial oppression. Some claim that Black lesbians do not have children, and therefore commit genocide against African-Americans. In short, some African-American people assume that Black and interracial lesbian relationships undermine "the Black family," the status of Black men, and the liberation of Black people. Some Black lesbians may feel outcast from their ethnic communities (Greene 1990).

African-American lesbians have a highly developed awareness of their devalued multiple identities, which require constant effort to integrate (Greene 1993a). They negotiate three rigidly defined and strongly independent communities, which fail to support significant aspects of their lives (Morales 1990). Concurrently, they manage racism, classism, sexism, and heterosexism of the dominant [white] culture, African-American communities, and lesbian communities (Greene 1993a). Like racism, heterosexual oppression is fed by stereotypes and myths about lesbians, bisexuals, and gay men. Heterosexuals invoke controlling images to justify denying social, political, and economic equality to sexual minorities. Often these negative images and beliefs are internalized by lesbians, which makes it difficult for them to cultivate a positive sense of self and create healthy relationships with other people. Self-authorization, a concept developed by Brown (1991), is a strategy of resistance for liberation that these women used to identify themselves as authorities of their own realities, to identify controlling images, to tell their own histories, and, ultimately, to claim their own lives. Josephine, who is a working-class Afra-American, describes how internalized heterosexism prevented her from acknowledging her lesbian identity:

> through school I always used to dream about women. And I thought, "I'm *not* supposed to be like this." I was in college when I first had an encounter with a woman. I was nineteen. It freaked me out. It took me a few years before I realized this is *what I am*.

Josephine eventually capitulated to her persistent feelings towards women and developed the capacity to accept herself as a lesbian. This demonstrates that while internalized homophobia is a consequence of heterosexism, she can "author her own identity," that is, choose to construct her own self-definition and affirm her own identity.

When asked to think about or identify with the terms butch and femme, almost all of the women rejected the image of lesbian couples as imitating the (correspondingly stereotypical) heterosexual roles of dominant/masculine and subordinate/feminine. By identifying these controlling sexual images, the respondents resisted internalizing them, and therefore claimed the authority to define their identities and the character of their relationships. However, one lesbian had internalized this model of roles in relationships. Carla also imposed her reality on others:

> We have arguments all the time about who's butch, because we both think we are. But she is feminine because she carries a purse and cries at movies. I [am] butch and when I look at other people, I'd say 90 percent of the time I look at them as butch or femme. You know if it crosses my mind, I'll identify them. Some people are hard to tell.

This exemplifies what Mehan and Wood (1975) have called an "incorrigible proposition": an unquestioned belief that cannot be proved wrong, even in spite of questionable or contradictory evidence. Carla believes there are two (and only two) gender roles in a relationship, and when someone does not neatly fit into one of her two categories, she adjusts the situation to fit her beliefs, rather than questioning her beliefs to fit the situation. She assigns each person to one of two possible categories, rather than acknowledging that this is a false dichotomy. When we internalize this heterosexist model, we impose inequality onto our view of all relationships.

Melanie, who is upwardly mobile and African-American, said a myth she would like to see destroyed is "that gay people are weak. We are not weak. We never would have survived if we were." Lauren, who is white and raised working-class, responded to my question about stereotypes [my emphasis]:

> I think [stereotypes come from] . . . a male-dominated society . . . men, dictate the norms. And they dictate our sexuality. But I think that's changing . . . *it's been to their detriment as well because it has dictated a rigid role for their sexuality.*

Herbert Blumer (1969) posits that symbolic interactionism is an approach to yield verifiable knowledge of human group life conduct. Reality can be sought and verified only in the empirical world.

Lauren's partner, Brenda, an Afra-American middle-class-raised woman, asserted:

> There's nothing abnormal [about us], we come in all sizes, shapes, and per-
> suasions. I think that people have a tendency, if you say "lesbian," to think
> of someone that is very masculine. I mean the reality by now should tell
> people that is not true ... but people get stuck in those places even though
> common sense and everything tells them differently.

This statement illustrates that, in spite of evidence to the contrary, it is
difficult to dismantle the pervasive controlling images that heterosexism invokes to invalidate these women's self-definitions. Josephine,
Melanie, Lauren, and Brenda used primarily two strategies of resistance: (1) self-authorization (described earlier); and (2) deconstruction, or exposing the ideological content of heterosexism by appealing
to their own experiences, common sense, or empirical reality.

Resisting Heterosexism within Families of Origin

Silence as Resistance

Lesbians routinely make decisions about whether or not to disclose
their sexual identities (Greene 1993b). Heterosexual oppression leads
many lesbians to remain silent about their identities to their families.
Since one's lesbian identity is not readily identifiable, heterosexuals
often presume and treat lesbians as if they are heterosexual. Garnets
and Kimmel (1991) suggest that even when lesbians are open about
their sexual orientation, this does not automatically invalidate heterosexist images because each individual can be discounted as anomalous.

Heterosexist attitudes often divide families from their lesbian and
gay members. Beverly Greene maintains that "[l]esbians ... need the
same strong connections with family members as anyone else. Strong
family ties may even be more crucial to lesbians ... given the hostility
and rejection they face in the outside world" (1993b, p. 77). Mays and
Cochran (1988, p. 61) report that "[m]uch research on Black Americans has discussed the importance of the Black family and social networks to the psychological well-being and survival of this group."
While most of the women reported having told their families about
their lesbianism and about their relationships with their partners, a

few women clearly chose not to "come out" to some family members. Brenda admitted:

> I haven't said a thing to my father. I guess he knows; I haven't decided whether I want to make a declaration or just let him assume. I haven't told my father that [my partner] was living here. I'll probably take the path of least resistance.

The choice to remain silent about one's sexual identity or relationship need not be interpreted as an expression of internalized heterosexism. Brenda sees her choice to remain silent as "the path of least resistance." Yet silence in this context transcends the false dichotomy of strategies that are destructive and those that liberate. Silence is not always complicity; when it is used to protect oneself, it is a way to resist. For some African-American lesbians, passing as straight is a strategy of resistance against heterosexual oppression. For many Black lesbians, heterosexual privilege may be the only privilege available to them, since it is unlikely that most can or would desire to pass for white, male, or middle-class.

For the women in this study, being in a relationship increases the pressure to come out to family members and the likelihood of being identified as lesbian. For African-American lesbians, "coming out to the family not only jeopardizes the intra-family relationships, but also threatens their strong association with their [racial-]ethnic community" (Morales 1990, p. 233).

Coming Out and Finding Social Support
Bonilla and Porter (1990) report in their study of attitudes towards homosexuality that Black homosexuals are not as openly rejected by family and community as whites are, but the moral stigma associated with homosexuality may be strong. Because lesbian unions are often hidden or not recognized, family members may perceive or treat their lesbian relative as "single." Families may not understand or may choose not to recognize that their lesbian family members have responsibilities to a primary relationship (Greene 1993b). Further, if the couple dissolves or has a problem, relatives may respond inappropriately to the situation, compared to marital distress in a heterosexual relationship (Greene 1993b, p. 78).

Most heterosexual couples can expect emotional support and concern for their relationships from their family members; however, the home is usually not a place where one's lesbian relationship is positively regarded or nurtured. Beverly Greene (1993b) argues that lesbians frequently form and maintain relationships in heterosexist contexts where there is little support. The potential danger is that couples may internalize these negative perceptions, which could (self-fulfillingly) disrupt the stability of their relationships. In this study, family members' responses to their lesbian family member's relationships ranged from limited acceptance to open hostility. Although nine respondents reported that parents and other family members gave the *least* support for their relationships, the other three women reported that families offered them *little or no* emotional support.

Eleven of twelve participants reported that siblings, cousins, friends, and other black and white lesbians offered the most support for their relationships, while grandparents and parent figures extended the least support. This is consistent with findings from Blumstein and Schwartz (1983) that (white) lesbian couples perceive greater levels of support for their relationships from friends and partners than from families of origin. Four general patterns (often overlapping) emerged in how parents and other family members responded to their lesbian family member's relationships. First, consistent with Edward Morales's (1990) study of ethnic minority lesbians and gays in the United States, some family members accepted their lesbian relative and her partner, but did not discuss their relationship. Patrice describes the limited support she receives for her relationship from her mother:

> She'll ask "How's everything with Rachel?" but that's about it. We don't talk
> about it. If Rachel and I have an argument, I don't talk to her about it
> because ... it doesn't sit well with her. As long as I'm happy, that's fine, but
> I know she doesn't care for it.

Patrice and Rachel belong to a Black Lesbian Support Group to get the social support they do not receive from their family members. This liberation strategy empowers them to find social support for themselves and also to support others negotiating similar relationship issues.

Second, some relatives were accepting of the relationship of the lesbian family member as long as it was not discussed. Greene (1990) asserts that Black family members may be more accepting than white family members of a relative's lesbianism as long as it is not "flaunted," that is, openly acknowledged. Third, some family members either failed to understand or chose not to recognize their lesbian family member's commitment to her partner. For example, even though Jane, an African-American woman, and her partner, who is also African American, were living with the partner's parents at the time, Jane described how her parents refused to accept the reality of her lesbian relationship by trying to fix her up with men. Finally, some relatives chose to ignore the lesbian relationship altogether by treating the lover as a friend.

Greene (1990) reports that Black lesbians were more likely to be involved with their families of origin than white lesbians. Mays et al. (1993) report that Black lesbians are more likely than white lesbians to remain part of their heterosexual communities and families, in part because of the importance of their racial-ethnic ties. Although all twelve women reported limited acceptance for their relationships by some family members, these couples remained connected to their families. This finding is consistent with previous research, and is ironic in light of the invective that Black lesbians undermine Black families or "sell out" their racial-ethnic communities. It is interesting to note that six of nine Black women and one of two white women are mothers. This is also ironic in light of the charge that Black lesbians are non-procreative and commit genocide against their own people. Many of these couples strategically resist heterosexism by coming out as lesbians to their family members, by remaining connected to their families of origin, and by actively encouraging their relatives to examine their heterosexism.

For interracial couples, race-, class-, and sex-based prejudice limits the degree of social support they receive for their relationships from family members. Melanie, who is Black, reported that she received the least support for her relationship from her partner's white parents:

> I hate to go over there. They have no respect for us. Her parents [say things to her] like "why don't you find a nice white boy to marry?" [Her mother's] nice to me because . . . I am not a stereotypical Black female who talks shit all the time, you know, who doesn't do anything. I work, and I try to pay my bills.

This statement illustrates the heterosexist, classist, and racist attitudes of the partner's white parents. Carla, Melanie's partner, stated that she receives support from her partner, "because we don't get it from our families." This couple draws strength from each other and from the people in their predominantly white lesbigay church, where they receive affirmation for their relationship, but at the cost of racism and classism.

Lauren, a white woman, describes how her family displays heterosexist and racist attitudes because of her relationship with a Black woman.

> [My brother-in-law] is a ... total bigot. Confronting him with my sexuality and him learning to accept me and whomever I [am with] was a big step for him. But a line has been drawn in the sand that [Brenda] is Black. He's so unwilling to accept that, we changed our tradition of Christmas this year. He said "I will not have Christmas with a nigger."

Lauren employs two strategies here to resist oppression: first, by recognizing and confronting heterosexism directly; second, by avoiding a hostile environment and creating her own holiday tradition. While the first strategy of resistance clearly challenges heterosexism and is one of liberation, the second resistance strategy exemplifies again how resistance is neither a destructive choice nor clearly a strategy to directly challenge racism. Yet it is resistance, because Lauren refuses to subject herself and her partner to bigotry. Both Lauren and Brenda are currently involved in antiracism work, a clear strategy of resistance for liberation because they are both actively engaging others in the process of healing from racism.

Two of three interracial couples reported that strangers often stare at them in public because of racism and heterosexism. Angela, a white woman, described how even when people smiled at her and her African-American partner to show support, she felt uncomfortable because she knew that others were able to identify them as an interracial lesbian couple. Barbara Smith, a prolific writer, describes how interracial lesbian couples are marked in a racist and heterosexist society, and thereby provides an explanation of how racism shapes heterosexism.

Speaking from experience, I think it's easier for two Black women who are lovers to be together publicly than it is for a mixed couple. To me, that's a dead give-away because this is such a completely segregated society. Whenever I had a lover of a different race, I felt that it was like having a sign or a billboard over my head that said—"These are dykes. Right here." Because you don't usually see people of different races together in this country, it was almost by definition telling the world that we were lesbians. (Smith and Smith 1983, p. 207)

Finally, the interracial couples in this study resisted heterosexism and racism by choosing to love across societal boundaries. They traverse the boundaries between segregated communities, Black and white, lesbian and straight, working and middle class.

Resisting Heterosexism in Black Communities

Although there is little empirical social scientific research on Black communities' attitudes towards lesbians (Mays et al. 1993), there is evidence that Black lesbians perceive themselves to be oppressed within the Black community because of heterosexism. However, the assumption that Black people are more heterosexist than white society is itself racist and empirically unsubstantiated. Rather, heterosexism often manifests differently in African-American communities than in white society. Some Black people think homosexuality is a "white phenomenon" and largely absent among African-Americans (Morales 1990). Thus Black lesbians may be viewed as sellouts to their racial heritage, which contributes to the invisibility of lesbians in African-American communities. The sense of shame may be less about "the family name" and more about "the race" (Morales 1990).

Heterosexism affects Black and interracial couples differently in Black and white communities. The participants in this study identified heterosexism in their racial-ethnic communities and how it affected their relationships, and described the resistance strategies they employed to cope with intolerance and discrimination. Consistent with Loiacano's (1989) research on identity development with Black gay men and lesbians, eight of nine African-American women maintained that being identified as a lesbian changed their degree of involvement in their Black communities. For the Black women in this study who had revealed their lesbian identities to others in their communities, the coming-out experience changed how they perceived their sense of acceptance *as Black women*. However, they did not see themselves as "sellouts" to white society or as contributing to race suicide against Black people, but rather identified heterosexism as the problem. In doing this, they employed the strategy of self-authorization. Melanie, a twenty-four-year-old, upwardly mobile African American, describes her choice to move away from the community in which she grew up:

> I don't live in my community anymore. I went to high school with a girl . . . [who also is] gay. She's teaching and living in [a Black] county and I knew I couldn't. I had to get out. The community is too small. Everyone who is Black is involved in the church. Everyone knows everyone else and you can't hide your business, at all.

Although Melanie no longer resides in her community, she still identifies with it as her community. Patrice, African-American and middle class, describes the choices she and her partner made because of heterosexism in her community:

> Man, my people. In the Black community, it's pathetic. Because of ignorance, that's what it is. There are some people you just choose to disassociate with. That is what we have chosen . . . to disassociate ourselves with people and we have a few friends . . . [heterosexism] is a problem. Some people are okay about it. But that's only a few. Very few.

Both Melanie and Patrice chose to limit their ties to their communities as a way to resist. Although Clarice and her partner, both working class and African-American, are out to their families and friends, Clarice described how their visibility in their neighborhood as a couple is threatening to some males in their community. Clarice describes what she calls a "common" occurrence in her neighborhood:

> A lot of guys approach us. They want to go to bed [with us]. I guess [our lesbianism] entices them because they see women who will have nothing to do with men. I've even had [men] say they will rape me.

Clarice also stated that both she and her partner take karate lessons to protect themselves from violent attacks and sexual harassment. This strategy of resistance helps them to feel safer and also transcends the false dichotomy of strategies that are destructive and those that liberate, since there is nothing inherent in literally "fighting back" that is liberatory, that is, that challenges the legitimacy of heterosexism.

All nine African-American women remained involved in their racial-ethnic communities to some degree and reported the importance of Black communities as a reference group and social support against racism. However, none of the African-American women in this study chose to reveal themselves as lesbians to all parts of their communities. Most feared being ostracized in their churches, fired from their jobs, rejected by people they knew, or violently attacked. That these women resisted oppression—through the strategies of silence, self-authorization, deconstruction, fighting back, directly challenging heterosexism and racism, and loving across segregated communities—while remaining connected to communities of great importance to them, suggests a commitment to racial uplift and community-building.

Black women rely on their racial-ethnic communities as a support from racism that pervades American society. In contrast, the two white women did not describe a commitment to white racial-ethnic communities and do not necessarily view white society as a support for their racial identity in the same way. For the white women in this study, heterosexism does not threaten their relationship to their racial-ethnic communities because of their white-skin privilege. The racist social context in which white people exercise racial privilege over African-Americans imposes extra burdens on African-Americans to be included and supported in their racial-ethnic communities. African-American lesbians are no exception to this.

Nevertheless, heterosexism in both Black and white communities limits the full participation of their lesbian members. In African-American communities, these women often lack support for their partnerships and their identities as Black women; this is especially true for those partnered with white women. Black women in interracial relationships may be especially likely to be accused of selling out to white society or "sleeping with the enemy." For the Black women in interracial couples, their *lesbianism* does not estrange them from their identities or communities, although *heterosexism* attempts to achieve this. Gomez and Smith powerfully articulate the "insidiousness" of how heterosexism targets Black and interracial lesbian couples:

> Homophobia is particularly dangerous for Black lesbians because it is so insidious. But as Black gay women, we haven't been interested in removing ourselves from our families or communities because we understand the importance of that connection. We straddle the fence that says we cannot be the uplifters of the race and lesbian at the same time—that's what makes it so dangerous for our emotional health. But ... I think that our ability to keep the family intact is what is going to ... help preserve the Black community. As lesbians, we have so much to teach the Black community about survival. (1989, p. 518)

Conclusion

This study has shown some of the ways that heterosexism impacts the relationships of Black and interracial lesbian couples in everyday life, and how they resist oppression. The couples in this study face prejudice and discrimination from their families and in their communities. However, these couples are not only casualties of heterosexist discourses, practices, and social structures in American society, they are warriors in the struggle for liberation. While it is important to understand the various manifestations of heterosexism, it is equally important to articulate the ways in which heterosexism is actively contested and subverted. Social interaction and institutions are gendered spaces; subsequently, they represent both sites of domination and places of liberation. This study found that in the face of oppression, Black and interracial lesbian couples challenge the multiple discourses that attempt to appropriate their accounts and invalidate their relationships with claims about who they are. The strategies of resistance they invoke to counter heterosexism begin with their own narratives of liberation as they become tellers of their own stories, asserting their own subjectivities. These couples fight back, survive, build in their communities, keep families together, and create their own families and communities—all of which contribute to social and institutional transformations.

Heterosexism keeps lesbians invisible to one another. The couples in the present study represent a crossroads as they negotiate and traverse the boundaries between segregated communities, lesbian and straight, Black and white, male and female, and working and middle class. The social norms that dictate the ways in which races, classes, sexes, and sexualities relate to each other perpetuate inequality and prevent lesbians (and all members of society) from collectively organizing against their shared and diverse forms of oppression. Heterosexist belief systems are ideological; that is, socially constructed/humanly defined. The effects of heterosexism are a material reality. By making explicit the assumptions underlying heterosexist ideology and by invalidating them, these couples demonstrate that heterosexism can be challenged.

The controlling images of lesbian sexuality are pervasive in everyday life and contribute to the subordination of all women in our society. By focusing on Black and interracial lesbian relationships, we have been able to expand our understanding of heterosexism by showing how it is constructed on the basis of race, social class, and gender. Like scientific concepts, reality "has a career, changing its meaning from time to time in accordance with the introduction of new experiences and replacing one content with another" (Blumer 1969, p. 161). Research that expands our knowledge of the realities of lesbian relationships will help to create new frameworks that reject the ethnocentrism of Western theories and concepts marginalizing nonwhite women and preventing them from defining their own subjectivities. Further, recognizing the different experiences of Black and interracial lesbian couples enriches the literature on lesbian relationships and the literature on sexual relationships. An understanding of the social construction of sexualities necessitates an interrogation of lesbian sexualities in all of their diversity.

References

Bell, Allen P. and Martin S. Weinberg. 1978. *Homosexualities: A Study of Diversity among Men and Women.* New York: Simon and Schuster.

Berg, Bruce L. 1989. *Qualitative Research Methods for the Social Sciences.* Boston: Allyn and Bacon.

Blumer, Herbert. 1969. *Symbolic Interactionism.* Berkeley: University of California Press.

Blumstein, Philip W. and Pepper Schwartz. 1983. *American Couples: Money, Work, Sex.* New York: William Morrow.

Bonilla, Louis and Judith Porter. 1990. "A Comparison of Latino, Black, and Non-Hispanic White Attitudes Toward Homosexuality." *Hispanic Journal of Behavioral Sciences* 12: 437–452.

Brown, Lyn Mikel. 1991. "Telling a Girl's Life: Self Authorization as a Form of Resistance." *Women & Therapy* 11: 71–86.

Frye, Marilyn. 1983. *The Politics of Reality: Essays in Feminist Theory.* New York: The Crossing Press.

Garnets, Linda and Douglas Kimmel. 1991. "Lesbian and Gay Male Dimensions in the Psychological Study of Human Diversity," in *Psychological Perspectives on Human Diversity in America,* ed. J. Goodchilds. Washington, DC: American Psychological Association, pp. 143–192.

Gomez, Jewelle and Barbara Smith. 1989. "Talking About It: Homophobia in the Black Community." *Feminist Review* 34: 47–55.

Greene, Beverly. 1990. "African American Lesbians: The Role of Family, Culture, and Racism." *BG Magazine* 6, 26.

———. 1993a. "Psychotherapy with African American Women: Integrating Feminist and Psychodynamic Models." *Journal of Training and Practice in Professional Psychology* 7: 49–66.

———. 1993b. "Human Diversity in Clinical Psychology: Lesbian and Gay Sexual Orientations." *Clinical Psychologist* 46: 74–82.

Krestan, Jo-Ann and Claudia L. Bepko. 1980. "The Problem of Fusion in the Lesbian Relationship." *Family Process* 19: 277–289.

Loiacano, Darryl K. 1989. "Gay Identity Issues among Black Americans: Racism, Homophobia and the Need for Validation." *Journal of Counseling and Development* 68: 21–25.

Lorde, Audre. 1984. *Sister Outsider.* Freedom, CA: The Crossing Press.

Mays, Vickie M. and Susan D. Cochran. 1988. "The Black Women's Relationship Project: A National Survey of Black Lesbians," in *The Sourcebook on Lesbian and Gay Healthcare, Second Edition,* eds. M. Shernoff and W. Scott. Washington, DC: National Lesbian and Gay Health Foundation, pp. 54–62.

Mays, Vickie M., Susan D. Cochran, and Sylvia Rhue. 1993. "The Impact of Perceived Discrimination on the Intimate Relationships of Black Lesbians." *Journal of Homosexuality* 25: 1–14.

Mehan, Hugh and Houston Wood. 1975. *The Reality of Ethnomethodology.* New York: Wiley.

Morales, Edward S. 1990. "Ethnic Minority Families and Minority Gays and Lesbians." *Marriage and Family Review* 14: 217–239.

Robinson, Tracy and Janie Victoria Ward. 1991. "'A Belief in Self Far Greater Than Anyone's Disbelief': Cultivating Resistance Among African-American Female Adolescents." *Women and Therapy* 11: 87–103.

Schneider, Margaret S. 1986. "The Relationships of Cohabiting Lesbian and Heterosexual Couples: A Comparison." *Psychology of Women Quarterly* 10: 234–239.

Smith, Barbara and Beverly Smith. 1983. "Across the Kitchen Table: A Sister to Sister Dialogue," in *This Bridge Called My Back: Writings by Radical Women of Color*, eds. Cherrié Moraga and Gloria Anzaldúa. New York: Kitchen Table Women of Color Press, pp. 113–127.

4

Sexual Harassment from the Perspective of Asian-American Women

EDITH WEN-CHU CHEN

A lot of times when I am around men, especially those who are not Pilipino, I am very self-conscious of how I might appear to them. It's not that I fuss over my looks or feel I should alter them in any way. I am concerned by how they perceive me as a Pilipina. I can't help but feel as if I'm being seen as exotic. And with exotic, the idea of being erotic. I am very aware that I am seen as foreign in this country, despite the fact that I was born and raised here. I am seen as an Asian girl as opposed to being seen as American. I am always afraid of being solicited like my mom and aunt when they were coming home from a movie.... And it is upsetting to think that so much can be determined about me without my having to say anything.

—Audrey de Jesus, Pilipina female college student, written for a class assignment for the class, Women of Color in the U.S., Winter 1996

The above quote highlights how the sexual harassment experiences of Asian-American women, like other women of color, are embedded within a complex and interconnected system of gender and racial subordination. Despite the growing contributions to the literature on sexual harassment, most of the feminist and social science scholarship on sexual harassment has ignored the role of race and the qualitatively different experiences of women of color (for further discussion, see Collins 1990; Crenshaw 1992; hooks 1984, 1995). This is partly because sexual harassment has been conceptualized solely as a problem resulting from gender hierarchies, with little attention to how racial hierarchies interact simultaneously with gender systems.

As the result of framing sexual harassment mainly in terms of gender relations, most of the studies concerning sexual harassment have focused on the experiences of white women. The little attention given to the sexual harassment experiences of women of color has focused on African-American women (Bell 1992; Collins 1990; Crenshaw 1992; hooks 1995). While Asian-American women, as women of color, share similar experiences with African-American women, they nevertheless also have distinct experiences. As a modest contribution to the growing social science research on women of color as well as on Asian-Americans, this chapter is a preliminary examination into how Asian-American women experience sexual harassment. In the next section, I will review some of the literature concerning Asian-American women and sexual violence. Then I will present some perspectives of Asian-American female college students on sexual harassment. As discussed later in the analysis, the respondents of this study suggest that Asian female racial stereotypes, patriarchal cultural traditions, immigrant status, and institutional barriers are just some of the factors that are salient to the sexual harassment experiences of Asian-American women.

Asian-American Women and Sexual Violence

Asian-American women share a similar position with African-American women and other women of color, all being subordinate members of a racial and gender hierarchy. Like other women of color, Asian-American women have often been stereotyped by the mass media, literature, popular accounts, and educational and religious institutions as sexually available, legitimizing the sexual exploitation and unwanted advances from white men (Mullings 1994). Misrepresentations specific to Asian-American women include prostitutes, geishas, and "good, faithful, uncomplaining, self-effacing, gracious servants, who will do everything and anything to make them [men] feel comfortable and carefree" (Wong 1980; also see Chow 1987 and Jen 1992).

Others have suggested that Asian-American women, particularly those of immigrant and refugee backgrounds, are victims of cultures that subscribe to patriarchal values and practices (Homma-True 1990; Lee 1988; Rimonte 1991). For example, many East Asian societies are still influenced by Confucianism (Fairbank et al. 1973). This philosophy stresses a "rigid hierarchical order of human relations based on age, sex, and inherited social class.... This philosophy was established as an ethical and moral system to govern all social relations in family, community and society" (Rhim 1978, p. 25). Women are supposed to be subordinate to men, and respect and obedience to people of authority are emphasized. Similarly, "marriage by capture" or the kidnapping and raping of a woman are still practices that persist in Southeast Asian and Philippine cultures (Rimonte 1991). Asian "culture" is often used to explain the tolerance by Asian-American women of unwanted sexual advances.

Very little research has been conducted on the particular experiences of Asian-American women concerning sexual harassment. Most of the literature that I have encountered was either anecdotal or dealt with the more severe forms of sexual abuse such as domestic violence, which was largely intraracial. What are the perspectives of Asian-American women on the more mundane, "acceptable," but nevertheless just as serious forms of sexual abuse, such as sexual harassment? Do Asian-American women believe their experiences to be unique or similar to those of white women?

Methods

The data for this chapter come from questionnaires that were given to two undergraduate Introductory Sociology classes and one undergraduate Asian-American Studies History class at the University of California at Los Angeles during the winter quarter of 1992. Originally, 298 surveys were collected from these three classes. For this chapter, I include only the data from Asian-American women respondents, who include 61 Asian-American women of Chinese, Japanese, Korean, Pilipina, South Asian, and Vietnamese ethnicity. Of the 51 questions in the survey, this chapter focuses on the open-ended question: "Do you think that the sexual harassment experiences of Asian-American women are different from Anglo-American women? How?"

The rationale for selecting only Asian-American women respondents for analysis comes from the insights of standpoint epistemologies (see discussion by Chang 1993, pp. 1277–1283). Standpoint epistemologies critique paradigms and theories that claim to be "objective," "neutral," or "universal," but which are often based upon a white male reality. In contrast to this so-called "objectivist approach," standpoint epistemologies privilege the perspectives of subordinated groups by claiming that they have "access to understanding about oppression that others cannot have" (Bartlett 1990, p. 872). Patricia Hill Collins defines a black women's standpoint as "those experiences and ideas shared by African-American women that provide a unique angle of vision on self, community, and society" (Collins 1990, p. 22). While Asian-American women share with African-American women racial and gender subordination, it is important to identify and understand the commonalities as well as the qualitative differences that Asian-American women share with them, other women of color, and white women. As legal scholar Robert Chang notes, "Asian-Americans suffer as Asian-Americans and not just generically as persons of color" (Chang 1993, p. 1247). Hence this chapter privileges the voices of Asian-American women as a way of understanding the oppression that is particular to Asian-American women.

Data and Analysis

Most Asian-American women (69 percent, n = 42) in this study stated that they thought that Asian-American women did experience sexual harassment differently from Anglo-American women, while eight (13 percent) of the respondents stated a "maybe" to the question. Eleven (18 percent) of the respondents stated that they did not think that the sexual harassment experiences of Asian-American women differed from Anglo-American women. It should be noted that even amongst those who noted the aspects of Asian-American women's experiences that differed from white American women's, a few were also quick to point out the commonality of sexual harassment that all women face.

Although the Asian-American women in the survey mentioned a variety of ways in which their experiences of sexual harassment would differ from those of white women, the two most common reasons were stereotypes and cultural traditions.

Stereotypes

The most common response (52 percent, n = 32) was that Asian-American women's experiences differed from white Americans' in the way they are (mis)perceived by the harasser. According to the respondents, men, especially non-Asian-Americans, commonly view Asian-American women as "exotic," "submissive," "passive," "docile," "man-serving," and "easy prey." As one Asian-American woman put it:

> Yes, I think Asian women are stereotypically seen as the passive "I'll do any-
> thing you ask" kind of person. A few men have assumed that just because I
> am Asian that I would treat them like a god of some kind and give them
> massages and bring them drinks. Sexual pressures are also higher because
> Asian women tend to be seen as doing anything to get higher or maybe even
> "well I have to obey my boss" kind of thing. (Third-generation Japanese-
> American woman)

As the respondent below noted, however, it is important to link the ideas and actions of individual men to the institutions that perpetuate racial and sexist imagery of Asian-American women. The history of U.S. military dominance and occupation in Asian countries such as Japan, Vietnam, Korea, and the Philippines has also often meant the sexual domination over Asian women in desperate economic conditions (Jen 1992; Lai 1988). Perpetuated by the media, the notions of Asian women as subservient and "a special breed of sexual creatures" become transplanted to the United States and are imposed upon Asian and Asian-American women alike. Although recently there have been attempts to present more balanced depictions of Asian-American women in television, film, and popular magazines, racist and sexist images continue to be recycled.[1] Despite the media fiction, these damaging images have a real impact on Asian-American women, as told by the respondent below:

> I think Asian-American women are much more likely to be harassed than
> Anglo-American women because of poor images presented to the general
> public. While today's Anglo-American women can be viewed as hard-work-
> ing, tough, persistent, career-minded etc., Asian-American women are still
> seen today as sex toys, cute, subservient, man-serving. Personally, I find that
> non-Asian males (Blacks and whites especially) are most likely to harass
> Asian-American women because they view Asian-American women as very
> sexual beings who are suppose to be good in bed and known for being good

at sex. I think the prostitute image is still alive and the exotic ideal pervades men's minds. I also think that men view Asian-American women as easier to command in every way. (Second-generation Chinese-American woman)

Unfortunately, the exotic sexual prostitute image of Asian-American women remains salient. Several respondents reported personal experiences with this imposed image. The same woman recounts:

I was standing at a bus stop and was approached by a teenage white boy and a teenage Black boy. The Black boy tended to follow the white boy's lead, which was to say things like, "I want to lick your pussy" and "I could rape you right now," not to mention "you Orientals are all prostitutes—good at sex." (Second-generation Chinese-American woman)

Because the respondents perceive that men view Asian-American women differently from Anglo-American women, many suggest that Asian-American women would be sexually harassed more frequently.

These prevailing racial stereotypes affected the partners some Asian-American women chose in their dating relationships. For example, one Asian-American woman stated that because of the assumptions white men often made about her, she preferred to date Asian-American men. She expresses her annoyance with some white men below:

Yes, especially from the Anglo-American men. A few times I've experienced this, I find them forward in asking for dates, sitting at the same table with me, rudely trying to get my attention. I usually don't want to make a scene and they automatically connote this to my being interested. It's annoying. Also, I had a friend who was stopped on a street corner in Westwood during her break from work at an accounting office. In not so many words, he asked if she were a hooker. Because of this, I much rather have relationships with Asian men. (Second generation Chinese-American woman)

The woman above was very cognizant of these stereotypes, which led her to choose Asian-American men as dating partners. It should be noted that many of the respondents for this survey are drawn from an Asian-American History class, in which issues of race and racism are being brought to the attention of students. Also, students who take ethnic studies courses may have a heightened awareness of racism to begin with.

It is unclear however, if dating Asian-American men will protect Asian-American women from intraracial sexual harassment. While dating Asian-American men may offer some protection from anti-Asian racism, it does not necessarily protect Asian-American women from sexism. Giuffre and Williams (1994), in their excellent study on restaurant workers' definitions of sexual harassment, suggest that since heterosexual, racially homogamous relationships are privileged in our society, unwanted sexual advances from men of the same race may not be seen as sexual harassment, but part of acceptable, normal, and everyday behavior. In addition, as other women of color have noted, women of color may be hesitant to call our brothers on sexual harassment since we, living in a society that can be hostile to people of color, often want and need their support.

Cultural Traditions

While the most common way that Asian-Americans perceive their experiences to be different from Anglo-American women is in the way men view them, 16 percent (n = 10) of the respondents mentioned that Asian-American women might handle sexual harassment differently from their Anglo-American counterparts. Some respondents suggested that rather than being a stereotype, Asian-American women are a product of a culture that promotes women to be accommodating and passive. As one Asian-American woman states:

> The most fundamental difference I think results from the traditional belief of Asian females who tend not to make trouble—they'll prefer to accept the harassment then. (1.5-generation Chinese-American woman)

Similarly, another woman states that older generations of Asian-American and immigrant women may be more likely to accept dominating male behaviors:

> I think that Asian-American women are traditionally more submissive and passive—my grandparents live with me and though I respect my grandmother immensely, she puts up with a lot from my grandfather and never

says a word. When he speaks disrespectful to her and commands her to do things, she calmly takes it while I never do. Similarly, I think Asian women who are more traditional and fit the stereotypical mold would be more quiet and less inclined to report incidents of sexual harassment as well as submit to such pressures. I think it would be hard for women of any race to report such incidences, especially if the perpetrator is one who is highly respected, but I think it would be harder still for Asian women because of their backgrounds and cultural roles. (Second-generation Korean-American woman)

While it is important to identify the cultural traditions that harm Asian-American women, it is also important to recognize the context in which these traditions are maintained. Given the acceptability and commonplace of gendered racism against Asian-American women,[2] Asian-American women may hesitate to fight sexual harassment. For example, some of the respondents suggest that institutional barriers may limit Asian-American women from speaking out against sexual harassment. As one Asian-American woman notes:

I also feel Asian-American women may not publicize the experience of being sexually harassed because they feel inferior against the white system. (1.5-generation Korean-American woman)

Hence, being a minority in a white and male-dominated system can make it difficult for Asian-American women to report sexual harassment, whether or not they possess these cultural values.

Other responses include that Asian-American women are newcomers to this country and therefore do not know about the laws against harassment. Another person suggests that since Asian-American women are relegated to less prestigious jobs, which are more prone to sexual harassment, they may be sexually harassed more often than Anglo-American females. There were also those who did not see Asian-American women's experiences of sexual harassment differing from white American women's. Rather, the respondents attribute individual types of personalities and situations that lead certain women to be harassed more than others.

Conclusion and Discussion

Most of academic and popular discourse has conceptualized sexual harassment as an outcome of gender inequality. Yet the preliminary examination of Asian-American women's experiences tell a more complicated story. Racial inequality is as much a dimension of the sexual harassment experiences of Asian-American women as is gender inequality. White and non-Asian men, holding stereotyped notions of Asian-American women, may subject Asian-American women to more extreme sexist attitudes and behaviors, which the men would not expect from their white or non-Asian counterparts. Furthermore, a society that privileges whites, men, and English speakers may make it difficult for Asian-American women to fight against any type of sexual harassment, whether it be intra- or interracial.

In addition, these findings have several implications for the relationships between racism, "culture," and sexism. While the operation of sexual-racial stereotypes about Asian-American women was the most common perception by Asian-American women of factors that distinguish their experiences from those of white American women, an Asian patriarchal culture that tolerates these behaviors was also mentioned by the respondents. Yet we must critically examine the relationship between the sexism within the Asian-American community and the racism and sexism of the larger society. Similarly, Chicana feminist Emma Perez criticizes whites who blame "machismo" for the oppression of Chicana women:

> Many Anglos, particularly white feminists, insist that the men of our culture created machismo and they conveniently forget that the men of their race make the rules. This leads to problematic Chicana discourse within feminist constructs. When white feminists ardently insist upon discussing machismo, they impose phallocentric discourse. By "centering" and "focusing" on the penis, they deflect from their racism. This evasion is both racist and heterosexist. (Perez 1991, p. 163)

As many women of color have noted, future studies dealing with gender inequality must also actively deal with racial inequality. This means considering not only how race shapes the gender inequalities that women of color face, but also how whiteness shapes how white women experience sexism (for example, see Frankenberg 1993; Giuffre and Williams 1994). Furthermore, as stated by Asian-American scholars and activists, we must reconceptualize racial inequality beyond black/white paradigms so that discussion of racism also includes issues relating to immigrant status and being a cultural minority (Chang 1993; Hune 1995; Sethi 1994).

Acknowledgments

This research was completed with support from the Graduate Affirmative Affairs Office of the University of California at Los Angeles, the American Sociological Association Minority Affairs Program, and the National Institute of Mental Health. Special thanks to Barbara Zsembik, Joe Feagin, and Carol Ronai for helping me rethink and rework my master's paper. Also much appreciation and gratitude to Gilda Ochoa, my friend and colleague, and Eunice Chen, my sister, who took the time to read, discuss, and listen to several versions of this paper.

Notes

1. For an excellent documentary illustrating the depiction of Asian and Asian-American women in American cinema, see Deborah Gee's 1988 video *Slaying the Dragon*.
2. Examples of U.S. institutionalized gendered racism against Asian and Asian-American women include the promotion of sex tours in Asia, the Asian mail order business, and the continuing damaging images of Asian and Asian-American women in the media, as mentioned previously. Margaretta Lin and Cheng Imm Tan have also written about how many battered women's shelters have turned away Asian-Pacific-American women due to language barriers or out of sheer racism (Lin and Tan 1994).

References

Bartlett, Katharine. 1990. "Feminist Legal Methods." *Harvard Law Review* 103 (4): 829-888.

Bell, Ella Louise. 1992. "Myths, Stereotypes, and Realities of Black Women: A Personal Reflection." *The Journal of Applied Behavioral Science* 28 (September): 363–376.

Chang, R.S. 1993. "Toward an Asian-American Legal Scholarship: Critical

Race Theory, Post-Structuralism, and Narrative Space." *California Law Review* 81 (October): 1241–1322.

Chow, Esther Ngan-Ling. 1987. "The Development of Feminist Consciousness Among Asian-American Women." *Gender and Society* 1 (3): 284–299.

Collins, Patricia Hill. 1990. *Black Feminist Thought: Knowledge, Consciousness, and the Politics of Empowerment.* Cambridge, MA: Unwin Hyman, Inc.

Crenshaw, Kimberlé. 1992. "Whose Story Is It Anyway? Feminist and Antiracist Appropriations of Anita Hill," in *Race-ing Justice, En-gendering Power: Essays on Anita Hill, Clarence Thomas, and the Construction of Social Reality*, ed. Toni Morrison. New York: Pantheon Books.

Fairbank, J.K., E.O. Reischauser, and A.M. Craig. 1973. *East Asia: Traditions and Transformation.* Boston: Houghton Mifflin Company.

Frankenberg, Ruth. 1993. *White Women, Race Matters: The Social Construction of Whiteness.* Minneapolis: University of Minnesota Press.

Giuffre, Patti A. and Christine L. Williams. 1994. "Boundary Lines: Labeling Sexual Harassment in Restaurants." *Gender & Society* 8 (September): 378–401.

Homma-True, Reiko. 1990. "Psychotherapeutic Issues with Asian-American Women." *Sex Roles* 22 (7/8).

hooks, bell. 1984. "Black Women: Shaping Feminist Theory," in *Margin to Center.* Boston: South End Press.

———. 1995. "Seduced by Violence No More," in *Debating Sexual Correctness: Pornography, Sexual Harassment, Date Rape and the Politics of Sexual Equality*, ed. Adele M. Stan. New York: Delta.

Hune, Shirley. 1995. "Rethinking Race: Paradigms and Policy Formation." *Amerasia Journal* 21 (1 & 2): 29–40.

Jen, Andrea M. 1992. "Empress, Geisha, and the Asian-American Woman," *Face* (November/December): 18–19, 86–90.

Lai, Tracy. 1988. "Asian-American Women: Not for Sale," in *Changing Our Power: An Introduction to Women's Studies*, eds. Jo Whitehorse Cochran, Donna Langston, and Carolyn Woodward. Dubuque, IA: Kendau-Hunt.

Lee, Inn Sook. 1988. "Korean-American Women's Experience: A Study in the Cultural and Feminist Identity Formation Process." Ed.D. dissertation. Columbia University Teachers College, 1988.

Lin, Margaretta Wan Ling and Cheng Imm Tan. 1994. "Holding Up More Than Half the Heavens: Domestic Violence in Our Communities, A Call for Justice," in *The State of Asian America: Activism and Resistance in the*

1990s, ed. Karin Aguilar-San Juan. Boston: South End Press.

Mullings, Leith. 1994. "Images, Ideology, and Women of Color," in *Women of Color in U.S. Society*, eds. Maxine Baca Zinn and Bonnie Thornton Dill. Philadelphia: Temple University Press.

Perez, Emma. 1991. "Sexuality and Discourse: Notes from a Chicana Survivor," in *Chicana Lesbians, The Girls Our Mothers Warned Us About*, ed. Carla Trujillo. Berkeley: Third Women.

Rhim, Soon Man. 1978. "The Status of Women in Traditional Korean Society," in *Korean Women: In a Struggle for Humanization*, eds. Harold Hakwon Sunoo and Dong Soo Kim. Memphis, TN: The Association of Korean Christian Scholars of North America, Inc.

Rimonte, Nilda. 1991. "A Question of Culture: Cultural Approval of Violence Against Women in the Pacific-Asian Community and the Cultural Defense." *Stanford Law Review* 43: 1311–1322.

Sethi, Rita Chaudhry. 1994. "Smells Like Racism: A Plan for Mobilizing Against Anti-Asian Bias," in *The State of Asian America: Activism and Resistance in the 1990s*, ed. Karin Aguilar-San Juan. Boston: South End Press.

Wong, G. 1980. "Impediments to Asian-Pacific American Women Organizing," in U.S. Department of Education, Office of Educational Research and Improvement, National Institute of Education, *Conference on the Educational and Occupational Needs of Asian-Pacific-American Women*, August 24 and 25, 1976. Washington, DC: GPO, October 1980, p. 93.

5

Tuna Memos and Pissing Contests

Doing Gender and Male Dominance
on the Internet

KIMBERLY J. COOK AND PHOEBE M. STAMBAUGH

Introduction

With the recent revolution in computer and communication technologies, the Internet is emerging as an important social sphere, where the needs, interests, and actions of a few men structure the social life there. Like many other social arenas, the Internet is heavily populated by men; yet women are increasingly entering the world of cyberspace and their presence is transforming this masculine domain. Despite the fact that most women in the United States do not have access to the Internet (Smith and Balka 1988; Kramarae and Taylor 1993), for those who work in government offices, educational settings, and scientific laboratories, entering the Internet is now an everyday activity. Electronic messaging has become another tool for connecting with other women (Smith and Balka 1988). Recognizing the potential of electronic mail, women's groups are establishing networks of their own, making the Internet a potentially potent site of resistance to male domination in various other social settings (Smith and Balka 1988).

In spite of its potential, women on the Internet encounter many of the same challenges typically faced when pioneering within other male-dominated settings. For instance, institutions supporting access to the Internet report a growing number of complaints about incidents of unwanted sexual advances, the presence of violent pornography, and sexual harassment (Peterson 1994). In addition, women who participate in male-dominated discussion lists and chat lines find the attitudinal climates "chilly" and occasionally hostile to women (Hall and Sandler 1982; Sandler, Silverberg, and Hall 1996; Truong 1993). As we approach the twenty-first century, the presence of women and women-centered communities on the Internet promises to transform the politics of gender in both virtual and actual social arenas.

In this chapter we focus on the problem of male dominance on the Internet. Like Dorothy Smith (1977), we define male dominance as situations where the presence of men overshadows the presence of women in ways that denigrate, dismiss, or define our interests, knowledge, and lived experiences. According to Smith, the reproduction of male dominance is accomplished through circles of men,

> whose writing and talk has been significant to one another [and] extends back in time as far as our records reach. What men were doing has been relevant to men, was written by men, about men for men. Men listened and listen to what one another say. A tradition is formed, traditions form, in a discourse with the past within the present. (1977, p. 137)

As we will discuss, "doing gender" (West and Zimmerman 1987) and the reproduction of male dominance in masculine culture are accomplished in much the same way on the Internet as in conventional reality. In this electronic setting, we observe how everyday interactions on an electronic mail discussion list called "SASH-L" (Sociologists Against Sexual Harassment) reproduce male dominance, despite resistance to it.

Gender is a salient aspect of social life on the Internet. Until recently, role theory conceptualized gender as something belonging to or assigned to someone, a product of expectation or outcome of interaction (Chodorow 1978). Challenging that view, "doing gender" theorists perceive gender as an ongoing activity or accomplishment (Martin and Jurik 1996; Messerschmidt 1993, 1994, 1995a, 1995b; West and Zimmerman 1987).[1] From this view, interaction does not express "natural" differences between men and women, but constructs them (West and Zimmerman 1987). West and Zimmerman state that "gender is not a set of traits, nor a variable, nor a role, but the product of social doings of some sort" (1987, p. 129). Furthermore, in our culture, rituals of dominance and deference are used to "do gender" and distinguish men from women (Messerschmidt 1993). Activities that privilege men, their ideas, or their experiences, or those that silence women's voices, suppress our knowledge, or ignore our lived experiences reproduce male domination (Smith 1977). Robert Connell (1987) and others (Messerschmidt 1993, 1994, 1995, forthcoming) theorize that women and men accomplish gender based on culturally supported or challenged ideals of masculinity and femininity. Connell defines hegemonic masculinity as the dominant ideal of a man who is strong and independent, self-sufficient, and heterosexual, which is "constructed in relation to women and subordinated masculinities" (1987, p. 186). Emphasized femininity is defined as the dominant ideal woman who is social rather than technologically proficient, frail and deferential to men, nurturing and supportive in many social settings, including the office and the home (Connell 1987, p. 187).

Messerschmidt (1994, 1995b) extends this examination to discuss "opposition" masculinities and femininities, where men and women do gender differently by challenging the dominant cultural ideals of gender. The presence of a women's movement and the advent of a men's movement have sparked a significant effort to challenge these hegemonic definitions of masculinity and emphasized femininity (Connell 1987; Messerschmidt 1993), which therefore challenges the consequent male domination. Some feminists point to the Internet as a particularly potent site of resistance, an arena where male domination can be successfully challenged and transformed (Smith and Balka 1988). In fact, some futurists suggest that in cyberspace, conventional ideals of gender as well as traditional rituals of dominance will soon become immaterial—if not obsolete (Pavela 1994).

Employing this "doing gender" approach, we posit that the advent of electronic messaging does not make gender irrelevant on the Internet but, rather, expands the resources that men and women draw upon to accomplish gender, confirming that gender and sex categories are *omnirelevant* (West and Zimmerman 1987). As in any other social setting, most renegotiate masculinity and femininity on the Internet. Although, some do not indicate a category, by using gender-neutral surnames, making sex categories either nonexistent or easily masked; "netizens" often write as men and women, and are accountable, through electronic discourse, to their self-identified sex categories (West and

Zimmerman 1987). This paper expands these theories by applying the concepts to electronic communication rather than conventional face-to-face interaction. We examine two situations—where masculinity and femininity are constructed in an electronic environment and where male domination is reproduced and resisted—as resources for doing gender. We conclude with a look to the future by examining the promise of an Internet *for* women (Smith 1977).

In the following section, we begin our analysis by briefly describing what activities are possible on the Internet, how social interaction occurs there, and how gender, male domination, and resistance are accomplished in this electronic forum.

The Internet as a Social Arena

In its brief history, the "Net" has been analogized to telephone, mail, and even highway systems. While communication researchers and legal theorists conceptualize the Internet as a conduit for communication (Kramarae and Kramer 1995), those who socialize there commonly talk about it as a place (cyberspace), a specific location to which they are transported daily via modem (Wood 1994).

Most enter this social setting from their home or office, where the primary mode of interaction is electronic mail or "e-mail." As of 1995, about 35 million people in the U.S. use e-mail (Peyser and Rhodes 1995) and if subscription trends continue, by the year 2000 several hundred million people worldwide will have electronic mail accounts (Kramarae and Kramer 1995). Electronic mail discussion lists network people with shared interests. Discussants make comments about a topic, which are then mailed by a "listserv" to all the other subscribers. Replies to their comments are then distributed in a like manner.

As a frontier, the Net invites exploration by the technologically curious, computer thrill seekers, as well as those simply inept in conventional social encounters. As a result, many behaviors considered socially unacceptable or even defined as illegal in conventional social spheres are allowed to flourish in this electronic environment (Dibbell 1994; Levy 1995; Wood 1994). In the virtual world, traditional mechanisms of informal social control often fail to regulate social behavior. Moreover, many legal principles and practices used in conventional settings do not transfer to virtual society; thus liability remains a slippery slope

(Cosentino 1994; Kramarae and Kramer 1995; Peterson 1994). With little institutionalized recourse, internetters must manage interpersonal conflict on their own.

Male Domination on the Internet

The Net is largely a masculine domain. The Net itself—the hardware and software that comprise it—is a product of the lived experiences and imaginations of computer programmers and software engineers—occupations overwhelmingly populated by men (Kramarae and Kramer 1995). Thus a few elite men have structured what activities are possible as well as what actually occurs on the Internet. Consequently, the majority of those who subscribe to Internet services are men (Kramarae and Kramer 1995), and a recent Prodigy survey describes the typical on-line subscriber as male, professional, married with children, and with an above-average income (Neubarth 1995). The Internet marketplace caters to the needs of those who can afford the personal computers and software to socialize on the Net, and significantly more men than women have the education and resources to do so (Balka 1993).

However, there are some Internet locations that are gender-balanced, and some places cater specifically to the needs and interests of women. Studies of discussion list behavior find that even when men are not in the majority, male domination occurs (see, for example, the participant observation studies of Susan Herring 1993, 1994, and of Herring, Johnson, and DiBendedetto 1992). Analysis of mixed-gender discussions find that men pose more new topics and post more and longer messages than women. For example, on a discussion list where women were in the majority as subscribers, a single man dominated the discussion by posting 146 of the 353 messages that comprised one week's discussion (Balka 1993). Observations of another discussion group found that while the subscription list was gender-balanced, only 2 percent of the women, compared with 19 percent of the men, actively participated in discussion (Herring 1993).

Male domination on the Internet is not achieved simply by the numbers of men relative to women who participate in virtual society, but by gendered styles of communication that accomplish hegemonic masculinity and emphasized femininity, which in turn facilitate male dominance. In both conventional and electronic society, some men signal their masculinity and therefore define themselves as men by engaging in activities that objectify, demean, and harass women (Messerschmidt 1993). As a result, on the Internet women are discovering many of the same problems of exclusion, objectification, and dehumanization (Kramarae and Taylor 1993; Truong 1993) that occur in conventional society. Those pioneering in this masculine domain report enclaves where anger toward women is openly expressed and misogynist views celebrated. On some bulletin boards and discussion lists, obscene jokes, antiwoman banter, and antifeminist rhetoric define the space as "male-only," discouraging women from settling in, much less fully participating. On the other hand, the Internet also provides a setting where men can express "profeminist" perspectives.

Some women take to the Internet repertoires of resistance strategies developed through their lived experiences socializing in other hostile climates. As in real settings, in virtual reality some women handle male domination with silence, confrontation, exit, and complaint (Gruber 1989). For example, in discussion groups where women or their ideas are treated with hostility or suspicion, women "lurk" in silence, watching the discussions without public comment. Also, when signing on to chat lines where men have been known to "hit on" women, some women mystify their gender by signing their messages with gender neutral or masculine nicknames (Truong 1993). According to West and Zimmerman, "any occasion, conflicted or not, offers the resources for doing gender" (1987, p. 140). Despite the capability to disguise one's gender, sex categories are assigned to people who are still accountable for gender under that assignment.

Many women also use electronic messaging to confront acts of male domination. However, doing so risks being "flamed" (Cosentino 1994). A flame is a widely distributed message on an electronic network that serves as a personal attack on someone within that community. Highly emotional, a flaming message serves to shame, humiliate, or otherwise poke fun at another person. Flames typically use sarcasm or ridicule for personal insult, which invite more flames; this results in "flame wars." While flames have been analogized to real world hazing (Cosentino 1994), flame wars are like school yard tussles, or barroom brawls. Flames towards those who confront sexist or harassing behavior—and especially when those retorts are flagrantly sexualized—are particularly intimidating to women when they are in a minority. The effect extends beyond the flame's target, serving notice to those who are lurking that challenges will be met with verbal warfare. Some women identify sites where flames are common, label them "dangerous," and then avoid them. Once a place on the Internet becomes a hostile climate, some women simply "vote with their feet," signing off or unsubscribing from that service. Finally, women are complaining to their discussion list moderators and electronic mail postmasters in increasing numbers, demanding institutional intervention (Peterson 1994).

Even though the Internet is a masculine domain, feminists and women's groups are turning to electronic messaging as a means to resist male domination in other social arenas (Herring, Johnson, and DiBendedetto 1992). On the Net, women can now easily find and participate in an array of concerted efforts to resist sexism and harassment in their homes, schools, or places of work. These woman-centered spaces create a sense of community among women and facilitate the mobilization of resources among women's groups. These lists share a common goal: to apply the strength of electronic messaging to empower women and to develop arenas where women's voices are heard, ideas given merit, and lived experiences privileged.

SASH-L is one such women-centered community. It is an electronic mail discussion list established by women where men and women collaborate in a variety of ways to identify and respond to sexual harassment in their everyday lives. In the analysis that follows, we postulate that some men accomplish hegemonic masculinity via electronic interaction, and thus dominance is established. We also note that some women resist those efforts, accomplishing "opposition" femininity. However, many women do gender through silence, resignation, or flight from hostile climates, thereby accomplishing emphasized femininity.

Data Collection Methods and Analysis

Our analysis draws upon both our direct observations as participants on the SASH-L discussion list and our interpretation of comments made by others in this social setting. As charter subscribers of SASH-L, we have observed the list's growth and development since its establishment in November of 1992. In addition, our "insider" roles as organization cofounder (Cook) and list moderator (Stambaugh) afforded us access to various face-to-face conversations and electronic messages about SASH-L to which other SASH-L subscribers were not privy. In addition to our firsthand observations, we rely on recorded observations from two other sources—the discussion list's public archives and the list moderator's private logs. Each documents three years of discussion and social interaction on SASH-L. We examined these logs with a particular interest in discovering and analyzing points of gendered conflict and significant change. After reading the log files for the three years of SASH-L's existence, we identified two discussions that had significant consequences for the focus of the list. Before proceeding with a detailed discussion of these two events, we contextualize them with a brief description of the SASH-L environment and the character of that community, and explain how discussion occurs there.

The SASH-L Discussion List

In November of 1992, the electronic mail discussion list called "SASH-L" or "Sociologists Against Sexual Harassment" was established as a forum for "developing meaningful responses to the sexual harassment problem" (SASH Third Annual Conference Program, 1994). The discussion list was a product of a daylong workshop on the particular problem of sexual harassment in the academy and in the discipline of sociology. Held in conjunction with the Society for the Study of Social Problems' annual meeting, SASH was supported with donations from the Society for the Study of Social Problems, some sections of the American Sociological Association, the Women and Crime division of the American Society of Criminology, and several anonymous individuals.

The first annual program encompassed a range of perspectives on the problem, and included the presentations of students, faculty, university administrators, attorneys, and representatives from various state and local agencies. At the workshop's conclusion, those in attendance established an electronic mail distribution file and used it to continue the discussion on the Internet. Since then, SASH-L's list of subscribers has grown, expanding well beyond the original conference organizers and participants to include many outside the academic community. Currently, about three hundred people from fourteen different countries subscribe to SASH-L. Discussions include commentary from lawyers, women's studies scholars, public health officials, and affirmative action officers—to name only a few of the many professional groups represented there. The gender composition of the subscription list is 71 percent women, 19 percent men, and 10 percent gender-neutral or concealed. Originally moderated by one woman, SASH-L is now co-moderated by one woman and one man.

In the first three years (1992 to 1995) of SASH-L's existence, relations on the list moved through various stages. Initially, men and women interacted without discernible conflict, sharing specialized knowledge or lived experience and personal stories of harassment, and seeking advice about how to make complaints. Those with personal and professional experience provided expertise to other subscribers about legal issues. In short, SASH-L was a supportive and collegial woman-centered environment. On one occasion, the topic of discussion was the SASH-L environment itself. Those who subscribed to other lists noted how uncommonly harmonious the list's atmosphere was, and some declared it a haven from other virtual arenas where protracted debates were common and sustained "gender wars" occurred.

The harmony and cooperation ended when two conflictual discussions occurred and were characterized by gendered dynamics of dominance and opposition in each. The first involved an incident the SASH-L subscribers dubbed the "the infamous tuna memo." The second situation, described as a "pissing contest," began as a discussion about "asymmetrical" or "consensual" relationships but escalated into a debate among a few men who dominated the arena. The following two sections describe the events surrounding these discussions with a particular eye to how men and women accomplish gender electronically.

The Tuna Memo

The "tuna memo" sparked the first real debate on the SASH-L discussion list. That discussion brought to the surface divisions within the community that had never before been apparent. About sixteen months after SASH-L's debut, a controversy erupted on another discussion list. The discussion involved an inflammatory message in which a man complained about having to attend a sexual harassment workshop. A subscriber to both discussion lists forwarded the controversial memo to SASH-L and opened a discussion about it there. The writer stated:

Here at [my university] they are about to treat us to another spate of seminars on sexual harassment. I plan to go because I always enjoy a good fight. The radical feminists will be there passing off their anger and ideology as either legal norms or ought-to-be. The white males will be there smug in their power, wondering what the women are bellyaching about.... If the women want to be treated as equals, whether they learn to enjoy the kind of teen-age pubescent humor that we unevolved males enjoy, they at least have to realize that our deviance from their norm is no more socially debilitating than is their endless coffee-break clatching about who's pregnant, who's engaged, and ... whose child performed what cute (or intolerable) act the other day.... All of this set my wife and me to thinking about jokes. Remember all those really awful, tasteless, disgusting jokes that men tell about women, their body parts, their times of the month, their scent on occasion—something about tuna fish—you know the kind! What is the female equivalent of this form of sexist humor? As much male-bashing as is going on these days, surely there is a body of "female mirth" over how disgusting men are, their body parts, their scent on occasion, etc. Where do I look in the library, the folklore collection, or elsewhere, to satisfy this bit of curiosity?

Clearly this messenger was "doing gender" by identifying himself as a heterosexual male, who subordinates women's lack of "ribaldry" to men's ability to enjoy "teen-age pubescent humor." For some women, the message evoked a powerfully visceral reaction. After reading it, one woman wrote "I am SHOCKED. I thought I was pretty seasoned to hostility but this really shakes me. Anybody [on this list] feel that way?" Replies described the memo as "dangerous," "hostile," and "intimidating."

Having defined the situation as serious, the discussion turned toward developing a meaningful course of action. A range of proposals were discussed, including: (1) informing the author's affirmative action officer; (2) making a complaint about the author's behavior to his departmental chair; (3) contacting his university's president and letting him know how his school is being represented; (4) sending letters of support and advice to the women in his department; and (5) direct confrontation of the jokester himself.

At this juncture, the discussion became a debate in which men and women disagreed about the seriousness of the situation and what should be done about it. Gender differences were not in whether or not they thought the memo was inappropriate but, rather, in how they experienced it. For example, while the women who commented on the memo described it as an assault, the men who responded saw the memo as "sexist," "sick," or "just plain stupid." Criticizing the list of proposed action plans as "knee jerk reactions," one man claimed the list was becoming a "lynch mob." Another attempt to minimize the problem trivialized the memo, describing it as only a "freak side show," from a "guy with a pathetically defective attitude." While the vast majority of the list observed the discussion in silence (only 11 percent of subscribers participated), one woman resisted their efforts to reframe the issue. She retorted:

> [The tuna memo] is NOT an annoying side show that merely proves a point. It is dangerous, oppressive action that women (and men) need to fear, be angry at, and to not tolerate.... To do nothing is to say we have no power to change what is harmful to us. I am certain that any response from us will cause him to say "those radical feminists can not take a joke." But if we do not use what little power we have to try to change our world, for what have we opened these lines of communication????

Similarly, using her personal experience of victimization as the source of her authority, a woman who rarely spoke commented:

> As someone who is in an ongoing situation of sexual harassment and who is trying to keep her career from being destroyed while at the same time being slowly killed inside.... I find the tone of this discussion extremely disheartening....

Yet, while the women who discussed the memo shared a sense of outrage (with different meanings), not all agreed on a course of action. For example, one seasoned internetter examined the list of proposed confrontation tactics and, finding them impractical, exclaimed:

> I'm beginning to wonder if I'm the only person in this list who has been through a flame war! You can't go blustering around in a storm of righteousness every time you get offended on the Net....

Learning that his memo had become infamous on SASH-L, the author flamed the entire SASH-L community, posting a racial/ethnic/sexist slur on another network, calling the SASH list a bunch of "Shiite Serbian Sociologist Sex Police." In an attempt to head off a flame war, the moderator intervened, asking subscribers not to use the SASH-L forum to respond. At that point, the "tuna memo" discussion abruptly ended.

Observing this discussion, we see how several women on SASH-L used this electronic forum to share their experiences and, in so doing, identified the "tuna memo" as another act of male dominance experienced in everyday life. Using electronic messaging, they brainstormed ways to make their voices heard and their experiences acknowledged, thus constructing specific types of opposition femininities. Yet differences in their experiences of victimization as well as their socialization to the Internet created disagreement among women about how to respond. Ironically, even in this woman-centered environment, they encountered resistance from some male "allies," who discounted their experiences and discredited their plans for action. Nevertheless, some women pressed on and wrote letters of protest to officials at the university from which the "tuna memo" was originally distributed. Finally, the debate shattered the sense of gender harmony previously enjoyed by the SASH-L community. Subscribers emerged from the disagreement as more of a "serial"—a collective united only by subscription rather than by experience, values, or politics—rather than a community (Young 1994). Through this dialogue, the women on SASH-L accomplished opposition femininity. Some men accomplished hegemonic masculinity in the tuna war, even some of the profeminist men on SASH-L who dismissed the memo as trivial. The writer of the memo and these men could be responding to their masculinity being put "on the line" (Morgan, cited by Messerschmidt 1993, p. 84) by the sexual harassment workshops required by universities and other workplaces.

The Pissing Contest

About one year after the "tuna memo" discussion, a male subscriber expressed concern about the emergence of university policies addressing "consensual sexual relations between professors and their students." The discussion began with an examination of the consequences of romantic liaisons between professors and students. But, as the conversation continued, the controversial issue of institutional policies regulating intimate relationships between junior and senior faculty arose. Soon, points of disagreement were discovered, lines were drawn, and the discussion became a debate. Two days into the argument, some of the women participants abandoned the topic while more men joined in, eventually dominating the discussion. Of the 58 messages posted about asymmetrical relationships, 33 were signed by men. In fact, three men were responsible for more than 72 percent of the volume of mail on this topic.

Most men and women agreed that banning relationships between faculty and students was a reasonable policy but disagreed with a ban on junior/senior faculty relationships. The conversation focused on the issue of personal and sexual autonomy and discussants explored the positive and negative aspects of institutional regulation. Battle lines were drawn around policies banning intimate relationships.

The debate erupted into a flame war when one man characterized those who were in favor of restricting junior/senior faculty intimate relationships as bigots:

> In terms of prior lines of communication, I think that [he] hit a core nerve in this area: hit a basic truth that we generally avoid when he stated that "to suggest that people should seek out those who are similarly positioned smacks of classism and bigotry." To argue that we should seek out only persons similarly positioned so that power differences are obliterated appears to me to be outright bigotry. How could any academic person, any "ethical," any "humanistic" person feel comfortable advocating that in matters relating to intimate relationships—stick to your own kind?

In response, a self-described profeminist man who disapproved of intimate relationships between junior and senior faculty members called those opposing institutional regulation "aging white men" whose "real" agenda was not to protect the rights of women but rather to preserve their sexual access to them. One of the wounded then returned fire, calling him a "sexist," an "ageist," and a "racist," at which point the target claimed he was being unfairly and incorrectly "demonized" by the men who were against regulation.

The flame war turned nasty when an antiregulationist challenged his opponent's sexuality and manhood by claiming he could not act on his sexual feelings when placed alone in a room with an attractive woman. In turn, the target defended his masculinity by saying that keeping his pants zipped only demonstrated how secure in his (hetero)sexuality he was. The profeminist man who supported regulation was being held accountable for his opposition masculinity by those others who were accomplishing hegemonic masculinity by deriding his "subordinate" masculinity (Connell 1987).

After one of the debaters posted three messages in one day—one of them exceeding three single-spaced typed pages—the moderator received five complaints from women, three of whom asked her to intercede. In her plea for intervention, one woman complained about mail volume, noting "that these lengthy exchanges have been between men. . . ."

SASH-L subscribers employed a variety of tactics to reclaim the forum. Two attempted to douse the flames by changing the subject. For example, one man interrupted the debate with a request for "ideas for making effective good posters depicting sexual harassment and appropriate responses to it." A woman who had been compiling a bibliography for the SASH-L archives squeezed in a progress report and asked subscribers to submit citations. Others attempted to negotiate a ceasefire. For example, a profeminist man who had watched the debate in silence informed the brawlers that the list was a "woman's space" and recommended that "men could learn a lot by listening" to women. The moderator attempted to negotiate an agreement to limit the number and length of messages. However, the pissing contest continued unabated.

Rather than compromise, three men continued to filibuster and turned their hostility toward the women on the list, sarcastically chiding them both for speaking up and for being silent. One man insinuated that harmony on a discussion list and complaints about adversity were odd:

> I really don't mind staying away when I am not wanted but am I really the only one who is surprised and amused by the preceding message? Is it that difficult for sociologists to "digest" a three screen message? . . . Don't the

members of this group enjoy the world of debate? Isn't difference of opinion more satisfying and in the end more productive than intellectual solidarity?

Another male flamethrower attempted to bait those who watched in silence:

> Guess what, I am bewildered too. A few SASH members complain and then there is silence. I have absolutely no idea what the preponderance of members think; and not until they give us their opinion will you and I know.

One woman who rarely contributed justified her silence by describing how the flames affected her sense of safety and well-being. She explained:

> I must admit, my defensiveness has been triggered by some of the posts and I think "ouch!"—why would I want to add anything to the discussion as I am just going to get hurt—that happens enough elsewhere. . . .

The majority of the women on SASH-L were silent through this battle, and as such were "doing gender" that reinforced emphasized femininity. A few of the women who spoke out against both the content and tone of the debate were "doing gender" that challenged both hegemonic masculinity and emphasized femininity. Another woman argued that while debate and contention were common on other lists, on SASH-L "we do not have to do what the people on other lists do." Finally, a third woman angrily compared the debate to a "pissing contest," a competition of insults where the winner is the one who talks louder and longer than the rest.

Acting upon women's complaints, the moderator intervened a second time and in private suggested that the antiregulationists set up their own discussion list dedicated to this issue. Following her advice, the three men capitulated and formed their own discussion list, and for two months the "asymmetrical relationship" debate lay dormant.

The flames were rekindled however, when a SASH-L subscriber offered the newly formed discussion list's mission statement for discussion. The pissing contest began again as one man accused another of "cranking up the old propaganda machine." He in turn sarcastically accused the other of being "patriarchal" in his analogies. As the personal epithets and barbs once again began to fill the electronic mailboxes of the list's subscribers, many responded by "voting with their feet." For example, in one week alone the moderator received an unprecedented 23 requests from subscribers asking for her assistance in signing off the list. In an effort to stop the exodus and prevent future flame wars, the moderator directly confronted the men, requesting them to take their exchange off SASH-L, and revised the focus statement of SASH-L to prohibit future debates.

The "pissing contest" discussion illustrates how the problem of male domination can emerge even in a "woman-space" like SASH-L. In spite of numerous interventions by both SASH-L subscribers and the list moderator, five men succeeded in dominating the forum by accomplishing hegemonic masculinity for nearly four months. In the process they filled the mailboxes of SASH-L subscribers with personalized sarcasms, slams, and unfounded accusations.

Most subscribers, the majority of whom were women, watched the fight in silence. A few attempted to negotiate a truce, and others confronted the antagonists directly. Still others complained, and finally many exited the hostile environment altogether. While the subscribers succeeded in reclaiming their forum, the conflict had significantly transformed the space they had regained. Harmony came at a particularly high price, as list members' ability to confront and transform the controversial issue of sexual harassment is limited by the ban on debate. While at present there is little conflict, SASH-L is now characterized as an arena for exchanging information, ideas, and tactics for battling sexual harassment in conventional settings.

Toward an Internet *for* Women

In this chapter we have examined how people accomplish gender in cyberspace, how everyday acts of male domination occur, how people identify them, their responses, and the problems encountered when opposing male dominance. In the "tuna memo" discussion, we saw how one man used electronic messaging to construct his masculinity by widely distributing a demeaning and degrading joke about women's body odor. For some women the memo was nothing less than a virtual assault on their gender (Holderness 1993); yet, in defining the situation as they experienced it, their efforts were met with resistance from men within their own community, who discounted their sense of danger and quest for empowerment. The "pissing contest" illustrates how the discourses of a few men can dominate even a "woman-space." In this scenario we saw how a few men disrupted the SASH-L community with adversarial communication styles honed by their participation in rough-and-tumble discussions on other male-dominated lists. Despite their tenacity, they did not hold the forum for long. Women and men successfully resisted the efforts of these subscribers to transform the list into an adversarial arena. SASHers "held the fort" by ignoring them, negotiating with them, confronting them, and finally by asking them to leave.

As the presence of male domination transformed the environment, the space recovered is not what it was before these discussions. While SASH-L remains a "woman-space"—a forum where women's voices and ideas are heard and their experiences acknowledged—women who choose to speak do so at the risk of challenge by both men and women. In addition, efforts to facilitate a safe environment where women can feel free to speak their minds have paradoxically produced unprecedented amounts of silence.

Thus the questions to which we now turn are: How can women-centered communities be sustained on the Internet, and what contributions can they make? Despite the challenges women face on the Internet, feminists and women's groups are increasingly using electronic messaging for activism and accelerating social change. For example, when four undergraduate men used their university electronic mail accounts to distribute widely a list of "75 reasons why women should not have freedom of speech," women on the Net forwarded the list to other women via women-centered discussion lists, and in those forums they discussed such strategies as sending "thank you" notes to the authors and complaints to the university's electronic mail postmaster and affirmative action officer. Their protests succeeded in temporarily overloading the university's mail system, and the university responded by taking administrative action.

More broadly, in "woman-spaces" like SASH-L, men who "listen in" learn about women's experiences of male domination, integrate that knowledge, and take it with them to other sites on the Internet and to conventional settings as well. Thus their experiences on women-centered lists structure their behavior in a variety of social settings. Also, in electronic communities like SASH-L, women gain strength from a sharing of experience but also observe the range and diversity of experiences among women. By listening and learning from each other, we expand our repertoires for handling acts of male domination in both our virtual and actual worlds. Thus, on women-centered lists men and women are learning new ways to reproduce and construct gender besides the traditional rituals of dominance and deference.

There are some potential pitfalls, however. Internet communication is largely the domain of the privileged. Therefore, predominantly privileged women use the Internet as an arena for resisting male domination, while women who are chronically marginalized are less likely to reap the benefits of global telecommunication in their everyday lives.

In this chapter we have argued that the Internet is an emerging social arena. We conceptualize electronic messaging as a form of social interaction through which men and women do gender differently. It is, however, a predominantly masculine domain, designed and used by men. Increasing numbers of women are pioneering and settling this vast frontier, and as we do so, the politics of gender and how it is accomplished will become increasingly salient, rather than transcended.

The Internet has not been the magical forum that rids the world of male domination. Male domination will be achieved in any social sphere where men and women accomplish hegemonic masculinity and emphasized femininity. As Messerschmidt argues (1993), action combating modern sexism must be multifaceted. We must organize around the larger political issues and examine our personal means of doing gender. To do so lends empowerment to others, while curtailing the overpowering tendencies toward hegemonic masculinity (Connell 1987, pp. 183–188). To the extent that computer technology is imbedded in economic, political, and cultural structures of domination, our ability to empower women electronically will depend on the extent to which we overcome these barriers or use them as springboards for the true democratization of social life. An Internet *for* women is a forum where we can speak, hear our ideas, and validate our experiences. It is a place where women feel safe, supported, and empowered, where feminist women and profeminist men can promote an alternative feminist discourse. In spite of the resistance encountered, SASH-L and similar lists struggle toward such a vision. Allowed to thrive, free of hegemonic masculinity, they promise to transform the problem of male domination in both virtual and conventional realities.

Notes

1. We would like to thank the following people for moral and intellectual support: Mona Danner, Nancy Jurik, James Messerschmidt, Marianne Nielsen, Martin Schwartz, Nancy Wonders, and the editors of this book.

2. Messerschmidt must be seen as a "structured action" theorist who places West and Zimmerman's notion of "doing gender" in a structural context. For a more detailed discussion of this approach, see Messerschmidt 1993.

References

Balka, Ellen. 1993. "Women's Access to On-Line Discussions about Feminism." *Electronic Journal of Communication* 3: 193.

Chodorow, Nancy. 1978. *The Reproduction of Mothering: Psychoanalysis and the Sociology of Gender.* Los Angeles: University of California Press.

Connell, Robert W. 1987. *Gender and Power.* Stanford, CA: Stanford University Press.

Cosentino, Victor. 1994 "Virtual Legality." *Byte* (March): 278.

Dibbell, Julian. 1994. "A Rape in Cyberspace," *Village Voice* (December 26): 36–42.

Frissen, Valerie. 1992. "Trapped in Electronic Cages? Gender and New Information Technologies in the Public and Private Domain: An Overview of Research." *Media, Culture and Society* 14: 31–49.

Gruber, James. 1989. "How Women Handle Sexual Harassment: A Literature Review." *Social Science Research* 74 (1): 3–7.

Halberstam, Judith. 1991. "Automating Gender: Postmodern Feminism and the Age of the Intelligent Machine." *Feminist Studies* 17 (3): 439–459.

Hall, Roberta and Bernice Sandler. 1982. *The Classroom Climate: A Chilly One for Women? The Project on the Status and Education of Women.* Washington, DC: The Association of American Colleges.

Herring, Susan. 1993. "Gender and Democracy in Computer Mediated Linguistic Communication." *Electronic Journal of Communication* 3.2, Special Issue on Computer Mediated Communication, Thomas Benson, editor.

————. 1994. "Gender Differences in Computer Mediated Communication: Bringing Familiar Baggage to the New Frontier." Keynote speech delivered at the American Library Association Annual Convention, Miami, Florida, 1994.

Herring, Susan, Deborah Johnson, and Tamra DiBendedetto. 1992. "Partici-pating in Electronic Discourse in a 'Feminist Field,'" in *Locating Power*, Pro-ceedings of the 1992 Berkeley Women and Language Conference. Berkeley: University of California.

Holderness, Mike. 1993. "Assault on the Interface: Sexual Harassment is the Latest 'Virus' to Infect New Technology." *Times Higher Education Supple-ment*, December 24. London, UK.

Kramarae, Cheris and Jana Kramer. 1995. "Net Gains, Net Losses." *Women's Review of Books* XII (February): 33–35.

Kramarae, Cheris and H. Jeanie Taylor. 1993. "Women and Men on Electronic Networks: A Conversation or a Monologue?" in *Women, Information Technology, and Scholarship*, eds. H. Jeanie Taylor, Cheris Kramarae, and Maureen Ebben. Women Information, Technology, and Scholarship Collo-quium. Urbana, IL: The Center for Advanced Study, pp. 52–61.

Levy, Steven. 1995. "Stop Talking Dirty to Me." *Newsweek* (October 16): 84.

Martin, Susan and Nancy Jurik. 1996. *Doing Justice, Doing Gender: Women in the Law and Criminal Justice.* Thousand Oaks, CA: Sage Publications.

Messerschmidt, James W. 1993. *Masculinities and Crime: Critique and Recon-ceptualization of Theory.* Lantham, MD: Rowman & Littlefield.

————. 1994. "Schooling, Masculinities and Youth Crime by White Boys," in *Just Boys Doing Business? Men, Masculinities and Crime*, eds. Tim Newburn and Elizabeth Stanko. New York: Routledge.

————. 1995a. "From Patriarchy to Gender: Feminist Theory, Criminology, and the Challenge of Diversity," in *International Perspectives in Criminology: Engendering a Discipline*, eds. Nicole Rafter and Frances Heidensohn. Lon-don: Open University Press.

————. 1995b. "Managing to Kill: Masculinities and the Space Shuttle Chal-lenger Explosion," in *Masculinities* 3: 1–22.

Neubarth, Michael. 1995. "Virtual El Dorado." *Internet World* (June): 8.

Pavela, Gary. 1994. "What Internet Means." *Synthesis: Law and Policy in Higher Education* (Winter/Spring): 397–399.

Peterson, Rodney. 1994. "Harassment by Electronic Mail." *Synthesis: Law and Policy in Higher Education* (Winter/Spring): 402–403, 416.

Peysor, Marc and Steve Rhodes. 1995. "When E-mail is Oops-Mail." *Newsweek* (October 16): 82.

Sandler, Bernice, Lisa Silverberg, and Roberta Hall. 1996. *The Chilly Classroom Climate: A Guide to Improve the Education of Women.* Washington, DC: The Association of American Colleges, the Project on the Status and Education of Women.

Smith, Dorothy E. 1977. "A Sociology for Women," in *The Prism of Sex: Essays in the Sociology of Knowledge,* eds. Julia A. Sherman and Evelyn Torton Beck. Madison: University of Wisconsin Press.

Smith, Judy and Ellen Balka. 1988. "Chatting on a Feminist Computer Network," in *Technology and Women's Voices,* ed. Cheris Kramarae. New York: Routledge & Kegan Paul, pp. 82–97.

Stanko, Elizabeth. 1990. *Everyday Violence. How Women and Men Experience Sexual and Physical Danger.* London: Pandora Press.

Truong, Koai Ann. 1993. "Gender Issues in Online Communications." CFP, version 4.1.

West, Candace and Don H. Zimmerman. 1987. "Doing Gender." *Gender and Society* 1: 125–151.

Wood, Lamont. 1994. *The Net After Dark.* New York: John Wiley and Sons.

Young, Iris. 1994. "Gender as Seriality: Thinking about Women as a Social Collective." *Signs* 19 (3): 713–738.

The Body

as a Gendered Space

Dialectical Linkages

Part II highlights the sexual and physical abuse of womens' bodies as gendered spaces. The bodies of women, through sexist discourses, become appropriated by men for their use. While identity is frequently used as a weapon in these instances, the paramount reality is that the women have no control over what is happening to their bodies, because of the institutionalized sincere fictions that support men and their abusive agendas.

tammy ko Robinson, in Chapter 6, "Autoethnography on Memory: Disclosure and Silence," takes us on a different journey through domestic violence, using her childhood experience with violence between her parents, her participation as an adult in a domestic abuse shelter, and a critique of the movie The Piano. *The dialectical linkages in Dorothy E. Smith's chapter apply here as well. Robinson's account blurs the boundaries of personal experience and other texts to weave a tale of domestic abuse that leaves us asking: "What about the children?" Does solving the problem between couples engaged in spousal abuse solve the problems of the entire family?*

In Chapter 7, "Wife Abuse and Family Idealizations: The Violent Regulation of Family Regimes," Dorothy E. Smith draws on published materials to demonstrate how the right-wing call for men to return to and become heads of families may accelerate wife-battering. The new "men's movement" asserts that men have an obligation to claim their rightful identities as heads of households. In extreme cases where men become obsessive, the discourses of family idealizations and masculinity become sincere fictions that legitimate the physical abuse of women. In cases where the women buy into the identities promoted by these particular family idealizations, they find themselves cut off from access to the economic/political arena. The battering of their bodies negatively impacts their identity or self-esteem; thus they are unable to construct alternate idealizations that would allow them to leave. In turn, lack of access to the economic/political arena keeps them in harm's way and also creates low self-esteem.

In Chapter 8, "Discursive Constraint in the Narrated Identities of Childhood Sex Abuse Survivors," Carol Rambo Ronai uses a layered account to describe her own and nine other womens' experiences with childhood sex abuse. Through discursive constraint, sincere fictions are offered by men to little girls to control their identities, and thus their bodies, for the purposes of having sex with them and of keeping them quiet about the abuse. In turn, the abuse perpetuated on the girls' bodies continues dialectically to feed back on their adult identities and their economic/political situations. These gendered spaces negatively impact the choices these women make and their life chances. Ronai also suggests that the dominant social science discourse of "objectivity" (that is, leaving one's own experiences and emotions out of one's research) acts as a weapon to silence women about the reality, pain, and impact of their own sexual abuse. In this manner, the male-dominated research community becomes a partner with mainstream society in ignoring and perpetuating sexual abuse.

We visit the topic of sexual harassment again in Chapter 9, "Defining the Situation: Sexual Harassment or Everyday Rudeness," by Melissa J. Monson. Through participant observation and interviews, Monson explores two major facets of harassment: the ways in which it manifests in public and the strategies female clerks use to cope with it. Customers are observed engaging in harassment, such as calling a clerk a "dumb broad" or "slut," in seductive behavior, such as making references to a clerk's anatomy, and in sexual imposition, such as swatting a clerk on the backside. Rather than defining the behavior as sexual harassment per se, most of the female clerks constructed this male behavior as rude or in poor taste. In the dialectics of domination, the gendered space of identity is constructed in the video store by sexist discourses that prescribe differential normative gender role expectations for the participants. As in the Smith chapter, we again see men engaged in abuse and women accepting it based on the sincere fictions each has internalized about gender roles.

In each of these chapters, the body becomes a gendered space due to the effects of identity and the economic/political arena as gendered spaces. By focusing on the body as a gendered space, we discover the subtle ways in which it can be appropriated through sexist discourses. The lived experience of being an appropriated body, in turn, genders a woman's identity. In all of these chapters, at various points, the women come to a place where they define their weakness and lack of control over their bodies' destinies as feminine. To be feminine is to be weak. Thus living with the abuse serves to support the sexist discourses they draw upon to define their identities, and gives them the sense that they are living out their appropriate gender roles.

6

Autoethnography on Memory

Disclosure and Silence

tammy ko ROBINSON

> The fact that we are here and that I speak these words is an attempt to break that silence and bridge some of those differences between us, for it is not difference which immobilizes us, but silence. And there are so many silences to be broken.
>
> (Lorde 1984, p. 44)

*　　*　　*

There is a silence where hath been no sound. There is a silence where no sound is made. I am listening to the mind's voice within Ada, a mute woman who is married off by her father to a stranger, and transported along with her piano and her daughter to her new husband in New South Wales. As the lead character in Jane Champion's gothic film *The Piano*, Ada endures physical and verbal abuse, and silence—a silence with which many women identify. The silence comes from the depths of our pasts, so deep that when we try to recover it, we are enveloped by vast nothingness that we, as women, become accustomed to. And, like Ada, who plays her piano instead of speaking, we learn at a young age to find a substitute for our voices. Some call this coping mechanism a sign of passiveness, and others, a sign of unspeakable pain. In the movie, silence was used as a lullaby for women, women who were once children, who had their consciousness and subjectivity put to sleep, much like Michael Taussig's account of *Imbunches*: children whose mouths were sewn shut and their senses blocked by fear, according to an old Chilean story (1987).

I wish to learn through the difficult process of self-disclosure how this silence, as Audre Lorde would say, immobilizes us, and how it can be broken by women who wake up to the nightmare of sexism. Only by replacing our mind's voice with something that is heard, loud and clear, in the most public of spaces, can women resist their construction as the other, of being twice silenced. I wish to displace the subjective power I possess as a writer and as a volunteer at a domestic abuse shelter by submerging myself and various texts into the drift of retelling in order to rewrite the relationship of desire(s), power, and discourse. By transgressing the boundaries of privilege and domination, disclosure and silence, fiction and reality, I take part in a movement to strengthen a community committed to collectively working, inside and outside, towards ending violence. In this paper I use a "layered account" format to accomplish this (see Clay, chapter 2 and Ronai, chapter 8 in this volume).

* * *

Domestic violence is a social problem that affects individuals and families in their intimate relationships. The Domestic Violence Center staff believes that the root cause of battering comes from the system of patriarchy, a social belief that men have the right to control their own lives, as well as the lives of their partner and children.... Women do not cause, deserve, or enjoy abuse and are entitled to a violence free life. (Children and Families of Iowa Volunteer Handbook)

* * *

Self Disclosure—*Use caution.* (These words are handwritten on the worksheet included in my orientation packet.) Self-disclosure involves the advocate's sharing of personal information about ideas, feelings, and life experiences in keeping with the client's interests and needs. In formulating self disclosing responses, the advocate identifies previous experiences from her own life which contained similar emotions and issues to those expressed by the client. (Children and Families of Iowa Volunteer Handbook)

* * *

The warning below is the last piece of advice spoken to me before I leave the domestic violence center as a volunteer in training, having completed twenty-three hours:

You would be amazed at what people can use against you. We caution you against using self-disclosure in order to protect yourself, even about what seems like the littlest things, the littlest details. For example, I always wear my wedding ring; I don't wish to hide the fact that I'm married. Sometimes women look at it and ask me if I am married, or they see the picture that I have of my husband on my desk. When they've seen it, they already know that the answer is yes. But it's almost as though by asking me, they are setting me up for the next question which is: "How can you help me or understand if you haven't been in an abusive relationship?" ... Well, I haven't been, but I anticipate their questions and I tell them that whether or not I have been doesn't matter, because I feel as though my job is to help them. And I feel as though I can still do that even though my relationship with my husband isn't an abusive one. You have to be prepared for these questions. In fact, one time we had one of our staff, who thought that she was doing a wonderful job consoling a client by telling her about her positive relationship, as a way of showing her that not all men are bad guys, get a complaint at the end of her client's stay here. We always have our clients fill out reports on their stay . . . to see what works, what doesn't work, and they let us know. Well, this client took this staff's words as a way of bragging, as a one-up on you type of thing. And she didn't want to hear or know about it. So you see, we have to be very aware of our status as volunteers and as workers here. We have to remember that we are in positions of power, what little power there is, and are viewed as such by the clients. . . .

Afterwards, as I read back through the orientation folder, my supervisor's story replays itself and resonates with the voice of bell hooks:

It is necessary for us to remember, as we think critically about domination, that we all have the capacity to act in ways that oppress, dominate, wound (whether or not that power is institutionalized). It is necessary to remember that it is first the potential oppressor within that we must resist—the potential victim within that we must rescue—otherwise we cannot hope for an end to domination, for liberation. (1990a, p.187)

* * *

Cornel West opens his book, *Race Matters*, with W.E.B. Du Bois' proclamation that "The problem of the twentieth century is the problem of the color line." Over the telephone, my mother echoes similar sentiments as we discuss racism in the United States, and this becomes, for us, an unusual moment of shared clarity. Merle Woo offers me an understanding of our moment in her "Letter to Ma" from the *This Bridge Called My Back* anthology: "Together we have lived one hundred and eleven years in this country as yellow women, and it is not enough to enunciate words and words and then to have them only mean that we have been keeping each other company." What I have taken away from Woo's text is not illustrated in the configuration of the words nor in their sentiment so much as in the form of communication the author chose. The dialogue between Woo and her mother takes place in a letter, just as dialogue between the field and the sociologist takes place in the ethnographic writing—writing that serves as textual replacements, as almost a forced dialogue. I not only ask: "This is what I'm writing—can you verify if this is what really happened, do you remember it this way, too?" but I also say: "Look Mom, it is necessary to talk about this among others, this isn't just threatening to bring scandal to our private lives."

My mother was one of three survivors in her family of seven during the years of Japanese occupation of Korea, she married an American officer after the Korean War, she endured the racism of the seventies and eighties in the United States. Because of this, we always say that my mother had a difficult childhood and that I had it easy in comparison. Sometimes, however, there is just no clear comparison.

I have loved my father, both as a father and a friend. I believe that my mother loves my father, or must have at one time to have married him, although I can't remember her telling me so. When I was little, she would often say: "Your father is a good man. You should marry someone like your father," and then she would list his attributes, almost as though they could be counted on one hand. "He doesn't get drunk, he doesn't gamble, he isn't out all of the time, he doesn't cheat on me, he's not like other women's husbands. I've seen other husbands who are really bad. Your father would be perfect, except he has a bad temper." As she told me this, she would quickly mitigate it with: "Oh, but at least his temper is not as bad as a Korean man's temper. You must never marry a Korean man."

I would often think about what Korean men were like, as though they were a subspecies, and once I asked my father to describe them to me. He answered: "They are spoiled rotten. Why are you asking?" I just told him, "Mother said not to marry a Korean man." As I remember this, I can see him taking a deep breath before carefully saying, "Well, of course you wouldn't want to marry a Korean man. He would expect you to be his servant, you wouldn't like it, Tammy. And I think that in your mother's case, she is probably referring to a bad childhood experience, because I think growing up, that her brother used to beat her."

In response to the advice offered by both of my parents, I defiantly thought that I might just marry a Korean man some day. How could either of them tell me who I was or was not going to marry? Especially since both showed me by example that violent tempers could run through all colors.

* * *

Mi takuye oyasin / We are all relatives.

* * *

I hated *The Piano*. After it was over, Shari and I walked quickly outside the theater to her car, and sat there quietly as the engine warmed up. It was a very cold New Year's Eve. I broke the silence that had followed us out of the theater by asking: "Can you drive? Will you be all right?" She nodded, and I breathed a sigh of relief. "Good . . . because I know that I can't drive right now, but I need to get out of here." Yes, she nods again. It was the ending to the movie that had left us both disturbed. She, Ada, had betrayed us.

"I'm glad that I saw it with you," she says to me. "David asked me to see it with him, but now I realize that I couldn't have." "No," I reply. "It would have hurt you too much. It would have been all too real, with him sitting next to you. He used to understand, but not anymore." "No," she agrees. "Not anymore. My mother wants to see this movie, and she'll ask me about it. How will I explain it?"

"Tell her it is a good movie," I say. "Tell her that she will think it is a good movie, but that she won't like the ending. Liking the ending would valorize it, but liking the movie is okay because it validates several lives." "Yes," she nods again, taking to what I say. "I see now why Ada chooses life in the end." "Yes, the movie isn't just for us, it's to teach us history." As I say this, I cry softly, my thoughts still troubled by how Ada's freedom and voice were bought and sold, troubled by the women we left in the movie theater, crying on their *husband's* shoulders, and troubled about thinking of what to say to Shari's mother. I am bothered by the idea of learning my mother's history through a fictionalized story of a Scotswoman from a movie she would never watch.

> Feminist struggle to end patriarchal domination should be of primary importance to women and men globally not because it is the foundation of all other oppressive structures but because it is that form of domination we are most likely to encounter in everyday life. (hooks 1990a, p.187)

In writing about my memories I am often tempted to stop, almost afraid that disclosure is not a way to heal or transform. But to stop now is to reinforce traditional writing where women and our experiences are treated as objects to be hidden away. Hélène Cixous says in *The Newly Born Woman*:

> She does not exist, she can not-be; but there has to be something of her. He keeps, then, of the woman on whom he is no longer dependent, only this space, always virginal, as matter to be subjected to the desire he wishes to impart. (1986, p. 65)

I take that back, about my mother loving my father. She did say it a couple of times, that she loved him, but she would always add: "But not as much as I love you. I love you more than I love him. If your father was to die, I would be okay, but if you were to die, I wouldn't be able to go on living." Of course, I wasn't able to say the same to her because if my mother were to die, I would remember her and live on, just as she had lived on with the memory of her parents' deaths. And I didn't think about my own mortality or suicide at such a young age—not then.

That was before the questions and the physical abuse came. My mother began asking me who I loved more, my father or my mother? How could I explain that I loved them both differently? I didn't have the words, so I would say that I didn't know. "What do you mean?— you don't know?!" She would yell at me, and then she would answer the question for me. "I see, you love your father more than you love me. But remember, if it wasn't for me, you wouldn't be here with us now; it was because I wanted a child; it was because I was lonely that we adopted you. Your father didn't want to have any more children, but I told him that I wouldn't leave Korea without a girl. And so he went to the orphanages and he picked you, and you had pretty eyelashes and big eyes, so I said okay." It was after this that I saw her drinking and her getting angrier more often.

*   *   *

"Empathy keeps the focus on the person with the problem and on that person's anger, pain, and individual needs." I read this in the manual, and I think that I have crossed over, losing the objectivity I am supposed to maintain. I am angry at myself for my reaction to *The Piano*. I felt thankful that Ada lost only a finger, and I forgot to be horrified that her husband lost control of his temper. He had no right to be so angry, I think now, as I wonder whether I am now loudly voicing my anger for *her*. This anger frightens me and disturbs my reading of both Márquez's book and of Champion's film, for women everywhere, mothers and daughters, become somehow implicated in these violent crimes against women.

*   *   *

"The time has come for you to be tamed," he told her.
Victoria Guzman showed him the bloody knife.
"Let go of her, white man," she ordered him seriously. "You won't have a drink of that water as long as I'm alive." (García Márquez 1982, p. 8)

*   *   *

There was one particular time when things were really awful—when I remember her yelling at my father: "You have no right to tell me what to do! When you come home, you take away my fun, my freedom!" I remember a friend of hers had picked her up and taken her out, and that my father, as he does on rare occasions, made us dinner that night.

She must have come home around ten o'clock or so, because I hadn't been in bed for very long when I heard them yelling at each other, or rather, her yelling. I heard my father asking her if leaving us had made her happy, but of course, my father didn't just ask. No, when he is very angry, his tone is dark, very controlled, and never loud. It starkly contrasts with my mother's tone; when she is angry or frightened, she gets extremely loud.

I remember her screaming at him, repeatedly asking him if he was trying to kill her. He answered this only by questioning whether or not she was drunk. She screamed that it didn't matter, and then I heard banging and yelling, so I ran out into the hallway, but I was held back by my mother's friend. She shoved me into the extra bedroom and closed the door, and all I could hear was running and my mother's screaming. What seemed like several minutes and several screams later, my father ran into the room where I had been put, slammed the door, and leaned against it. I was nearby, huddled in the dark; I whispered: "Are you okay? Is Mother okay?" But he didn't have to answer. I could hear her outside the door, banging on it, collapsing against it, breaking into sobs. I heard her friend speaking in Korean, trying to calm her down, telling her that it was okay. I heard my mother say that she wanted to kill my father. I remember looking at my father, seeing him holding his hand—he was bleeding. My mother had cut him with the butcher knife.

My father and I didn't speak to each other for a while, but eventually he said: "Don't worry, Tammy. Your mother's drunk, and everything that happened tonight happened because she's drunk." I listened, not saying a word. He said: "Some people make funny drunks; your mother makes a really mean drunk." I cannot recall ever seeing my mother drinking after this incident, nor have we ever spoken about how the knives from the kitchen disappeared for a while.

A couple of days later, I saw my mother sitting outside, and when I approached her, she asked what had now become her regular interrogation: "Do you love me?" I said: "Yes, of course—you're my Mother," and I waited for her to say some more about how she loved me, but instead she said: "I don't believe you. I don't understand you. You're a coldhearted child. Mothers and daughters are supposed to share a strong bond, but you're closer to your father. You love your father more." I must have started crying then, but that detail was inconsequential, because she continued on: "If you loved me at all you would have helped me the other night and given me support and protection." In defense, I told her: "Andy's mother pushed me into the room, and I asked Dad if you were okay," although I didn't add that I had thought it was her who had gone after him with a knife. But she told me to go away, that she didn't want to hear any of it. She told me to go inside and close the door. Feeling helpless and not wanting to anger her anymore, I did what she told me to, and for the second time in a few short days, I heard her crying on the other side.

*   *   *

I have a fear of crying, of always crying on the nights after my Saturday shifts at the center. I worry that I am listening to stories that I have been trying to forget all my life; I worry that I am listening to a story I never asked to hear. I am left with a sick wonder at Marquez and Champion for creating these characters who become complicit agents in perpetuating their own abuse; I wonder at *The Piano* and how the audience knew of the violence that was to happen to Ada before it was committed; and I wonder at myself and Ada's daughter for being aligned with our partial memories, and for losing the ability to talk the language of our mothers. And as I read our lives into this novel or into that movie in order to avoid committing similar mistakes, I realize how tight the tensions are between condemnation and liberation.

*   *   *

"What do all of you do to relax when you're stressed? I ask you this because this is very important to keep in mind while you're working here. We don't want our staff or our volunteers burning out. This job can become a twenty-four-hour thing if you *let* it," my supervisor says during training.

"Aren't you going to bed, Jessie?" I ask him.

"No, I want to listen to this record one more time before I give it to Molly to put away," he answers. He looks up at me and says, "Why? Are you tired?"

"Yes, I am very tired," I reply.

"Well, you better go now to the front desk to see where they're going to put you. You should see if they can give you a room upstairs," he says matter-of-factly, but it's the closest to nice he's been all evening.

Oh no, I think to myself, he doesn't understand that I am a volunteer here, that I get to go *home* now.

*   *   *

... you do well not to gaze too closely on the beings who give you nightmares. Idealize only toward the lovely and the beautiful: that is woman's work. (Balzac in a conversation with George Sand, quoted in Sand 1991, p. 218)

*   *   *

Rules on community living:
(1) no physical or emotional abuse
(2) no smoking
(3) maintain client confidentiality and the secret location of the shelter.
    (Taken from a sign posted in the shelter)

*   *   *

"Jonnie, hey buddy, where do you think you're going?" I hollered after the three-year-old as he pattered barefoot down the long white corridor. He was running from the room where we were doing projects with the other kids. One never knew where he was running to.

I didn't catch up with him until he had turned the corner. There, his mother and an advocate sat in the dark, peeking through the slatted blinds. Jonnie was climbing his mother's leg onto her lap.

"Jonnie no," his mother said, "go back with the other kids."

"Come on Jonnie," I pleaded, not knowing what was going on, "let's go back and make puppets."

Jonnie didn't want to come with me, though, he wanted to see what was behind the blinds. I did too, but I also knew the kind of monster that it could be.

Jonnie made it up into his mother's lap and the advocate waved me towards the window. "Look out at that car. Does it say Mercury? Does that man have a mustache?"

It was dark outside, winter dusk, and the lot was illuminated by yellow halogen lights. The car was at least eighteen years old and the age showed. It was a green heap of rust and dents, the kind of seventies coupe with a loud muffler that scares me whenever I come up against one on my bike. There was a figure inside, obviously a male figure, but I couldn't make out any characteristics.

"I don't know, I can't tell. Do you want me to go outside and see?"

"No, no, just take Jonnie back," she said, then added in a lower voice, "we've already called the police."

"Jonnie come on!" I struggled to pick him up as he wiggled and kicked. "You really don't want to get too close to the window."

"What's out there?"

"It's nothing Jonnie, just cars." I didn't feel good about lying to the kid, but what else could I tell him. "Come on Dish-man, let's go back with the others."

Jonnie gave up his futile struggle and ran ahead of me, back down the corridor to the brightly lit dining room where chaos was at reign. I followed behind, relieved to see Jonnie heading not to the window but to a table of kids instead.

I don't remember which volunteer I was talking to when the first few kids ran to the window, threw aside the blinds, and looked out. What I do know is that the next several minutes were spent trying to keep the kids away from that window, and explaining what was happening to the other volunteers. All this time some of the kids were getting really excited, running in circles, and talking about "the man out there, there's a man . . ."

I felt so angry that I had to explain to a particular volunteer that it was more important to keep the kids away from the window than to continue cutting paper.

It seemed like hours but it couldn't have been more than two minutes. During the pandemonium the advocate walked over and took me aside.

"Would you please take these keys and bring the van around to the back door so that people can leave if they need to?"

"Of course, are the police coming?"

"Yes."

I suddenly remembered what had been nagging at me from the first time I looked out at that car.

"You know, I think that same car was sitting out there when we came to work today."

"Really? Well, we don't know who it is but the police will tell us when they get here."

I took the keys and walked the entire length of the building to the front door. I stepped outside into the quiet night. Thinking of it now, I really don't remember being scared. I think that I was more upset that this kind of thing had to happen, that this man could cause so much fear, and that these kids are too innocent to understand the danger, even though they are survivors.

I climbed into the high van, turned on the headlights, and drove slowly past the green car. The man inside was blond, with lots of hair and yes, a mustache. I didn't see a make on the car. I pulled the van into the parking space and went back inside.

The police arrived shortly afterward and this set the kids off again. By this time we were trying to keep the kids calm, and appealing to the older kids to be responsible by keeping the younger ones away from the window. I managed to look outside once, the cops had the man up against the hood of his car and they were frisking him. After ten minutes or so, the flashing lights disappeared from behind the windowscreen, and Jonnie started to cheer: "He's gone! The man's gone!"

We let the kids believe that but we still kept them away from the window, for we knew differently. The man was not gone. The police had questioned him and found out that he was waiting for his wife, who was in a counseling session. Her session was dealing, as it did every week, with domestic violence, specifically wife-beating. Even though he is her abuser, there is nothing that the police can do in this situation—she asked him to be there. I didn't understand. The advocate explained: "Apparently this woman is in counseling on a court order. She really doesn't want to be here. In fact, she has apparently been disruptive in other meetings."

"But she's endangering everyone's safety, she's breaking confidentiality," I said, still not understanding.

"That's probably her point."

*   *   *

This story about a woman who endangers other clients in the community shows how we can explicitly hurt one another on the outside; however, it does not show how those who do want counseling and those who counsel are still implicitly silencing one another from the inside. For example, it has been the current trend in feminist texts and feminist practice in the family violence shelters to focus on wife abuse. However, maintaining this focus has produced the undesirable effect and tension of workers dislocating or ignoring the transference of violence experienced or witnessed by children, not just outside but inside the shelter, which translates into a lack of counseling facilities or programs designed for children especially for this problem. This political move becomes even more complicated when different sources produce differing reports on parental violence.

For example, in *Feminist Perspectives on Wife Abuse*, feminist sociologists assert that "children of battered wives are more often beaten by their fathers than by their mothers." (Bowker 1988, p.158) Contradicting this information was data I received from Children's Advocacy training, which stated that if the woman is in the cycle of violence and has a child, it is eight times more likely that she rather than her abuser will abuse the child, thus accounting for more than 58 percent of the children in abusive families. At the shelter, we act on the belief that if the woman is treated, the mother-child relationship will improve, thus somehow justifying why the advocate does not do anything or ask any direct questions that could lead to a CPI (Child Protection Investigator's) report and eventually cause the mother to lose custody of her child.

By not asking, or finding ways to deal with children as survivors, the full needs of both the mothers and the children are not being met in the domestic abuse shelter. In making the claim that when we are writing as feminists, in writing in a feminine language that talks about the abuses done to our bodies, we need to add to the agenda, the prospect of talking about our bodies as potential sites that can give abuse. Minh-ha states, in her book *Woman, Native, Other* (1989):

> Touch me and let me touch you, for the private is political. Language wavers with desire. It is "the language of my entrails," a skin with which I caress and feel the other, a body capable of receiving as well as giving: nurturing and procreating. (p. 37)

The Piano is an example of an account that does not disclose the possible effects of domestic violence on the child. Kathi Maio, in a review in *Ms.*, claims that by "choosing whom to love, Ada brings down the wrath of the patriarchy" and since "She literally snatches life back from the depths and applies her will to finding a new voice," *The Piano* relates "a feminist story. Then, or now." Of this reviewer I ask: When did the feminist story separate itself from children's advocacy?

Why is it that the audience never sees whether or not Ada's daughter—what was her *name?*—dances again? Why? It is as though the young child's trauma and guilt are not to be addressed, now that we are offered the image of Ada leaving the piano that has become no longer hers, at the ocean's bottom, soon to be happily remarried to the man who first bought it from her. The narrative suggests that for one victim of domestic violence, myths such as codependency, low self-esteem, passivity, victimization get rather half-convincingly dispelled at the movie's end by one word—"survivor." As I recall the image of Ada leaving the piano at the ocean's bottom, I realize that the film is correct in that there should be an alternative to annihilation for the main character:

> It is at one and the same time the restitution of something that has been levied from the associative flux; the reproduction of the process of detachment from the signifying chain; and a residuum that constitutes the subject's share of the whole. The desiring machine is not a metaphor; it is what interrupts and is interrupted in accordance with these three modes. (Deleuze and Guattari 1987, p. 41)

*   *   *

> What a death. What a chance. What a surprise. My will has chosen life. (Champion 1993)

*   *   *

As I negotiate my coming to and entering of these contiguous terrains of advocate and survivor, I wonder: Is the desiring machine only temporarily interrupted? How can one be secure with their mode of being where the power ascertained from the culture of terror can still be felt and seen? How can I forget what brings the children and myself to the shelter? The endings to both *The Piano* and to *Chronicle of a Death Foretold*, as well as the framed pictures of men on the desks of the advocates, which remain painfully segregated from those in the social room, down the hallway, where there are pictures of women standing alone, photographs of women holding children, and pictures of young girls and young boys holding hands, cause me to ask who the movie's ending was productive for, and how the ending erases the memories of what has happened. What will Ada's daughter remember—silence and pain or the healing of self-disclosure?

Note

Derrida says that the meaning of signs lies in the relationship with everything that is absent, and so it goes for this text. "Thank you" to the names who have not been mentioned here, yet constitute a share of my life and my work.

References

Bowker, Lee. 1988. "On the Relationship Between Wife Beating and Child Abuse," in Kersti Yllo (ed.), *Feminist Perspectives on Wife Abuse.* Newbury Park, CA: Sage.

Bradford, Colleen. 1994. "Survivors of Violence Supported." *Des Moines Register*, April.

Jan Chapman Productions. 1993. *The Piano.* Directed by Jane Champion, MIRAMAX Films.

Cixous, Hélène. 1986. "Sorties," in *The Newly Born Woman*, translated by Betsy Wing. Minneapolis: University of Minnesota Press and Manchester: Manchester University Press.

——— 1981. "Sorties: Where is She?" translated by Ann Lidle, in Isabelle de Courtivron and Elaine Marks (eds.), *New French Feminisms.* Minneapolis: University of Minnesota Press and Brighton: Harvester.

Culbertson, Roberta. 1995. "Embodied Memory, Transcendence, and Telling: Recounting Trauma, Re-establishing the Self," in *New Literary History*, pp.169–95.

Deleuze and Guattari. 1987. *A Thousand Plateaus.* Minneapolis: University of Minnesota Press.

hooks, bell. 1990a. "Feminism: A Transformational Politic," in Deborah L. Rhode, (ed.), *Theoretical Perspectives on Sexual Difference.* New Haven, CT: Yale University Press.

———. 1990b. "Third World Diva Girls: Politics of Feminist Solidarity," in *Yearning: Race, Gender, and Cultural Politics.* Boston: South End Press.

Lorde, Audre. 1984. "Transformation of Silence," in *Zami, Sister Outsider, Undersong.* New York: The Crossing Press and W.W. Norton & Company, Inc.

Maio, Kathi. 1994. Review of *The Piano*. *Ms.* IV, p. 84.

Márquez, Gabriel García. 1982. *Chronicle of a Death Foretold*. New York: Ballantine Books.

Minh-ha, Trinh-T. 1989. *Woman, Native, Other*. Bloomington: Indiana University Press.

Sand, George. 1991. *Story of My Life: 1804–1876*. New York: State University Press.

Taussig, Michael. 1987. *Shamanism, Colonialism, and the Wild Man*. Chicago: The University of Chicago Press.

West, Cornel. 1993. *Race Matters*. Boston: Beacon Press.

Wheeler, Scot. May 1994. Personal communication recounting an experience at the shelter called *Green Car*.

Woo, Merle. 1983. "Letter to Ma," in Cherrié Moraga and Gloria Anzaldúa (ed.), *This Bridge Called My Back*. Latham, New York: Kitchen Table Women of Color Press.

*Documents used from the Children and Families
of Iowa Volunteer Handbook:*

Domestic Abuse Intervention Services (Children and Families of Iowa)

Domestic Violence Fact Sheets (National Women Abuse Prevention Project)

Domestic Violence Statistics

Iowa Cares (Winter 1991) (Iowa Children's and Family Services)

IowaCASA Newsletter (Spring 1994) (Iowa Coalition Against Sexual Assault)

How Society Shows that It Tolerates Violence

Power and Control Wheel (Domestic Abuse Intervention Project)

Virginia Protection Newsletter (Spring 1986) (Child Welfare Services, Virginia Dept.)

Volunteer Express Newsletter (March 1994) (National Coalition Against Domestic Violence VOICE)

7

Wife Abuse and Family Idealizations

The Violent Regulation of Family Regimes

DOROTHY E. SMITH

These pages explore the uses of violence to enforce an idealization of a family regime of male dominance and female subordination. The literature on wife abuse is full of brief quotations in which women and also, to some extent, men speak about violence, why it is used, and their reactions. Interspersed with the interpretations of the researchers are fragments spoken from the worlds they seek to understand. The literature tends to individuate the problem by attaching attributes such as need to control, dependency, and so on to typified "batterers" or battered. But many of the quotations from people's own accounts tell of events and feelings fully articulated to the social organization of family life. Indeed, they are as much stories of the social organization of men's and women's family relationships, and the part that force plays in them, as stories of individuals. Focusing on the individual batterer deflects attention from the social organization within which force is used.

The argument here is not a causal one. Rather, it is that family regimes are the work of those involved: they are ordered, successfully or not, by culturally standardized idealizations; in the "wife abuse" literature, we find men using force, and women responding to men's use of force in realizing of such idealizations as a local regime.[1] The use of force is not aberrant. It is one of the resources that "comes to hand" in regulating the everyday doings of family life in relation to idealizations of what family should be.

Family life is often represented as a sphere of freedom, a space of privacy in which people can be "themselves" in relationships of intimacy with others. But in reality advertising, movies, books, schooling, women's magazines, college courses in child development and psychology, and high school courses in home economics 120

create pervasive idealizations of family. They are more than prescriptions, rules, advice, recommendations that individuals take to themselves. Such family discourses generalize idealizations—the kinds of house, furniture, clothing, kitchen equipment, car, children, economic and sexual roles of husband and wife, and so on. They create a point of view outside people's actual lives from which the latter come under scrutiny, not only by those who live them, but by others who also participate in these relations. A public standpoint is created, in relation to which anyone's family life is examinable. It is an organizer of relationships among people who are neighbors, who are teachers in children's schools, who are health care professionals treating family members, and so on.

The idealizations are designed in various ways quite outside the local practicality of family living. Advertising offers images of the family living room, bedrooms, and kitchens that are hard to sustain. They are aimed at selling furniture and kitchen devices and are otherwise indifferent to the practicalities of putting together a household conforming to the standardized images they have created. Discourses of parenting have evolved in academic contexts, often developed by professional men who have had little experience of the practicalities of the mothering they have sought to govern, and they have expanded their prejudices into influential theories. Churches as communities that create a shared moral universe construct idealizations of family and family life out of the theologically transformed interests of the mostly male leadership.

Public discourse is increasingly dominated by an ideology of family that represents the decline of the traditional male-headed family as eroding the moral basis of the society. Issues of poverty become redefined as moral problems: the defective, female-headed family is both symptom and cause (for example, Wilson 1987). A typical example is in a column in the *New York Times* on random killings in Denver:

> The availability of guns is a big part of the problem, but there are so many
> other factors. Families have deterioriated, disintegrated, collapsed. Girls too

young to see R-rated movies are having their second and third child. Boys
growing up without fathers and with children for mothers learn in the street
how to behave. Poverty, welfare, and drugs have corroded the soul of urban
America and neither the government nor the people most affected have put
up anything like a valiant fight. (Herbert 1993)

Of course, there is no factual basis for the implication that families in
the United States consist largely of teenage single mothers with male
children who have no one to teach them how to act (mothers clearly
being viewed as incapable of this function). The ideology of familism
is so well entrenched that the writer feels no need to back his statements with evidence.

Along with this is a new men's movement that is oriented towards
men's recapture of their authority in the family. In the absence of the
everyday practical welding of masculine authority in the family to the
conditions of wage-earning, contemporary men's movements seek a
new commitment to making the traditional idealization a design for
living. Tony Evans, a leader in the Promise Keepers movement (a men's
movement) urges men to take back their leadership of the family
whether their wives consent or not, and women to give back leadership
to their husbands "for the sake of . . . our culture" (Minkowitz 1995, p.
69). Though men's movements disavow violence, the use of physical
force is one resource available to men in enforcing a family regime in
which men are enjoined to be dominant. We must be concerned that
these new or renewed idealizations enjoining men to impose their
dominance on family life legitimate implicitly, though not explicitly,
the use of force when other means of asserting men's authority over
their wives fail.

Marriage

Entry into marriage constitutes the local regime to be regulated with
respect to cultural idealizations of family and gender roles. Angela
Browne (1987) reports that "[s]tudies of abused women have found
that the majority—73 percent to 85 percent—do not experience
physical assault until after they have married the abuser" (p. 47). Some
accounts suggest that men view marriage as according them a special
responsibility for enforcing the idealizations of the regime, hence
legitimating their use of violence. At a public hearing, a woman testi-

fied that:

> [m]y husband hit me on his lawyer's advice. Several years before the inci-
> dent [with which he was charged], according to my husband, his lawyer had
> advised him that the best way to dominate a wife is by being sexually aggres-
> sive, and, if that failed, by beating her. (Stacey and Shupe 1983, p. 34)

From New Zealand comes an explicit statement of a man's use of
force to establish his authority. It is from a study of men involved or
planning to be involved in a "stop violence" program.

> PA:[2] Can you explain what discipline means in your relationship?
> GAVIN: Well it's [pause] well just respect and manners and that I s'pose
>   y'know. A woman who's gonna put up when they shut up, so to speak.
> PA: For her to put up and shut up?
> GAVIN: Yeah. (PA: Okay.) Um, so for her not to undermine [laughing] my
>   authority and ohh I don't know.
> PA: Your authority?
> GAVIN: Saying, you know, meaning "what I say goes," you know "no we're
>   not bloody going out tonight. We're staying at home." "Ohh I wanna go
>   out" [laughing]. "No, we're not. I don't wanna go." Y'know. Or like Fri-
>   day night she said, "Ohh I don't really want you to go out." "Well fuck,
>   tough, I'm going." Y'know. And I went out. That's my authority . . .
>   (Adams et al. 1995, p. 389)[3]

Related to this are accounts of men's use of violence in the early days
of marriage to enforce idealized gender roles.

> Joan had expected [when she and Randy got married] that she and Randy
> would share responsibilities "fifty-fifty," but Randy didn't recognize any
> obligation to help with the children or housework. He made that attitude
> clear in their first year of marriage when Joan asked him to carry out the
> garbage and he responded by dumping it on her and all over the living room
> couch. (NiCarthy 1987, p. 181)

Another account of the early days of a marriage shows us a man using
force to assert his right to his wife's household services as well as to

supervise how and when they should be done:

> Sharon and Roy Bikson had been married about two months. It was sum-
> mer, and Sharon stacked the dishes in the sink after the evening meal: she
> decided to take a bath and then do the dishes later. Roy told her she should
> do them now, but she replied that they would be fine there, or why didn't he
> do them? Sharon started to leave the room when Roy—suddenly furious—
> grabbed her. He spun her around and began to slap her face repeatedly.
> Sharon jerked free, but Roy caught her and pushed her down, hitting her in
> the chest with his fists and slapping her. She attempted to say something to
> him, but there wasn't time to get her breath. [Later she told him that she'd
> never done anything to deserve that.] Roy said he knew it, but that she had
> brought it on herself: she was too rebellious. Washing the dishes was
> woman's work, not something a man should do. (Browne 1987, p. 51)

In these instances at least, men's violence is used to enforce a gender
regime established by marriage.

In the Family Regime, Who Regulates?

Marriage founds each particular family regime. Women and men bring
to it understandings of responsibilities for its regulation. In the quota-
tion above from New Zealand, the man justifies his use of force in
terms of his special responsibilities as a man. Edward Gondolf's study
of men who batter describes an association of men's role as governors
of the family regime with the use of violence:

> The men feel that they deserve some privileges in return for maintaining
> order; that is, they expect some concessions, respect, and rewards for their
> job of managing themselves and others. If a man should fly off the handle
> now and then, he should not be made to feel guilty or be accused. After all,
> he has a difficult role to bear as controller, manager, and provider, or so the
> batterer's logic goes. (Gondolf 1985, p. 82)

In many accounts, it is clear that while assaults may flow from a
man's anger, this does not mean that they are not systematic or
intended to control or enforce the specifics of a man's will. An act sat-
urated with emotion is not necessarily lacking intention or authority.

Though Stacey and Shupe do not report that they explored the bases of men's justifications, their study shows a strong relationship between the severity of violence and men's sense of being justified. "Half the men felt the battering was justified (even if they apologized)" (Stacey and Shupe 1983, p. 96).

In the somewhat scarce accounts from men, we find as a common theme their sense of having a right to use violence to get their wives to comply to their idealizations of family life:

> MIKE: [But why would you hit her if she was going to be all the emotional support that you would have?] Simply because she wasn't seeing things the way that I would. I wanted her to fall into a role model, but if she got out of that role model, that's not what I wanted. . . . I guess the only way that I could get her back in line was to hit her. . . . [Why do you think the physical abuse came up then. . .?] Well, like I said before, it was just a way to get her to conform to what I wanted. (Tifft 1993, p. 87)

> MR. R.: I just don't like to have to go through that [beating his wife], you know, but I have to bring out my points or try to bring out to her the things that could be better or beneficial to the whole family if she would just change her ways. (Stacey and Shupe 1983, p. 97)

In the second of these, "Mr. R." assumes both right *and* responsibility to "discipline" his wife in the family interests. It is he who judges what is "beneficial to the whole family."

Women, too, may share the idealization of men's special responsibility for the family regime, though reports of this tend to be from an older generation. One of the women Dee Dee Glass talked to described her mother as believing that "women need a man to keep them under control by being physically violent," and that when she is beaten, it is because she deserves it. As a result "she can't make a decision on her own at all" (Glass 1995, p. 90)

Here, however, is a contemporary account, in this case illustrating the religious legitimation of a male-dominant family regime:

> Now the only time he gets a little rough is when I do something wrong. Like the other day when I went by to visit with my mother across town and didn't

tell him about it first. My mother has been sick for a long time now and I was the only one around to look in on her. . . . So he gets a little rough. But I forgive him. I really do believe that the man should be the head of the family, though. That's what it says in the Bible, and I believe in the Bible. (Stacey and Shupe 1983, p. 105)

There are also many accounts of men whose violence, verbal and physical, sustains their detailed management of family life. Scarf (1988)[4] describes one family situation in which the husband took over complete and detailed financial control:

I have to ask him for money every day. We have a joint checking account, but he goes over it every day, and he practically has a heart attack if I paid for something without his permission. (Scarf 1988, p. 162)

Descriptions of the man's assumption of direct or supervisory control over the details of family living in relation to idealizations of roles, household practices, and family economy are typical. In one family, wife and husband

followed strict, stereotypical male-female roles—the wife doing all the household chores, the husband none. When they went out, he drove. He decided where they were to live, what furniture to buy, and how the money was to be spent. (Scarf 1988, p. 179)

Kay describes her husband as

the type of person that did not like me to make a decision for myself. If I decided to cut my hair and went ahead and did it, I would get into a lot of trouble. He would really get angry. If I decided that it was okay for the child to spend the night with a friend, he didn't like it. I didn't ask him first. If I go to the grocery store and I take a little bit longer than what I should have, he didn't like it because I was supposed to be where he wanted me to be at the exact time. I wasn't supposed to do anything that I wasn't told to do. (Tifft 1993, p. 87)

Violence is used to establish the man's desires as exclusive determinants of his wife's provision of personal services, which are enforced as simple complements of the man's desire.

He'd never come home at the same time, but I was supposed to have dinner—and not just *any* dinner—ready whenever. [He'd say] I never liked sex
enough, I never dressed as well as he wanted. Once he gave me a bloody
nose, then became angrier that I couldn't go out to a show with him because
it hadn't stopped bleeding. (Stacey and Shupe 1983, p. 69)

Chris was expected to have dinner ready the moment Wes stepped in the
door, whether that was at six o'clock in the evening or one in the morning.
If it wasn't ready or it had dried out he unleashed his rage. (NiCarthy 1987,
p. 114)

Alternative bases of subjectivity are displaced and subdued. "The man's
moods, definitions, attributions, and opinions dominate the environment" (Browne 1987, p. 80). The idealization embodied in the regime
he regulates legitimates his right to exact personal services as the com-
plement of her economic dependency on him.

Violence as Punishment

We have been concerned as feminists with why women who are beaten
do not leave their husbands. Both the realities of their general economic dependence, particularly when they have children, and descriptions of responses to trauma or fear have been described. In one study
(Graham et al. 1994), parallels are drawn between women's being
beaten by their male partners and the "Stockholm Syndrome." In a
bank robbery in Stockholm in 1973, two men held four bank employees hostage for five days. The employees developed "strong emotional
bonds" with the men holding them hostage and came to see the police
as enemies. It is suggested that women's responses to men who beat
them are of this kind. There is, however, an alternative and more
straightforward account: violence is understood as punishment, and
punishment locates a fault that should be changed.

Both men's and women's accounts suggest that beating is effective
in enforcing compliance to the man's assumption of his right to govern. Browne reports a study[5] showing that "men were twice as likely as
women to say that their relationships improved after the use of violence" (Browne 1987, p. 42). The accounts describe a heightening of
women's attentiveness to their husband's standards of service. Joan
reports how

[she] tried to adapt [to Randy's violence] by always serving dinner on time and never confronting Randy with anything unpleasant. (NiCarthy 1987, p. 181).

Women become fearful "of doing something he didn't like or neglecting to do something he wanted" (NiCarthy 1987, p. 140); they "monitor" "the abuser's whereabouts and state of mind ... anticipating his wants or frustrations" (Browne 1987, p. 79). Julie, whose husband hit her for the first time just after they were married, reported:

You never forget it when someone hits you that hard, and you never have to be hit that hard again to continue to be afraid. In fact, I don't think he ever hit me that hard again. But in the following years that we were together, I was always afraid that he would, and it kept me in line. (Barnett and LaViolette, 1993, p. 79)

In some acounts, we can see how the familial idealization works to legitimate the man's violence as punishment for something the woman has done wrong. If he is angry and violent, she must be at fault. If there is punishment, there has been a crime. Julie's story does not include an account of what she meant by "keeping her in line," but many, such as the following, record how violence leads to a woman's scrutinizing her behavior to detect where she might be at fault. Her self-scrutiny is structured by an idealization of family and gender roles. When, as in the following instance, she cannot figure out what she is being punished for, the violence makes no sense to her. It is simply bewildering:

At first, [Susan] felt sure they could work it out; in between the batterings, Don was so nice and good to her and she didn't want to give up on them. She kept asking herself, "What am I doing wrong? The house is nice ... I keep it up nicely ... I prepare food for him.... I'm not just sitting around ... I'm not having any affairs." (Browne 1987, p. 63)

Susan adopts the standpoint of the family idealization's gender role prescriptions: she asks herself about her housekeeping, her preparation of meals, her sexual loyalty. The beatings are incomprehensible to her *in these terms*. She looks for but cannot find the fault for which she is being punished.

The translation of violence into punishment leading to guilt is manifest in the following stories:

> At first I thought it was my fault that he was angry with me, but it wasn't my fault he hit me. But . . . the more abusive and the more distant he became, the more I actually internalised that and made it my fault. . . . it was my fault if the dinner wasn't ready. It was my fault if something went wrong. It was my fault that he had assaulted me. It was my fault that I'd upset him. It was my fault for nagging. (Glass 1995, p. 65)

When Dory reviews her experience of living with a violent husband, she too cannot understand her husband's anger because her self-scrutiny in terms of the idealization of the Jewish family tells her she has been a good wife. Even though Dory is confident that she did what she should have done as a Jewish wife and mother, she still sought an answer to his "uncontrolled fits of rage" (Scarf 1988, p. 176) in something she had done:

> I still miss him. I could never figure out what I did to make him so angry. I was such a good wife and mother. I was brought up in a Jewish home, and did everything I was taught. . . . (Scarf 1988, p. 176)

In some accounts, even extremes of violence, interpreted by the familial idealization, are seen as somehow the wife's fault.

> [Betsy] wept as she recalled the beating, describing it in graphic detail, how she felt as his fingers were digging into her flesh, at what point the wounds opened up and which ones bled and how she felt the blood dripping. "He told me that he had been trained in the army to kill with his hands. That he could break my neck and my back. He grabbed me around the waist and held me until it was hurting. He threatened to snap my back. He choked me until I couldn't breathe. He threw me on the floor and beat me some more. I lay there apologizing, and he stood over me yelling: "Look what you make me do to you!" When he stopped kicking me and beating me, and hitting me with his belt, he started to cry. Then he told me to get out, and he pushed me out the door and locked it. He had torn my clothes, and I was almost naked." . . . *Even then Betsy felt it was her fault. "I still believed that*

Jewish men make wonderful husbands, and I as a Jewish woman was doing
something so wrong that was causing him agony." (Scarf 1988, p. 172, my
emphasis)

The idealizations of the family at work in these accounts interpret
the man's anger and his violence as legitimate responses to a woman's
fault or as caused by "something she was doing wrong." As in the above
account, the man himself interprets his anger in the same way "Look
what you make me do to you!" This logic may well be shared by non-
family members to whom a woman appeals for help. A minister to
whom one woman appealed for help "scolded her for 'talking back' to
her husband" (NiCarthy 1987, p. 29).

Women are sometimes ashamed to disclose that wounds and
bruises have been inflicted by their husbands because they feel that to
have been beaten shows that they have been at fault in some way. As we
have seen in the minister's response just cited, this may be a realistic
appraisal of others' responses. A number of reports describing police
responses to domestic violence calls suggests that police may respond
in this way. Some of Suzanne Henry's police respondents in an Aus-
tralian study made such interpretations:

> From my experience, I think the woman should do more around the house.
> The woman demands a lot, but doesn't do her bit—and he retaliates. I'd feel
> the same. (Henry 1989, p. 78)

> I feel that a lot of women could've avoided the violence by being a bit more
> generous—doing a better job of the housework and taking better care of
> their appearance. (Henry 1989, p. 79)

Answering questions as to why women stay in violent relationships
needs attention to women's interpretations of the violence and how,
understood in terms of a family idealization, violence becomes punishment for faults she tries to rectify.

The Idealization of Women's Subordinated Subject

The idealization of women's role in the family constitutes a definite
structuring of her self. Some accounts describe this "self" or subject as

a total subordination of autonomous will and desire. The subject is displaced onto the others women serve. Among a group of women who came together to criticize their experience as psychiatric patients, I listened to a woman describing how she had learned as a girl that she was nothing in or for herself and that she existed only to serve men. And this she did, for twenty years and through several episodes of psychiatric hospitalization for depression. I've found echoes of what I think was her experience in accounts by women of what we might call, following Dana Jack (1991), the "silenced self." Jack describes, among married women suffering from a depressive illness, a pattern of suppressing their own desires and judgment and subordinating themselves to their husbands' and children's needs. Her work emphasizes self-silencing *as a daily and routine practice.* From another source, the following story by a woman who was abused as a wife illustrates Jack's notion. A woman who as a ten-year-old took over responsibility for cooking for a large family told the interviewer that she felt she "didn't exist. That there was nothing inside me" (Glass 1995, p. 23).

Kathy Nairne and Gerrilyn Smith see a relation between family idealization of women's selfless service and depressive illness in women. One woman they quote describes an idealization of women's displaced subject as one she sought consciously to realize:

> The idea of always putting someone else first is very central to my belief about the female: that it is the nurturing, appropriate thing to do; that the woman should be caring in a way which means putting someone else first to a point which is quite nonsensical. Even though I know intellectually that it's a pattern which has been handed down to me, I still *feel* "You as a female should be able to do this." (Nairne and Smith 1984, p. 51)

Belenky and colleagues (1986) describe an analogous form of consciousness that is characterized by the alienation of a woman's subjectivity and agency in the male figures in her family:

> I didn't think I had a right to think. That probably goes back to my folks. When my father yelled, everybody automatically jumped. Every woman I ever saw, then, the man barked and the woman jumped. I just thought that women were no good and had to be told everything to do. (Belenky et al. 1986, p. 30)

Force may be used by men to create this decentering in wives who express autonomy. One woman reports that her husband

> gradually started grinding me down, taking everything that was me. He didn't approve of my business, because I was making money. He criticised my friends, he criticised my family. He was nit-picky about my clothes. He would try and dress me how he wanted. He tried to take everything of me away. (Glass 1995, p. 80)

Eva Lundgren (1992) has written in this connection of men's "episte-mological privilege," that is, their right to define reality for women (see Scarf 1988, p. 165). Belenky and colleagues report a woman reflecting on why she stayed for ten years with an abusive husband:

> You know, I used to only hear his words, and his words kept coming out of my mouth. He had me thinking I didn't know anything. (Belenky et al. 1986, p. 30)

Women committed to such an idealization *are active* in subordinating their own desires and judgment to the man to whom they are married. In decentering themselves as subjects, they *become his agents* in governing themselves:

> Women often ask: "Am I giving enough? Am I being selfish? Am I being loving enough?" The phrase "to care for" comes to mean both the *emotion* of caring and *actions related to* care-giving—feeling love, and therefore "being there" for and doing for the other person. (Browne 1987, p. 79)

Discussion

These stories make visible men's uses of violence to enforce a family regime conforming to an idealization of family in which men dominate and women serve. As an idealization, it was formed at a time when the economic organization of North America provided a significant sector at least of the white male population with stable employment, enabling a "family wage," that is, a wage sufficient to provide for a family, and indeed at its apex in the 1950s at more than comfortable standards of living. This is the period that is sometimes known by regulation theorists as "Fordist," identifying it with a combination of mass production, typified by Ford's invention of assembly line production, and mass distribution. These were complemented by a mass media that, through advertising, images of family life in movies and on TV, and women's magazines, standardized consumer interest and demand, to complete the circuit.

This economic organization provided for the practical viability of family regimes governed by this "traditional" idealization. In some women's stories, women's experience of complete economic dependency as children and as young women is described as foundational to their dependency on the violent men they have married. A woman who has had no experience of independence, who has never been expected or expected herself to become independent, who has lived among women who are dependent, whose media-originated idealizations of marriage inculcate dependency experiences a seamless social reality. She has not known how to think about herself as someone capable of independence,[6] nor does she know know how to go about it:

> I was so lost. I knew I couldn't function, support myself and my baby. I wasn't strong. I had to hang on to him. He was the provider, he did everything for me. . . . (NiCarthy 1987, p. 175)

Though Gloria left Hal more than once, she went back because she

> felt dependent on him. She had never lived on her own and thought that violence and possessiveness were conditions of marriage. (NiCarthy 1987, p. 107)

Family idealizations provide the terms on which people's family lives are judged and on which they judge themselves, but their realization as a regime is subject to economic relations over which they have no control. More than one member of a family-household may have to find paid work to keep it going; the hours and demands of paid work and school of various family members do not necessarily coordinate; the relations of an economy determine who earns and how much, and the allocation of time between paid work and home. People do indeed construct or organize families together, but they do not do so under conditions of their choosing, and there is often little they can do to change the ways they are hooked into the larger society and the consequences it has for them. The onus of familial idealizations does not change but actual family regimes are assembled and operate in material realities that family members can do little to change or control. So people assemble and regulate family regimes out of the resources that "come to hand": differences in physical strength and in ability to control access to resources—money, food, shelter, goodies, leisure activities, and so on. The one who is more physically powerful has resources that can be used against the less powerful, men versus women, parents versus young children, adult children versus their elder parents.

Conventions of privacy protect actual family regimes against outsiders whose scrutiny might disclose a constant and normal failure to live up to the impossible. Privacy also protects the household as the backstage (Goffman 1959), where family members work to create the face that families present to themselves as well as to outsiders. The use of physical force is part of this backstage work for many families, and is deeply implicated in the organization of the family regime as a locally regulated practice of a family idealization.

The regulation of public discourse on the family from the right wing and the formation of indirect communities of men committed to traditional idealizations creates specific hazards for the women they partner. The traditional idealization, as a design for regulating actual family regimes, is no longer sustained by the organization of the economy. Unemployment is high—among some groups, extremely high. Many households must be supported by more than one earner. A basic contradiction emerges between the idealization and the actual conditions of its realization in practice. Men may be more or less disposed to violence, but if the family idealization they and groups they participate in accord them the right and responsibility to govern the local regimes constituted on marriage, the use of force becomes the major means of enforcement when resources such as a man's economic dominance are lacking. Its uses may be more normal than we'd like to think.[7] How can violence not come into play to enforce compliance to men's authority when that authority to control has become a matter of their identity and commitment as members of a men's movement or church that lays on them the idealization of male "responsibility" for family regimes?

Of course there is much to be learned once we begin to ask questions about family social organization and how it is hooked into public discourses. It is likely that some of issues I have raised in relation to wife abuse might be raised in relation to the uses of physical force towards children. A particular point of stress lies in the juncture between the private and backstage existence of a particular family and the face it presents to outsiders who share the idealization it is to be judged by. These relations have not been investigated, although the kinds of materials I've used here give some clues to them. Nor do we have explorations of the ways in which idealizations of family and of masculine roles in regulating family regimes enter into men's relationships with other men. We do not really know the extent of wife abuse or child abuse, though we have come to realize that it is greater than we ever believed. My fear is that in the present context men's temptation to resort to violence will be heightened by the gap between family idealizations enjoining traditional gender roles and the practicality of their realization under contemporary economic conditions.

Notes

1. This is not, of course, a generalized theory of male violence. Indeed I doubt there can be such a theory. I am specifically uninterested in violence motivated by obsessive jealousies and possessiveness, or other emotional perversions that are more appropriately explored as attributed of individuals.
2. PA is the researcher doing the interview.
3. In this case the couple were not married, but in explaining his title to authority, the man described a relationship that was a marriage in everything but having "signed a piece of paper."

    I'm the [laughing] bread earner, (PA: Yeah.) um, I'm the protector of this household. Um, when it comes down to it what I say goes. (Adams et al. 1995, p. 389)

4. Scarf's study is of special interest because it is the only one I've encountered that addresses the use of violence within a particular subculture. Hence it "localizes" men's use of force, and women's interpretation of it, in relation to that subculture's idealization of family.
5. The reference is to Murphy (1984).
6. Belenky et al. also emphasize how this organization of self may cut off

the capacity for representational and reflective thought (Belenky et al. 1986, p. 31).

7. A recent nationwide Canadian study (Mitchell 1993) showed that more than half the women surveyed had experienced violence from men and that 29 percent of women who were or had been married had experienced violence from husbands.

References

Adams, Peter J., Alison Towns, and Nicola Gavey. 1995. "Dominance and Entitlement: The Rhetoric Men Use to Discuss Their Violence Towards Women." *Discourse & Society* 6 (3): 387–406.

Barnett, Ola W. and Alyce LaViolette, eds. 1993. *It Could Happen to Anyone: Why Battered Women Stay.* Newbury Park, CA: Sage Publications.

Belenky, Mary Field, Blythe McVicker Clinchy, Nancy Rule Goldberger, and Jill Mattuck Tarule. 1986. *Women's Ways of Knowing: The Development of Self, Voice, and Mind.* New York: Basic Books.

Browne, Angela. 1987. *When Battered Women Kill.* New York: The Free Press.

Davis, Liane V. and Jan. L. Hagen. 1992. "The Problem of Wife Abuse: The Interrelationship of Social Policy and Social Work Practice." *Social Work* 37 (1): 15–20.

Glass, Dee Dee. 1995. *"All My Fault": Why Women Don't Leave Abusive Men.* London: Virago Press.

Goffman, Erving. 1959. *The Presentation of Self in Everyday Life.* New York: Anchor Books.

Gondolf, Edward W. 1985. *Men Who Batter: An Integrated Approach for Stopping Wife Abuse.* Holmes Beach, FL: Learning Publications, Inc.

Graham, Dee L.R. with Edna I. Rawlings and Roberta K. Rigsby. 1994. *Loving to Survive: Sexual Terror, Men's Violence, and Women's Lives.* New York: New York University Press.

Henry, Suzanne E. 1989. "Policing and Male Violence in Australia," in *Women, Policing, and Male Violence: International Perspectives,* eds. Jalna Hanmer, Jill Radford, and Elizabeth A. Stanko. London: Routledge, pp. 70–89.

Herbert, Bob. 1993. "In America: Killing 'Just for Whatever.'" *New York Times,* August 11, p. A13.

Jack, Dana Crowley. 1991. *Silencing the Self: Women and Depression.* Cambridge, MA: Harvard University Press.

Lundgren, Eva. 1992. "The Hand that Strikes and Comforts: Gender Construction in the Field of Tension Encompassing Body and Symbol, Stability and Change," in Maud L. Eduards, Inga Elgquist-Saltzman, Eva Lundgren, Christina Sjöblad, Elisabeth Sundin, and Ull Wikander, *Rethinking Change: Current Swedish Feminist Research*. Stockholm, Sweden: HSFR (Humanistisk-samhällsvetenskapliga forskningsradet), pp. 131–158.

McClintock, Anne. 1993. "Screwing the System: Sexwork, Race, and the Law," in "Feminism and Postmodernism," eds. Margaret Ferguson and Jennifer Wicke. A special issue of *boundary* 2 (19), (2): 70–95.

Minkowitz, Donna. 1995. "In the Name of the Father." *MS* 6 (3): 64–71.

Mitchell, Alanna. 1993. "50% of Women Report Assaults.'" *Globe and Mail*, November 19, p. 1.

Murphy, J.E. 1984. "Date Abuse and Forced Intercourse among College Students." Paper presented at the Second National Conference for Family Violence Researchers, University of New Hampshire, Durham.

Nairne, Kathy and Gerrilyn Smith. 1984. *Dealing with Depression*. London: The Women's Press.

NiCarthy, Ginny. 1987. *The Ones Who Got Away*. Seattle, WA: The Seal Press.

Scarf, Mimi. 1988. *Battered Jewish Wives: Case Studies in the Response to Rage*. Lewiston: The Edwin Mellen Press

Stacey, William A. and Anson Shupe. 1983. *The Family Secret: Domestic Violence in America*. Boston: Beacon Press.

Tifft, Larry L. 1993. *Battering of Women: The Failure of Intervention and the Case for Prevention*. Boulder, CO: Westview Press

Wilson, William Julius. 1987. *The Truly Disadvantaged: The Inner City, the Underclass, and Public Policy*. Chicago: The University of Chicago Press.

8

Discursive Constraint in the Narrated Identities of Childhood Sex Abuse Survivors

CAROL RAMBO RONAI

When we can't figure out what our own particular story is, we feel lost. (A Native American in an ad for MTV)

*   *   *

Let these three asterisks denote a shift to various temporal and attitudinal realms.

*   *   *

I have just come in the door, home from school. My father lies on rumpled, stained, grey sheets, his body rigid, masturbating. His feet flex with the oncoming orgasm, his toes splayed apart, revealing flaking, overgrown, yellow-green, toenails. The presence of his second grader is no reason to stop; this is nothing out of the ordinary.

I must find my way around him and get to my mother because we've got big problems: the social workers are on their way. I slowly put down my books and papers and find something to do in the entryway to make myself appear busy. I catch a quick glimpse to gauge how close he is to orgasm and determine it is safe to proceed past him and to my mother in the kitchen. If I go too early he may decide to stop masturbating and grab me. If I go too late and interrupt his orgasm, he may hit me. Likewise, if he catches me staring at him, he may either decide to involve me or get angry at my interruption. It has to be gauged just so, as does everything in our household.

I successfully make it over to my mother, who is heating spaghetti sauce on the stove, and whisper: "The social workers are coming and they will see him like that." My mother stops what she is doing, turns fearfully to my father and blurts out, "Carol says the social workers are on their way here."

My mother, who is borderline mentally retarded, does not have the finesse I do. We are working with very little time, but I would have waited until after the orgasm to tell him. My father screams at us, grabbing his clothes: "What did she say? Why are they coming here?" My mother responds, cowering: "Don't look at me! She just told me." Through gritted teeth, my father asks, "What did you say to them? What did you do?" I tell him: "They want to give us something called a voucher so I can buy shoes." "Did you tell them you needed shoes?" he asks. "They said I needed them," I reply. "Why did you say you would take them? Why are they coming over here?" I edge my way towards the door of the efficiency apartment, my mother following me. This is getting bad, he is ready to blow up.

My mother opens the door and I walk out. My father yells and my mother ducks. A pan of hot sauce sails out of our doorway, splattering red goo all over our neighbor's door across the hall. My mom and I stand there paralyzed, dumbfounded by such a public display of violence. This is unlike Frank; he never risks anything he could get caught for. "He could have burned us with that," my mother whispers. "The pan could have hit your head," I add.

In a minute my father emerges, fully dressed, and exits the apartment building growling, "Clean that shit up." My mother and I scramble to get the mess cleaned up, fearful of the neighbors getting home early or the social workers arriving. We don't want to explain this.

*   *   *

Using at-hand knowledge (Riemer 1977) of my own experience of childhood sex abuse, sociological introspection (Ellis 1991), and nine life history interviews with female survivors, I explore how collective discourse serves to produce and reproduce ongoing abuse in the everyday lives of survivors. This chapter is written using an ethnographic reporting format called a "layered account" (Ronai 1995; 1992), a technique that allows the researcher to incorporate as many resources as possible including theory, statistics, and accounts of lived experience and emotions. The goal is to evoke in the reader her or his own lived emotional experience (Ellis 1991) of childhood sex abuse and to explain the continuing impact of the experience on the adult survivor.

In this chapter, I will assume that life is a story we tell and retell to each other and ourselves as a means of triangulating our identity through temporal and social space (Bertaux 1981; Gubrium, Holstein, and Buckholdt 1994; Kohli 1986). By identity, I mean who we perceive ourselves to be in any given situation, moment, or scene, relative to others. By telling a story, we make identity claims. I, for instance, am telling a story here of being a survivor of childhood sex abuse and a sociologist. Others react to this claim through the filter of their own experience. Through their reactions, I construct a sense of whether my portrayal of self, my identity claim, is considered to be legitimate or not.

Identity emerges as a narrative dialectic with the past and with the audience. The narrative is emergent in character because the past is constantly being reinterpreted through the lens of the present. The story changes each time we tell it, depending on the context of the situation and the intended audience. Narrative is also intersubjective; at the same time we make identity claims for ourselves, we embed within our stories identities for others to claim. Through the medium of the story, we exist socially as individuals and intersubjectively as a collective. Also through the medium of narrative, both bodies and identities become the subjects of domination.

Others have the ability to threaten our opinion of ourselves by suggesting negative categories to define ourselves by. Childhood sex abuse is frequently perpetuated through "discursive constraint" (Ronai 1994), where an individual's behavior is constrained by the threat of having a negative category applied to his or her self. These categories are disseminated throughout society so effectively that they take on a taken-for-granted or "given" quality. Through an effective application of discursive constraint, a pedophile can physically control a child while sexual abuse is being perpetrated, or discursive constraint can serve to silence the survivor years after the abuse takes place.

*   *   *

He grabbed me by my small arm, practically pulling it out of the socket. "No," I said, firmly planting my feet and pulling away from him, "I don't want to." "Don't be a baby. You know you like it," he said, pulling me toward the bed. "I don't like it today," I said, flinging all my weight in the opposite direction in an effort to counterbalance his pull. If I put up enough resistance, sometimes he would give up, regarding the whole matter as not worth the effort. It wasn't working. My feet were dragging across the multicolored shag rug of the efficiency apartment, burning with the friction. "No," I screamed, flinging my bottom to the ground. I was still being dragged. I kicked at him and missed. He laughed affectionately, as if reacting to something "cute" I had done.

Upon seeing the violence I was willing to employ, my mother intervened and pulled on my other arm. "It's her bedtime, Frank, let her be," my mother stated. "Since when?" he asked, dubious of my mother's motives, forgetting to pull on my arm for a second. "It has always been eight o'clock, 'cause she has to get up to go to school in the morning," my mother replied, yanking my right arm, pulling me away from him. He thought about this for a moment, then pulled my arm and said, "That can't be right—it's too long to sleep." They pulled, back and forth, for several rounds arguing. Each time my mother pulled I leaned in her direction, hoping to break his grasp and run away.

Ultimately "logic" won out. "I'm her father and I'm setting a new bedtime, eight-thirty." I flashed a desperate look at my mother. "There's nothing I can do," she said, as she let go and turned. "NO!" I screamed, vibrating deep in my chest from the effort to keep the word airborne. "No, no, no," I whimpered as he dragged me to the bed, raking my panties down my legs, scratching long red welts with his nails. "No," escaped my lips, now barely a whispered sigh as he parted my legs and descended, face first between them. "You always like this once we get started," he said. "Not today," I replied, passively submitting in the most distracted, disinterested manner possible.

Later, he turned away from me and put something wet on his finger. He turned back and tried to place his finger inside my vagina. The pain burned, seared, straight up my middle and into my head. I stopped breathing; I remember the sensation of my lungs freezing, of attempting to breathe in only to get nothing. In that moment I lost all cunning; I was a blaze of raw animal, cornered, fighting for survival. The pain was excruciating and I had to get out of there. Instinct, panic, and my hatred for my father flashed, and I thrust out my leg as hard as I could. My father's head snapped back with the impact, a satisfying thud, as my heel connected with the side of his skull. I attempted to roll out of bed, away from him, to no avail. He was on top of me in an instant, pinning me with his left hand as he punched me matter-of-factly in the side with his right.

I say "matter-of-factly," because there was no anger in his face. He was interested only in controlling me. With that realization I calmed down, and he stopped punching me. Again he turned and put something wet on his finger. Again he put his finger inside my vaginal passageway. And again, the pain was unbearable and I kicked out at him. "Hold still, it can't hurt that much," he said. "It does," I moaned through clenched teeth, "it does," I repeated. "You're just being a big baby, now hold still," he said, again placing his finger inside my vagina, though not so far this time.

It hit me with an icy horror what this was about—he was considering intercourse. Why put his finger in there otherwise? He had sex with my mother while I was around all the time, but never with me. It was my turn if I wasn't careful.

He was trying to massage my vulva to make it feel pleasant so that I would like the finger inside. I decided that I would scream out every time he placed his finger in my vagina. My only chance of putting him off for a while was to convince him that I was, indeed, too small to take him. After a while he gave up, shoved me, and stated, "I still think you're just being a baby. I bet it doesn't hurt that much."

* * *

Calling me a "baby" was a tactic my father used to control the discourse available for me to define myself by. To cry, to object to the treatment I was receiving, was to resist my father's will. He countered my resistance through physical consequences and discursive constraint. By offering me a negative self-label, "baby," my father was attempting to delegitimate my conception of self, coerce me into doing his will and force my future silence.

* * *

I'm talking with Trisha, a white, forty-six-year-old woman who, after hearing me speak publicly about my history of child sex abuse, volunteered to be interviewed. She states, "I'm not sure I'm what you're looking for. . . . I was beaten and verbally abused. . . . I don't know if you call it child sex abuse or not."

I listen as Trisha recounts stories of her father and brother sexually abusing her older sisters; her father and brother treating her in a highly sexualized manner, calling her "slut," "prostitute," and "cunt" at nine years of age because she started growing breasts; and her uncle almost catching her to molest her. She recalls being picked up by a stranger in a car, being driven to a remote area, and "fondled." This story is inconsistent with her earlier confusion about her definition of being a child sex abuse survivor. I believe she is lying. I struggle to keep this doubt out of my presentation of self, angry for doubting her because the fear of not being believed is a mechanism that serves to keep child sex abuse victims silent.

Towards the end of the interview, I ask: "Has shame played any role in your life?" Trisha is dead quiet. She begs me to keep the interview confidential. I repeat that I will. She reveals she had sex with her brother:

> But I can't really call that child sex abuse. I was eighteen and he kept pestering me to have sex and beating me up for not letting him screw me and I made the decision and told him I would if he gave me three hundred dollars. I didn't think it would be so bad but it was awful. I'd say the turning point in my life. Everything was ruined after that. And later he got married and told his wife that I seduced him and she confronted me and told me she knew I seduced him and that I screwed him up for the rest of his life. God, the whole family must know his version of the story. It makes me sick, physically ill to tell it. Meanwhile, he's the *legitimate* one, not me. [her emphasis]

Trisha trembles telling me this, and repeats:

> I can't claim this is childhood sex abuse yet when I read about sex abuse victims I feel like I know what they mean when they describe how they feel.

I immediately empathize, and feel obligated to share with her an incident that occurred when I was fifteen years old. I tell Trisha, "I've got a story like that, a story I have never told anyone the way it really happened."

*   *   *

I went to see a Health and Rehabilitative Services (HRS) counselor about getting vocational training for my mentally retarded mother. Hugh was delightful for a girl who had never experienced a father. He had slightly overgrown white hair and an elfish beard without a mustache. He seemed grandfatherly, kind—someone I felt safe with. He was mischief, intellect, philosophy, light. He decided to treat me as an incest survivor before he dealt with my mother's issues. He made me feel good about myself and gave me a great deal of hope about my future. I adored Hugh. Hugh showered me with attention, bought me art supplies, drove me around, and took me out to eat. He even took me to the hospital and paid for it when I broke my foot. Through HRS, Hugh found a way for me, by the age of sixteen, to go to college.

One day Hugh asked: "Do you have any good bras?" The question was awkward but seemed legitimate because I was stuffing my breasts into small white triangles of cloth, wearing training bras when I needed a C-cup. I interpreted his interest in the topic as an embarrassing necessity that resulted from his counselor role. I said, "No." He gave me money to buy two bras and commented; "I hope your breasts haven't been damaged."

Later, we had several conversations about the harm that could be done to growing breasts that did not have proper support. Later still, he asked to examine my breasts to see if they were damaged or not. By now, I suspected he was sexually interested in me, but I was afraid he would sabotage my college money if I tried to stop him. Of course, maybe he was concerned about my breasts and I was just being a paranoid little girl—a baby.

With trepidation, I took off my shirt to let him see that I bought the bras. He cupped his hands around my breasts. I choked, laughed, and snorted at the same time, nervously spraying saliva as I did so. My emotions were so overwhelming I didn't know what to do. Hugh was trembling. He asked if he could kiss my breasts and I was paralyzed.

That moment stretched into forever. Why was I allowing this to happen? Why was I stupid enough to trust him? Did my letting him do this make me a whore? I knew what I was doing. Or did I? I wasn't doing anything. This is the way all men are, and I'd better get used to it. Or is this the way men react to me? Is this the price I pay for love and support from men? I was trapped by my internal dialogue and my knotted twisted shame, as I remembered that I had told and listened to dirty jokes with Hugh, that I had asked Hugh questions about sex, that I had told him what my father had done. I had brought this all on myself, I had miscommunicated to Hugh, making him think I wanted this when I didn't. It was all my fault. I was responsible. I had led him on. I wanted to cry. I wanted to stop existing because I didn't know how to go on living, being who I must really be to allow this to happen.

He reached down and kissed my breasts. He sucked a nipple while I sat there and let it happen. I caught a whiff of Old Spice aftershave mingling with his sixty-year-old-man musk. The aroma filled my nostrils, hit my stomach, and I was repulsed. My throat seized up, and for a second I felt as if my heart had stopped; I could not breathe. I wanted to throw up but nothing was coming in or going out. Finally, revulsion overpowered me. I pushed off backwards from him in the wheeled office chair and put my top back on. I did not look at him and neither of us said anything as we left his office together.

He tried this on several subsequent visits, until finally I told my boyfriend what was going on, and he went with me to my next visit. My boyfriend said only two words: "I know." Hugh sputtered that it wouldn't happen again, my college was secure, and concluded the session by saying: "Gee, I sure hope I haven't done more damage to her. She just seemed so different."

*   *   *

Trisha and I have stories that are of interest for at least two reasons. First, my need to share this story felt like a way to legitimate her status as a sex abuse victim. I was offering her my frame by sharing my story. As we talked she pointed out that I was underage when my experience happened. I countered that eighteen is an arbitrary age limit. What was important was how it made her feel.

I told her that I knew my story sounded wimpy compared to what she went through. I felt I had to be careful not to make too big a claim about what happened to me relative to what happened to her. We were operating off a "harm done" continuum, whereby her experience of abuse became more valid than mine because she had sex with her abuser whereas I only had my breasts fondled. This conversation reflected an economy of violation and validation. She legitimated my claim by invoking my minor status, and I legitimated her claim by invoking the seriousness of the act.

This language exists in the research literature as well. Many scholars organize the lived experience of sexual abuse in terms of severity based on levels of intrusion, duration, trauma, and the relationship between the victim and offender (Summit and Kryso 1978; Kempe 1984). In this vocabulary, our experience is less legitimate than others because our experience does not match the official authorities' definition of serious childhood sex abuse. Trisha was not a child when she had sex with her brother. My breasts were touched by a male counselor, nothing more. Also my father's primary form of abuse was to perform oral sex on me. Our abuse wasn't "so bad."

Second, both stories demonstrated discursive constraint. Trisha and I were attempting to find a language to frame these experiences for each other in such a way that we could live with ourselves. We needed to be validated as victims, as women who lacked power in these situations; otherwise, why did we allow these things to happen to us? But we both drew on another definition of the situation, one we internalized from mainstream discourse—we were both "whores."

Our statuses as legitimate survivors were in question because of personal gains we had derived from the situation. The possibility of having to face others calling us "whore," a particular fiction we did not want to have attached to our definition of self, served to keep us quiet about our experiences. In other words, our knowledge of how this category has been applied to other women in our situation served to constrain us by threatening the kinds of claims we were permitted to make about who we were. Our definition of self became problematic and made it difficult for Trisha and me to know how to act towards ourselves and our social worlds.

*   *   *

The self-constructions of the sex abuse survivor are often not taken as legitimate. Trisha, for instance, comments that she hates holidays and other family gatherings, because everyone believes her brother's account of events rather than hers:

> Anytime I have a complaint about anything, they wave me off saying, "There goes Trish again." In private, one of my sisters will admit her abuse to me. In public, she doesn't want them to treat her like they do me.

Selves that are not taken by others as legitimate are not listened to. Without legitimacy, the survivor does not have the power to contribute positively to her or his emergent definition of self. Those who are "authorized" to tell their legitimate, believable stories will have their sense of self confirmed by the external world. They are legitimate society members. Those who tell stories that are not believed, or stories people are not comfortable hearing, will have their identities, their self-constructions, brought into question. They will experience discursive constraint. Fear of not being taken as legitimate silences survivors, which, in turn, makes the discourse of child sex abuse infrequently heard. This, in turn, perpetuates the idea that these stories are strange, unusual, and not legitimate.

The survivor of childhood sex abuse experiences the loss of a complete identity. In everyday life, the stories that people take for granted as resources to share their identity with others are not readily available for the survivor. One twenty-four-year-old white participant, Daphnie, remarked:

> Everyone can sit around and talk about their childhood, but what am I supposed to do? I can't talk at all. I have to keep quiet or I'd spoil everyone's time.

A twenty-three-year-old Asian participant, Trina, commented:

> I just wish I could share this with people, that if they knew this they'd know why I get the way I get sometimes and cut me a break. But then again, if they knew, they wouldn't trust me anymore.

All of the subjects echoed a fear of being stigmatized; two were concerned that someone might consider taking their children from them; five stated they did not want to be thought of "that way."

In part, the definition of self for the survivor is that the self is not trustable. With too much criticism, or discursive constraint, coming from the victimizer and/or the society at large, life becomes problematic. Everyday events lack the "accomplished" quality that they appear to have for others. Survivors, in their most vulnerable moments, do not have the means by which to make decisions because they no longer trust their cultural proscriptions. This process of second-guessing oneself can leave the survivor feeling slow-witted, as if she were a visitor to a new culture.

There are, at times, good reasons for survivors to question their conclusions. Child sex abuse survivors have beliefs that reflect their unique experiences. Daphnie recounted the following:

> My father told me this was how men showed love and that he loved me more than my mother or sisters. Even though I sort of knew better, I sort of didn't. When a guy told me he loved me, I always felt like I was obligated to have sex with him, so I did, and ruined it or I broke up because I didn't want sex. I never got to have an innocent, puppy love relationship. I was making it not happen without even knowing it. Something was always missing, and I chased away what I wanted so bad.

For many, love and sex were intertwined. The "puppy love" relationship was elusive to Daphnie because her definition of showing love to men included sex. According to her account, Daphnie's boyfriends thought she was "easy," not lovable, and she developed a reputation as someone to have sex with.

The label "sex abuse survivor" serves as a placeholder to mark a problem spot in the identity of the survivor. It provides an explanation as to why the subject is having difficulty negotiating his or her social world, thus allowing him or her to work around it, but it does not treat the problem. Diana, an African-American striptease dancer and survivor, observes:

> I'm in therapy, just started. I know a lot of stuff I do, the dancing, promiscuity, whatever, are supposed to be because of sex abuse. I get angry easy. I don't always know how it affects things, but I guess it is good to know something is controlling you that maybe you wouldn't know about otherwise. I

don't always get how it is really connected though, you know, how it really makes sense that I get angry easy because of what happened then. But it lets me know there is something to work on, something to come back to later, by myself or with my therapist.

For Diana, the category "sex abuse survivor," with the attendant characteristics, serves to make life temporarily less problematic. Her stocks of knowledge now include information about being a survivor. When Diana once again becomes depressed or considers suicide, this frame offers her hope that one day she will "understand" herself and her behavior better. For now, her failures to negotiate her social world can be attributed to this category and sorted out later.

*   *   *

Instead of trying to disguise the socially constructed character of my project, the layered account allows me to demarcate a space whereby I can freely explore the kinds of experiences that contributed to my conclusions: my biography, my emotions, and my interviews with sex abuse survivors. Put another way, the research space has typically been a gendered space, specifically, a male space. Male standards of the emotionless, so-called objective scientific method have defined that space for centuries. Social scientists live with the threat of discursive constraint as do childhood sex abuse survivors. If they fail in their attempt to try to emulate "science," their identities as "real researchers" may become delegitimated.

As a result, social scientists are forced to be silent about the way their research ventures really evolve, and they come to simplistic, easy-to-convey, reductionist conclusions. These conclusions, in turn, have a potentially abusive impact on the women their studies are supposed to be helping. For instance, the self, the idea that we possess one, is a social scientist's construction. It also exists in mainstream society. Selves can be good or bad, organized or disorganized, whole or fragmented. All of my subjects referenced having selves, and all of them concluded something was wrong with their selves and claimed to have negative emotions about them. Ultimately, the language of the self can be a language of domination or discursive constraint. If we don't live up to the fiction of the ideal self, just like the ideal body or ideal family, then we feel as if we lack something we must try to achieve.

It is said that the sex abuse survivor is in recovery the rest of her life, permanently damaged (see Davis 1990; Giarretto 1982 for examples). Good mental health, the ideal self, remains out of reach of the survivor forever. Perhaps this should be reconsidered. I suggest that survivors, after learning the vocabulary or word game (Lyotard 1988) of surviving, must abandon the fiction of the ideal self, or they will feel forever empty, pursuing the impossible, looking for a centered, whole self that isn't there for them, indeed, never was there for anyone.

As feminists we must question the authority we give the scientific voice to authorize or define our lives. Whether the topic is "levels of severity" of abuse, mindless and heartless reporting formats, permanently incomplete selves, or other reductionist rhetoric that we take as given, we become simultaneously the oppressed and oppressors when we insist on perpetuating forms that have emerged out of a deeply patriarchal tradition. We are victims of discursive constraint anytime we make choices in our projects that will make them seem more "scientific." Simultaneously, the next person who reads our results will have it reinforced one more time that they must, really must, reproduce the same, old, stagnant, scientific model or else they won't be considered legitimate researchers.

Every time we speak or write we make identity claims for ourselves. Which identities shall we claim as writers and researchers in the late twentieth century? Will we let the discursive constraint of "science" continue to narrate our lives? Do we need to eliminate entirely the discourse of science from our social scientist identity? Or is there a way to decenter the authority of the scientific voice in such a way as to allow the scientific voice to be one of many voices we permit to contribute to our ongoing conversation? These questions and more will reach crisis proportions as we cross the threshold into the next millennium.

References

Bertaux, Daniel. 1981. "From the Life History Approach to the Transformation of Sociological Practice," in *Biography and Society: The Life History Approach to the Social Sciences*, ed. Daniel Bertaux. Beverly Hills: Sage.

Davis, Laura. 1990. *The Courage to Heal Workbook*. New York: Harper & Row.

Ellis, Carolyn. 1991. "Sociological Introspection and Emotional Experience." *Symbolic Interaction* 14: 23–50.

Giarretto, Henry. 1982. *Integrated Treatment of Child Sex Abuse*. Palo Alto, CA: Science and Behavior Books.

Gubrium, Jaber, James Holstein, and David K. Buckholdt. 1994. *Constructing the Lifecourse*. New York: General Hall.

Kempe, C.H. 1984. *The Common Secret: Sexual Abuse of Children and Adolescents*. New York: W.H. Freeman.

Kohli, Martin. 1986. "Social Organization and Subjective Construction of the Life Course," in *Human Development and the Lifecourse*, eds. Franz Weinert and Lonnie Sherrod. Hillsdale, NJ: Erlbaum Associates.

Lyotard, Jean-Françoise. 1988. *The Post-Modern Condition*. Minneapolis: University of Minnesota Press.

Riemer, Jeffery W. 1977. "Varieties of Opportunistic Research." *Urban Life* 5: 467–477.

Ronai, Carol Rambo. 1992. "The Reflexive Self Through Narrative: A Night in the Life of an Exotic Dancer Researcher," in *Investigating Subjectivity: Research on Lived Experience*, eds. Carolyn Ellis and Michael Flaherty. Newbury Park, CA: Sage, pp. 102–24.

———. 1994. "Narrative Resistance to Deviance: Identity Management Among Strip-tease Dancers." *Perspectives on Social Problems* 6: 195–213.

———. 1995. "Multiple Reflections of Child Sex Abuse: An Argument for a Layered Account." *Journal of Contemporary Ethnography* 23: 395–426.

Summit, R., and J. Kryso. 1978. "Sexual Abuse of Children in a Clinical Spectrum. *American Journal of Orthopsychiatry* 48: 237–51.

9

Defining the Situation

Sexual Harassment or Everyday Rudeness?

MELISSA J. MONSON

> Hell, yes I've been sexually harassed. What woman who's been alive more than five minutes on this earth hasn't?
>
> (Speer 1992, p. 253)

> My life is one big sexual harassment experience from the time I leave my house to the time I come back home.
>
> (Cheyenne Goodman 1992, p. 96)

Women are bombarded on a daily basis with an arsenal of whistles, catcalls, "oh baby"s, leers, ogles, pats, touches, grabs, gropes, and sexual innuendo: routinely trivialized into the all-too-familiar sex object role. In 1988, the United States Merit Protection Board predicted that 85 percent of all working women will be sexually harassed in their lifetime (Rhode 1989). One report indicates that 70 percent of female undergraduates experience sexually harassing behavior while in school (Lott, Reilly, and Howard 1982). A similar study (Farley 1978) found that 70 percent of women workers report having been sexually harassed while on the job.

Despite substantial evidence documenting the pervasiveness of sexual harassment,[1] there is a lack of reliable official statistics that systematically document this form of sexual exploitation. The ambiguity of conceptual and operational definitions of sexual harassment makes it difficult to maintain reliable statistics (Paludi and Barickman 1991). Given women's everyday experience with sexual harassment, it is puzzling that many women are reluctant to attach the label "sexual harassment" to unwanted sexual advances. For this reason, efforts to record the incidence of sexual harassment are calculated from lists of potentially harassing behaviors, rather than asking the respondents directly whether they had experienced sexual harassment. While this approach is useful in determining the frequency with which sexual harassment occurs, it does little to explain the divergence between statistical evidence and the process of labeling an act as harassment.

The research community has been called upon to "establish the basis on which particular situations in the everyday lives of working women come to be labeled sexual harassment" (Schneider 1982, p. 75). More precisely, the bases on which specific everyday situations are *not* labeled sexual harassment deserve attention. This observational study explains labeling processes used by female video store clerks about everyday experiences of sexual harassment.

The theoretical framework for this paper is informed by literature addressing internalized gender oppression (Benokraitis and Feagin 1995; Stockard and Johnson 1992). Gender oppression is internalized through the same process of socialization that other, more mundane aspects of gender are internalized through. That is, as girls learn socially appropriate gender roles, they also learn the relative social worth afforded to those roles and to femininity in general. Under the current conditions of patriarchy, this means a girl will learn that she is less valued and that she commands (is deserving of) less respect, thus she finds herself trivialized, dehumanized, and treated as an object. She finds that it is not just strangers that treat her with such indifference or even spite, but those who profess to love her as well. Her inferior position is reinforced on a microlevel through a series of everyday belittling or even hostile encounters, and on a macrolevel though institutionalized sex discrimination. She learns that to be a woman means to live with, to accept, and to internalize an inferior status. People whose lives are subsumed by social inequality tend to normalize individual and cumulative acts of repression, rather than defining them as violations of human dignity. While the literature does not explicitly connect sexual harassment with internalized oppression, the implication is that internalization of sexist gender roles discourages women from identifying themselves as victims of sexual harassment.

Introduction to the Research Setting

This research effort originated from my personal observations of sexually harassing behavior while waiting for service at a local video rental store. A male patron was overheard saying to a female clerk, while staring unswervingly at her breasts: "Those are nice, I'll take two." The young woman to whom the remark was directed blushed brightly, lowered her eyes, and finished the transaction without another word or further eye contact. The man continued to leer and grin broadly. Following his departure, the young woman continued to avoid eye contact with the next patron. When I arrived at the counter, the clerk's mannerisms suggested she had been unnerved by the encounter. "What an ass," I said. She looked up and I continued: "I can't believe guys get away with that garbage."

"Yea, well, you know," she said, beginning to relax a bit.

"Yea, I do know. And it is just not right. I mean you should not have to put up with that."

"Well you know, some men are just like that," she said.

The continuing discussion launched this project. Beth (a pseudonym) told me the type of interaction I had witnessed was commonplace. In fact, she said, "much worse has happened." She spoke of men making passes at her, calling her or her female coworkers derogatory names, patting her on the behind, rubbing into her, and making lewd gestures. During the conversation I made Beth aware of my professional research in the area of sexual harassment. Beth asked why the behavior she had been experiencing was a form of sexual harassment. She had asked an insightful research question. Most of the time sexual harassment refers to a manager or supervisor and a female employee. Little has been written about the harassment that women experience from patrons. Yet sexual harassment emerges in multiple, varied contexts that contribute to the objectification of all women in the U.S. daily. This project sheds light on one such context: employee-patron interaction in the retail/service environment.

Research Setting

My observations in this essay were made in a relatively small video rental store. The shop employs six full-time clerks, five of whom are female. Additionally there are two part-time employees, one male (the owner's seventeen-year-old son) and one female. The male owner occasionally works as a clerk when needed. The video outlet is located in a middle-class neighborhood in the Western United States. All of the employees are white, as is the majority of the clientele.[2]

Videotapes for rental were divided into four main sections. Along the back wall there were four shelves of newly released movies. The second major section was devoted to second-run movies. The third section was a small room in the back containing science fiction and horror films. The final section was where they sold music videos, CDs, and cassette tapes. There was no X-rated or adult section in the store.

Two television monitors were located on opposite sides of the store, showing movies. One of the monitors was located adjacent to the checkout counter, so that those standing in line could watch while they waited for service. The clerks chose the movies following only the guideline that there should not be "too much sex or violence. Or swearing." What counts as "too much" was arrived at by group consensus. Occasionally, a movie played that did contain sexual activity or profanity. "You can't catch everything," I was told. "If someone has a problem with it, then we have to change it."

Methodology

Nonparticipant observation was the main research tool used in this study, thereby allowing potential sexually harassing behaviors to be recorded independent of individual clerk perception. In light of predicted discrepancies between actual behavior and the subsequent evaluation of those behaviors as sexual harassment, this provides a critical research advantage. Observational studies also have the benefit of avoiding many of the problems associated with respondent recall by relying on written field notes rather than participant memory to document customer-clerk interaction. Additionally, systematic observation allows behavior to be studied as it occurs, thus improving the opportunity to analyze contextual elements of the research setting.

As unobtrusively as possible, I recorded observations made throughout the store. The majority of data collected emerged from observing employee-customer interaction at the checkout counter. Periods of observation varied, but were conducted primarily on weekday evenings and Saturday afternoons. It was during these times, according to the employees, that "problems with people" were most likely to arise.

Observations at the video store were supplemented with in-depth employee interviews. Although the interview schedule was open-ended, questions generally centered around observed employee-customer interaction. This allowed the processes by which actions are labeled or not labeled sexual harassment to be closely examined. Conversations were recorded with all of the full-time female workers but, due to conflicts in scheduling and time limitations, not everyone completed an in-depth one-hour interview.

Observing Sexual Harassment

The challenge of this project was to be able to recognize and document potential sexually harassing behaviors as they occurred. Fitzgerald and colleagues (1988, p. 157) provided an appropriate framework for such a task. Based on the earlier works of Till (1980), they developed a typology containing five distinct levels of sexual harassment:

1. Gender harassment: generalized sexist remarks and behavior;
2. Seductive behavior: inappropriate and offensive but essentially sanction-free sexual advances;
3. Sexual bribery: solicitation of sexual activity or other sex-linked behavior by promise of rewards;
4. Sexual coercion: coercion of sexual activity by threat of punishment;
5. Sexual imposition: sexual imposition or assault.

The benefit of using this scheme is that it defines sexual harassment in terms of specific behaviors, giving special attention to the perceptual gap that exists between the occurrence of an action and the labeling of that action as sexual harassment. In other words, this typology does not require the recipient to interpret the action as harassment, but instead allows the researcher categorically to document the action itself.

The types of sexual harassment observed in the video store were limited to "gender harassment," "seductive behavior," and "sexual imposition." There were no incidences of sexual bribery or sexual coercion. In part, this may be a function of the fact that sexual bribery or coercion imply an inherent power difference between harasser and victim. In the case of video store clients, there is no direct and little indirect power to hire, fire, or offer promotion to store employees.

Therefore, threats of professional reward or punishment in return for sexual favors are of little consequence. And, in fact, no such interactions were observed.

Gender Harassment

For the most part, customers were polite and cordial with store clerks. Dissatisfaction with rental service, movie prices, rewinding fees, movie selection, late fees, and related issues were the most frequent types of problems that arose. These disputes, while mainly nonthreatening in nature, did on occasion rise to the level of hostile confrontation. In the heat of specific confrontations, customers often resorted to gender specific name-calling. "Bitch" was the most commonly used derogatory expression. It was also the only gender-specific expression used as frequently by female clients as it was by male clients. "Dumb broad" and "slut" were also heard on occasion, but these terms were used exclusively by male customers.

References to the alleged inabilities of women workers were also frequent during the observation period. The women were called "dumb," "stupid," "ignorant," and "incompetent." With the exception of "dumb," a label used to describe Dan, the seventeen-year-old son of the store owner, on one occasion, these derogatory terms were used exclusively to describe female clerks.

Another type of gender harassment observed was sexual comments about actresses in the movies displayed on the store's monitors. A few male customers openly expressed their desire to have sex (in their words, "do," "bag," or "pop") with the actresses on the screens. They discussed at length the physical appearance of the actresses. Female customers also verbally fantasized about male actors, but their desires were not shared with male clerks. Male fantasies were shared with both male and female clerks, and at times accompanied with leering or ogling.

A final type of gender harassment observed was the unrelenting references directed at female clerks, such as "sweetie," "honey," "hun," "babe," "baby," "sweet cakes," "foxy," and "foxy lady."

Seductive Behavior

The main type of seductive behavior involved specific references to the clerks' female anatomy. Comments overheard included, "Hey baby, nice hooters," "great ass," "nice tits," and "nice pair." Other, less frequent examples of seductive behavior included making kissing sounds, suggestively licking lips, and repeated unwanted requests for dates.

Sexual Imposition

In only one instance was blatantly inappropriate touching of a clerk by a customer observed. An elderly male patted a clerk on her behind. When the clerk bent over to retrieve a movie box, the patron reached out and gave her a swat on her backside as he was passing by. "Hey there sweetie, better watch where you point that thing," he openly commented. Jane just laughed and went about her business.

Defining Sexual Harassment

None of the clerks defined the observed behaviors as sexual harassment. In their opinion, sexual harassment must go beyond the commonplace "rude," "inconsiderate," or "childish" behaviors that they encountered. As predicted, actions that were everyday occurrences were viewed as ordinary inconveniences rather than personal or social injustices. For these women, sexual harassment implies a direct quid pro quo threat. Because customers lack conventional economic power over employees, the potential for sexual harassment is seen as virtually impossible.

As Tracy explains: "Well it has to be more than just rudeness. Like when your boss says, 'sleep with me or you are fired.' Something like that."

Likewise, Sally added: "Yes, that is what I think too. Customers are rude, and have no business touching me or whatever, but they really can't do anything other than talk. Talk is annoying and it can really get you. . . ."

At this point Tracy chimed in: "Pissed off!"

Laughing, Sally continued: "Yes, pissed off. But that is just part of the job."

When I suggested that sexual harassment transcends the "put out or get out" type of situations, that it includes anytime anyone puts you in a defensive position, one that makes you feel less or wrong about yourself, or scared, or frightened because you are a woman, Jane joined in, saying: "Oh honey, that is most times. It has got to be more than that."

Defining an Ambiguous Situation

While not deemed sexual harassment, many of the behaviors observed were condemned by the clerks as being rude or generally obnoxious. Other behaviors were found to be less serious, either classified as unintentional on the part of the customer or as misinterpretation by the clerk; and some behaviors were not seen in negative terms at all. Instead, they were viewed as good-natured sexual banter.

Rudeness was distinguished from other types of behaviors by the mean-spiritedness and the malicious intent of the perpetrator. It included everything from spiteful to mundane gender-based comments, from leering to ogling, and from touching to groping. An action was considered rude when it was done with explicit hurtful intent.

As Tracy explains: "Some of them [customers] are down right nasty . . . you know, rude and yelling and that kinda thing. Like calling me 'bitch.'"

Beth added: "Ya, they come in like they own the place, giving orders, that kinda thing. Then the names start flying. Or they try and stare you down."

Tracy interjected: "Or look you over."

Beth continued: "Nice, eh? And these are grown people."

Despite the injurious objective of these actions, they were not perceived as sexual harassment, primarily because the behaviors were considered too common an occurrence to warrant a special label. By expecting "rude" treatment, the clerks rationalized the men's behavior as normal and therefore something to be endured, rather than changed or prevented. As Sally explains: "Rudeness is an everyday occurrence around here. The way I see it, if I fly off the handle over every little thing, I would go crazy. Or drive everyone else crazy . . . either way, what's the point?"

A second type of behavior was that which was described as inadvertent or having benevolent intent. For instance, the clerks generally believed gendered references (for instance, hun, sweetie, babe, and dear) were used not out of disrespect, but because: "They [the customers] don't know our names. They are just trying to get our attention." Here, gendered references had become so normalized that the women often did not even recognize that they were gender-specific. When asked why male clerks were not subject to the same treatment, I received puzzled expressions. "I never really thought about that before," Sally told me, "but anyway I would rather be called sweetie than ma'am anyday. I may be old, but I don't need a reminder!" The implication being that, while "sweetie" isn't necessarily flattering, it is less offensive than other gendered comments, and therefore, tolerable.

Intent was at times determined by familiarity with a customer, as in the case of the elderly gentleman, George, who patted Jane on the backside. Speaking of the incident, Jane said: "Oh that. That was just George. He's a sweetie. Comes in here just about every day." When asked if he always greeted her in such a friendly manner, Jane replied, "Oh that is just George's way. He is harmless really."

More often however, judgments about intent were grounded in subjective interpretation, based on preconceived stereotypes of age, dress, and physical appearance. Older customers were generally excused for questionable behavior because they ". . . grew up in a different time. That type of thing was normal then." Fashionably dressed and physically attractive customers were also taken to be less menacing. Tracy commented, "I am sure he just had a bad day, a guy that beautiful couldn't be that big a jerk." Sally added jokingly: "A guy that beautiful can be as big a jerk as he wants."

In a third type of situation, clerks went so far as to redraw their initial definition of an occurrence in order to make it seem less threatening. Both Beth and Tracy recalled instances in which they were very frightened by the touch of a male customer, but instead of defining the incident as sexual harassment they questioned their own judgment about what happened.

BETH: There was this one time about a year ago when this man came up from behind me and grabbed my breast. I didn't know what to do. He didn't say nothing, just kept right on walking. I thought maybe it didn't happen, like I just imagined it or something. I was real jumpy for the rest of the day.

TRACY: Mine wasn't that bad but it was still kind of scary, you never know what some people will do. This man just kind of rubbed up against me. We was [sic] in that back room. You know, where the sci-fi stuff is, and he was looking at movies. Well the next thing I know he is rubbing his whole body up against mine, and I am pinned in the corner. I don't know if he meant anything by it. He said, "excuse me" or something. It is just, well I was, ah, real freaked out for a second. Then I just says, "I got to get to work" and ran out of there.

In both of these cases, the women felt violated by the touch of a male customer; however, internalized doubts of their own ability to define the occurrence correctly prevented them from confronting the behaviors as anything more sinister than inconsequential contact.

The fourth type of situation described by the clerks was those marked by mutual participation and good-natured banter, rather than harsh words or reprehensible actions. The difference expressed by the women was rendered comprehensible after a short period of observation. On one occasion, when one of four young men approached a clerk with the words, "nice pair," referring to her breasts, Beth retorted in a joking manner: "Thanks, you too." This unexpected response caused embarrassment for the patron, as his friends began to hassle him. One taunted, "you know she's right John, I never noticed."

When asked about this interaction, Beth said, "It's totally different. That one guy [referring to the earlier incident noted above] was creepy. Those kids were just having a good time."

Sally concurred: "Ya, a little harmless play is kind of fun. It's those weirdos ya' got to watch out for."

Although this was the first encounter Beth and Sally could recall having with the young men, the exchange was judged to be in good spirits. Here again, the question of intent was largely determined by outward physical appearance.

Sally and Beth were asked how they could distinguish between a genuine "weirdo" and guys "just having a good time." Sally said: "Well, I guess it is just a feeling or something. I don't know, intuition maybe?"

Similarly, Beth commented: "Yes . . . you just kind of know."

When asked if the perpetrators had predictable physical characteristics, such as beady eyes, scars, or one eyebrow, the response was one of laughter. Sally replied: "Sometimes [more laughter] . . . mostly it is just a feeling. All those things your mother told you to look for." Beth added:

Yes, mom was right about something. Actually the old watch-out-for-strangers lecture is quite useful. It is usually those "you want some candy little girl" types you have to watch out for. But even then, it is usually nothing to get too upset about. Putting up with sh... crap is just part of the job ... part of life.

The clerks did not see the behaviors as operating within a context of sexual inequality. Rather the clerks viewed the behaviors as the individual actions of "mean," "well-intending," or "harmless" people. Although the actions were found to be commonplace and described as getting "kinda old," they were not fitted into a comprehensive definition of the workplace as a sexually hostile environment. Instead, the behaviors were normalized as being simply another form of rudeness that women are faced with daily.

Coping Strategies

During the observation phase of this research, the clerks never become overtly angry or hostile with a "rude" customer. They remained polite, referring to customers as "sir" or "ma'am" and attempted to defuse confrontational situations by employing one of three coping strategies.

The first and most commonly implemented strategy was the sharing of empathetic understanding. After rude customers vacated the store, clerks allowed themselves to vent some of their frustrations. Sometimes this was only a passing word to the others, as when Tracy said, "What a prick," about a customer with a rewind complaint. At other times, two or three of the women would commiserate while eating popcorn or drinking a soda between serving customers. These discussions often centered around the inappropriateness of customers' behavior. Downtime permitted clerks to compare experiences. The following is typical of such interactions:

BETH: What a jerk.

SALLY: Ya, I can't believe some people are just too rude.

BETH: You wonder where they were raised.

SALLY: I think there is a place that just turns out guys like that, just to make our lives miserable.

Tracy: Ya, a prick factory. [Everyone laughs.]

During these moments the women seemed to be constructing and reaffirming their definition of the situation. While they felt there was nothing they could do to stop the behavior, that didn't mean they regarded it as acceptable. In discussions among themselves, they blamed the male harassers. However, labeled as "jerks," "idiots," or "pricks," the harasser's actions could be dismissed more easily and not personalized or perceived as sexual harassment.

A second coping strategy was to play along, as when Beth made the crack about the young man's breasts. Playing along may also be seen as a way of building rapport with the customers. As Tracy explained, when asked about a comment she made about Julia Roberts's breasts: "Some of these guys are regulars. It is just kind of our little joke. Let's them know I remember them." However, when continually viewed as a joking matter, harassment appears less serious. It becomes normalized as just another example of "boys being boys," your run-of-the-mill, everyday occurrence.

The third coping strategy was to allow derogatory comments to slip by unacknowledged. Often clerks remained visibly unfazed by customer commentaries. Sometimes this was strategic; at other times the clerks simply did not notice. As Beth said, "It [rude behavior] gets to be so common that after a while you just don't hear everything anymore."

Sexual Harassment: An Everyday Occurrence

> When I remember the many moments during which I was sexually harassed, I wonder how any woman over the age of thirty could possibly be so protected or so naive to say she has never had similar moments. (Jewell 1992, p. 136)

The answer to this elusive question may be found by looking at the gender socialization process. Mickelson notes:

> When a person grows up in a culture which tolerates or even applauds the overt sexual behavior of one gender at the expense of another, it is often impossible for the individual to draw the line between the tolerable and the intolerable. (1992, p. 189)

In other words, when one lives in a society where women are treated daily as secondary citizens and sexual objects, one comes to accept that image as a given.

Like many women, the clerks at this video store felt embarrassed, violated, and angry about some of the actions directed towards them, but they did not feel it was anything unusual. Sexualized or demeaning behavior, while seen as "rude," was not described as sexual harassment. Rather, it was perceived as ordinary, mundane, something that women "just need to deal with." The men were perceived as just being themselves, having a little fun. If a patron's behavior crossed the line between good taste and inappropriateness, it was not seen as intentional and thus, in the words of one clerk, "should not be taken too seriously. If you go and get yourself all riled up over everything, well, uh, you'll just go crazy."

As demeaning treatment becomes normalized, women are less likely to become enraged and "all riled up." Instead, it becomes part of living, just another component of the daily indignity of life as a woman in a patriarchal society.

Conclusions

Although the video store clerks, like most women, expressed an interest in stopping the behavior, they found it more expedient to develop coping strategies to deal with the harassment they encountered daily. Given the current political, social, and cultural climate in the U.S., it is little wonder that women choose (either by intention or happenstance) not to see everyday acts of rudeness as sexual harassment. For the majority of victims, it becomes far more pragmatic to develop coping strategies that help them temporarily deal with the problem than to attack sexism on a larger scale. Regrettably, this course of action addresses the problem only one situation, one context, and one woman at a time, doing little to solve the fundamental problem that lies embedded within male-biased economic and political institutions.

Susan Carol (Sumrall and Taylor 1990, p. 231) warns, "A woman's denial is the ultimate enemy." Defining sexually harassing behavior as normal undermines efforts to prevent it. The road to the eradication of sexual harassment must start with the women's perceptions. Everyday experiences should not be dismissed as inevitable. They must be reevaluated and scrutinized. It must be persistently asserted that not only are certain behaviors not welcome, or appropriate, or right; they are often not legal, and women will increasingly not tolerate them.

Notes

1. See also Bond 1988; Adams, Kottke, and Padgitt 1983.
2. None of the sexually harassing behaviors documented in this study was instigated by men or women of color.

References

Adams, J.W., J.L. Kottke, and J.S. Padgitt. 1983. "Sexual Harassment of University Students." *Journal of College Student Personnel* 24: 484–490.

Benokraitis, Nijole V. and Joe Feagin. 1995. *Modern Sexism: Blatant, Subtle, and Covert Discrimination*, 2nd ed. Englewood Cliffs, NJ: Prentice Hall.

Bond, M. 1988. "Division 27 Sexual Harassment Survey: Definition, Impact, and Environmental Context." *Community Psychologist* 21: 7–10.

Farley, L. 1978. *Sexual Shakedown: The Sexual Harassment of Women on the Job.* New York: McGraw.

Fitzgerald, Louise F., S.L. Shullman, N. Bailey, M. Richards, J. Swecker, Y. Gold, A.J. Ormerod, and L. Weitzman. 1988. "The Incidence and Dimensions of Sexual Harassment in Academia and the Workplace." *Journal of Vocational Behavior* 32: 152–175.

Goodman, Cheyenne. 1992. "One Long Sexual Harassment Experience" in *Sexual Harassment: Women Speak Out*, eds. Amber Coverdale Sumrall and Dena Taylor. Freedom, CA: The Crossing Press, pp. 96–97.

Jewell, Terri L. 1992. "How to Teach One Dog a New Trick" in *Sexual Harassment: Women Speak Out*, eds. Amber Coverdale Sumrall and Dena Taylor. Freedom, CA: The Crossing Press, pp. 136–139.

Lott, B., M. E. Reilly, and D.R. Howard. 1982. "Sexual Assault and Harassment: A Campus Community Case Study." *Signs* 8: 296–319.

Mickelson, Jane L. 1992. "And if I Speak ... What Then?" in *Sexual Harassment: Women Speak Out*, eds. Amber Coverdale Sumrall and Dena Taylor. Freedom, CA: The Crossing Press, pp. 184–189.

Paludi, Michelle and Richard Barickman. 1991. *Academic and Workplace Sexual Harassment.* Albany: State University of New York Press.

Rhode, Deborah L. 1989. *Justice and Gender: Sex Discrimination and the Law.* Cambridge, MA: Harvard University Press.

Schneider, Beth E. 1982. "Consciousness About Sexual Harassment Among Heterosexual and Lesbian Women Workers." *Journal of Social Issues* 38: 75–98.

Speer, Laurel. 1992. "You Want to Do What to My What?" in *Sexual Harass-*

ment: Women Speak Out, eds. Amber Coverdale Sumrall and Dena Taylor. Freedom, CA: The Crossing Press, pp. 253–254.

Stockard, Jean and Miriam M. Johnson. 1992. *Sex and Gender in Society*, 2nd edition. Englewood Cliffs, NJ: Prentice-Hall, Inc.

Sumrall, Amber Coverdale and Dena Taylor, eds. 1990. *Sexual Harassment: Women Speak Out*. Freedom, CA: The Crossing Press.

Till, F. 1980. *Sexual Harassment: A Report on the Sexual Harassment of Students*. Washington, DC: National Advisory Council on Women's Educational Programs.

The Political/Economic Arena

as a Gendered Space

Dialectical Linkages

Part III focuses on the economic and political arenas as gendered spaces. While the topics in these chapters relate to the identities and bodies of the women in question, the substantive focus moves away, to varying degrees, from the personal toward collective experiences. These chapters bring us full circle in the dialectic of domination, painting for us the broader societal backdrop, the social, political, and economic contexts where people deal with sexist constructions of themselves and their bodies. Here we see how external forces crash into the microsocial lives of every woman. Here again we see the painful realities of class, racial group, and sexuality, often intertwined, shaping the experience of gender as it emerges in economic and political arenas.

Yanick St. Jean and Joe R. Feagin report on interviews with African-Americans in Chapter 10, "Black Women, Sexism, and Racism: Experiencing Double Jeopardy." Again we see how certain "things" often discussed separately in the literature are in actuality closely interwo-

ven as part of a larger whole. Black female and male respondents view the "integrated" workplace as still a white plantation mirroring a racist past and continuing the heritage of racialized suffering. The discourse of gendered racism, such as the sincere fiction that black women serve as "twofers" in filling workplace quotas (as women and as "minorities"), supports the historical effort by white Americans not only to inferiorize black women and men but also, through several linkages, to sabotage the black family. The gendered space of the workplace restricts or blocks economic mobility for black women and, through a domino effect, serves to oppress black men and black families—and, through enlarging circles of effects, black organizations and communities. Black identities, black bodies, black families, and black communities all suffer as a result of widespread discrimination as it is accomplished through the sincere fictions of gender and race in economic and political arenas.

In Chapter 11, "Higher Education as Gendered Space: Asian-American Women and Everyday Inequities," Shirley Hune urges the reader to consider another important group of women, Asian-Americans, and explores the experiences of Asian-American women in the sphere of higher education. The current era is often said to be one where sexism is no longer an issue, especially in academia, which is often assumed to be a very tolerant and humane place. Yet Hune shows not only that a masculine preference shapes the gender space that is the academy, but also that the identification of the targets of oppression involves a racialized marking off of women's bodies. These women face a dialectical repetitiveness of racism and sexism. The racist dimension is seen in the curious mixture of images and action tendencies termed the "model minority" stereotype. This imagery suggests an achievement of (at least) parity with white women on the part of Asian-American women. Yet the reality is that even college-educated Asian-American women still remain occupationally segregated (often in clerical work), underrepresented among doctoral students, undermentored in graduate programs, less likely to be promoted once in the professorate, and *generally restricted, if not silenced, by the interactive intertwining of gender and racial discrimination.*

In Chapter 12, "The Gendered Spaces in Ethnopolitical Life: Social Identities and Political Activism among Chicanos," Barbara A. Zsembik examines the gendered nature of ethnopolitical activism among Chicanas and Chicanos, locating it in the historical context of the cultural nationalism and women's movements of the 1970s. Again, in dialectical fashion, the past is part of the present. Contrary to assumptions that Chicanas are passive and subordinated to the machistas in their lives, we see women engaged in collective action for social change, and action in the public spaces of politics in the community and workplace. They endorse different political strategies from men, based in women's and men's separate ethnic and class identities, and private locations of the self. This chapter demonstrates the complex nature of these economic/political arenas as gendered spaces and the webbing into these spaces of ethnic-gendered identities.

In Chapter 13, "Which 'We' Are We?: The Politics of Identity in Women's Narratives," Barbara Ellen Smith examines the differential intersections of racial group, class, and gender in the narratives of three women who discuss the development of their careers as political activists. One thing to notice is how their class/race/gender identities link in complex and varying ways to political commitments. In their narratives they link identity formation to political action and resistance. Although racial group, class, and gender may be statuses equal in theoretical significance in terms of the consequences they have for women's lives, they are not equal in the discourses women use to mark off and make sense out of their experiences and perspectives. The three women accent different aspects of their three possible identities in complex and interactive ways. Racial and class experience shape whether a woman uses the discourse of gender to interpret political experience and activism.

Finally, in Chapter 14, we revisit the topic of sexual harassment, this time examining the effects of federal sexual harassment law on a rapidly growing segment of the workforce. In "Sexual Harassment for Whom?: The Case of Women in Part-Time, Temporary, and Independent Contractor Employment," Dula J. Espinosa uses one major court case (about Wendy Breen) to illustrate how some women in less than full-time employment are not protected from sexual harassment under current federal statutes. Even though it was concluded that Wendy Breen had been subjected to continual sexual harassment, including attempted rape, by her employer, she was not protected under federal law from sexual harassment. Even though she was very much under the control of her employer, because she was a real estate agent, the court construed her to be an "independent contractor," that is, someone who is self-employed and not covered by federal law. Here we see the way in which U.S. laws and courts are accomplices in "doing" sexual harassment. The economic/political/legal arenas are thus gendered spaces that use an aspect of a woman's identity—her work status—as a justification for the appropriation of her body against her will.

In this concluding section we accent the third of our gendered spaces, the political/economic arena. Identities, bodies, and political/economic arenas reveal multiple levels of sexism that are webbed together in an interactive process of daily living. We can now see why, to understand modern sexism fully, one must move away from a static, simple-matrix model and expand the conception of gendered oppression to include a dialectical understanding. This book's chapters underscore our conception of sexism as both a structure and a process full of layered, interactive, feedback-looping, accumulating realities. Lived sexism is an ever-moving dialectic of domination. Sexual domination is found at many points in time and in many places, some most unexpected, and it assuredly has a cumulative history. It rarely stands alone, linked as it often is to other forms of oppression. We also see, in all three sections, the imbedded possibilities and potentialities for human liberation from gendered oppression, for no system of domination lasts forever, and its targets, however oppressed, remain active agents who can and do move history from oppressive status quo to human liberation.

10

Black Women, Sexism, and Racism

Experiencing Double Jeopardy

YANICK ST. JEAN AND JOE R. FEAGIN

Introduction

From the beginning of their importation as slave labor, African-American women have participated in the labor force (Malson 1983). Initially confined to labor as manual and personal service workers, over the intervening decades black women gradually expanded the range of their labors outside the home to a variety of blue-collar and white-collar occupations. In recent decades they have made gains in white-collar occupations, often exceeding those of black men, especially in corporate America (MacLachlan 1993; U.S. Department of Labor 1994; Gaiter 1994). For instance, between 1984 and 1994 the percentage of black women in professional and managerial careers grew by 6 percent, from 16 percent to 22 percent, whereas the percentage of black men increased by only 3 percent, from 13 percent to 16 percent (U.S. Department of Labor 1994).

Today, the workplace outside the home remains an important sphere of life for black women. It is a major source of black family income. A study by the Economic Policy Institute reveals that African-American women with some college earn more than their male counterparts (Roberts 1994). Black women with a graduate degree have a higher labor force participation and earn slightly more than their male counterparts (Bernstein 1995, pp. 34–35).

Yet, the importance of the workplace for black women and their families does not mean that it is a place where their skills and abilities are nurtured or their contributions are fully acknowledged. Recent survey research and audit studies of U.S. workplaces have documented widespread discrimination against African-Americans (Bobo and Suh 1995; Turner, Fix, and Struyk 1991). Yet there is much more research to be done. There is remarkably little research on black women in the social science literature, and many existing references to black women in that literature are misrepresentations of their character, experiences, and realities.

In this chapter we examine critical aspects of workplace discrimination that are generally missing in the extant literature. We examine the *lived experiences* of black women in particular workplaces. Our analysis relies on the narratives of middle-class black respondents for insights into the situations of black women. We attempt to preserve their voices and respect the reality of the racial and gender barriers they describe. We consider the conditions in which these women find themselves at the moment and listen to their direct testimonies as we attempt a thorough understanding of these women's situations. Those who have endured best know the intensities of their wounds.

In examining these lived experiences in U.S. workplaces, we will see evidence of what Philomena Essed (1991) calls *gendered racism*—the discrimination faced by black women that stems from the intersection of race and gender. This is an example of *double jeopardy.* In our examination of lived experience we will also find accounts of what Feagin and Sikes (1994, p. 16) call the *domino effect* of racial hostility—for example, the impact on black men of bigotry directed at black women, and vice versa.

In addition, in our analysis we will glimpse signs of historical continuity in these women's lives. Experiences with gendered racism in the present often trigger reactions, including memories of past suffering. Individual and collective memories play a role in the negative impact of everyday discrimination (Feagin and Sikes 1994, pp. 15–18). Discriminatory white actions are often more than they at first appear. To paraphrase one black respondent: "whenever I hear the 'nigger' word, in the back of my mind I see a black man hanging from a tree." Part of the tragedy of modern racism is that white oppressors, consciously or unconsciously, intensify contemporary oppression because it is rooted in the legacy and memories of much past oppression. Past and present encounters with white bigotry help to transform black women and men into a community with a shared oppressive and heroic past, what has been called "a community of memory" (Bellah et al. 1985).

The African-Americans we quote below were part of a sample of 209 African-Americans interviewed in more than a dozen cities nationwide (Feagin and Sikes 1994, pp. 29–33). They were asked a number of questions about their everyday lives, including one inquiring: "Who faces more problems in achieving their job and other goals in America, black men or black women?" Examination of the answers of the 209 respondents brought to light particularly clear and insightful statements by thirty-seven of them. From these interviews we have drawn statements that best articulate the themes developed below.

Experiences in the Workplace

The workplace—where the black women quoted here spend a great deal of their time—is a logical starting point for understanding their lives. A few previous analysts have noted that black women appear to be more successful in the workplace than black men (Roberts 1994). One of our male respondents, a corporate manager, put it this way:

> Whenever there's a choice here in America, in all indications, if you've got a black male and a black female who are equal and qualify for a position, from all indications the black female will get it.

White managers usually make hiring choices, so it is their images of black women and men that really matter. The professional competence of black women is often less of a factor in the decision to hire them than is their image among whites as docile workers, which is in turn frequently coupled with a white image of black men as defiant or threatening (Dollard 1939; Gaiter 1994). These fictions make black women a more advantageous and safer choice for white male employers.

Essed (1991) suggests that black female employees are often not taken seriously. Instead of being rated strictly on qualifications, black women are often evaluated on the basis of what counts most for preserving the racial-gender hierarchy. Sometimes the evaluation is in terms of appearance, as this black woman noted:

A black woman is seen as a woman first, so consequently she is being evaluated on . . . how she looks. So, [employers] don't fear us [black women] as
much.

Another black female manager noted the matter of control:

I'm sure if I were a white male and I dominated a white woman, I'm sure
that I would think that I could also dominate a black woman. . . . Females
are females.

The alleged submissiveness of black women, which is often equated
with their femininity, buffers potential threats to employers and stands
as a serious consideration in many hiring decisions. One woman stated:

There's something about the femininity of black women that allegedly tones
them down no matter how radical they really might be, that [white males]
find more accepting.

The more feminine these women, white employers reason, the fewer
the professional and personal risks—an undisputable advantage that
black men, often seen as forceful and combative, cannot offer. This
point was underscored by another respondent:

Most people feel most comfortable when they're not threatened, whether it
be professionally or physically. . . . I think a white male will always feel like
he can physically handle a black female when it comes to a fist fight or a
confrontation. And I don't think they're sure of that when it comes to black
males.

One result of this image as weak and submissive is that important
decisions are made by whites in power for black women even without
their knowledge or consent, a point emphasized by a female executive:

I've had things said to me like: "We didn't give you a certain position
because we knew you had a child, and we knew that you would not want to
be that far away."

Although black women clearly disapprove of such treatment, they may endure these controlling practices as a consequence of their double status as woman and black. To retain their positions they must often cooperate and, consciously or through silence, reinforce the existing images. Black women are under survival pressures to acquiesce in their own exploitation, a point underscored by this male professional:

> I go back to my experiences with the school system. . . . Females were more . . . ready to accept the lower salaries than were males, and mainly because the female always had the . . . possibility of getting a husband, who . . . would take care of her, where her salary was normally second. So therefore, they take more crap, excuse my French. . . . They were more likely not to say anything. . . . The same thing is true even in industry and other jobs. Females—especially black females—they've been accustomed to not making equal salaries to males, and once they get those salaries, they were going to try not to do anything that would cause them to lose it.

Consequently, white employers often give priority in hiring to black women whom whites expect to be, compared with their male counterparts, naturally controlled both physically and professionally. "Black women," argued one respondent, are in the workplace "just because the white man did not want a black person in that position, and they feel that they can control *her* better."

Gendered racism takes many forms, including the expectation that "docile" black women will be less likely to express open resentment or resistance. To many white male minds, black women's physical characteristics signal weakness and inferiority, and professional characteristics are a lesser matter. Black women provide a unique advantage to white employers since they can be patronized. They may also be more likely than black men to give in to pressures to conform, and they contribute to the self-enhancement of many white male employers. However, for the women such working environments are places where falsified identities combine with suppressed mobility to remind them of their double jeopardy—inferiorization on the basis of both race and gender.

Specific Workplace Barriers

Concrete occupational ceilings, common perceptions that they are incompetent, and excessive demands merge with other workplace realities to thwart black women's efforts toward greater life achievements.

Occupational Ceilings. If superior qualifications and performance were the sole criteria for selecting black women as workers, their conspicuous presence in the workplace would be evidence of professional quality. Despite their visibility, black women's upward mobility is restricted, tracked, and evident only within certain occupations (MacLachlan 1993), a point accented in several interviews:

> There are particularly carved out and defined roles . . . that white America asks [black women] to get into. . . . The black female is moving a lot faster because they have these paths and everything directed for them.

If black women remain within the fixed space outlined by employers, certain rewards may follow. To survive they must endure most of the practices of the hierarchy, even limitations on mobility:

> I've seen people who were in this same management training program as myself who were white males, they have since almost tripled their salaries, and of course, their titles are much more, or better than mine. And . . . most of them, have less education . . . less experience than I have.

Occupational ceilings are undergirded by white male expectations about ease of control of women workers. White male stereotypes penetrate every work context, including academia. One male professional recounted his wife's experiences as a college professor:

> One of the first things [the dean] said to [my wife] when she started working there . . . was that he believed that the place for a woman to be was in the kitchen, barefoot and pregnant. (Laughs.) Yeah, he had preconceived ideas about what women should do. In fact, I don't think there was even one woman that actually got tenure in that whole department. Well, there was an older lady, but actually . . . I can't think of anybody . . . who stayed there past two or three years.

Having a doctorate does not protect a black female professor from being undermined professionally. The dean's remarks are evidence that even for "educated" white men, a woman's biological features may displace her accomplishments in the male mind.

The last respondent continued with more about workplace limitations:

> There was quite a bit of sexual discrimination, in terms of the fact that the faculty there were white males and they wanted to keep it that way. They would hire other white males who had credentials that certainly were not in any way in comparison to my wife's; my wife's credentials were much better than theirs. They had opportunities, they got to do things, they got money, they got whatever they needed to do their job, whereas she was, "We can't do that" or "We can't do this" and that kind of thing.

The respondent clearly sees his wife's barriers as *gendered* racism. Clearly, there was an ongoing, unchallenged "affirmative action" plan in operation for white men, who had the clout to reproduce themselves in the workplace and to block entry by dissimilar faculty members. Black women, perceived as nonconfrontational and cooperative, may be highly valued by white supervisors in situations where conformity is expected:

> In the case of her going up for tenure, her department head at the same time was also ... [candidate] to be dean of the college. And she knew that this guy was not very research oriented, and he didn't do a lot of other things, and she didn't think he was very good for her department. Well, she was on the search committee, which she should *not* have been since she was also going up for tenure at the same time, but he of course, I guess, felt that she was going to vote for him when the question was called as to whether or not he should still continue as part of the search. Well, she voted in confidence and said, no, that she didn't think he would be very good for the college. And, of course, when it came time for them to make a decision on her tenure, he said no, that she was not worthy of tenure. Yet, before that, in fact, he was the one who pushed her into going up for tenure. So she didn't get tenure, she was only going to have another year to be there, so we talked

164 | Yanick St. Jean and Joe R. Feagin

about it and decided she should fight for it. And so she took it to the provost, and she had to write this long paper about what actually happened in the department and that kind of stuff, and they found that he lied and he did a lot of other things, and they had to give her tenure.

In this case, the black woman did not act as anticipated and reportedly suffered reprisals from her white male superior. Note, too, that her decision to challenge the tenure review was reached in consultation with her spouse; this is evidence of the way in which discrimination and its impact become part of the collective history and memory of black families.

The respondent continued with one interesting final point about professional competence:

> An interesting thing is that the provost told her, "You will never do scholarly research." Yet, however, this same woman . . . just won a national award for the most original scholarly research in the nation last year! I don't know what that says, but I'd say there were certainly either racist or exceptionally sexist overtones.

This female professor was exposed to serious forms of differential treatment in her daily work activities. Yet the professional abilities that are sabotaged by white male decision-makers in some settings are exploited whenever that is beneficial. Despite obvious departmental partiality toward white men in the distribution of resources, this woman was rejected for promotion; this suggests that even with fewer means black women are expected to be highly productive.

Perceptions of Incompetence. White racist attitudes have long encompassed notions of black inferiority, laziness, and incompetence. Recent opinion surveys reveal that this is still the case (Feagin 1996). Because of these stereotypes, many black female employees find their abilities questioned or, perhaps, acknowledged grudgingly as if occurring by chance and not expected to last. One female administrator explained:

> The perception is that women in particular cannot manage. . . . Some barriers have been broken, and even though women are in some of these positions and they have been successful . . . comments are still made that, "Well, she's

still hanging in there." Like it's expected that she's not gonna be successful. I
think that's just a perception of America that women cannot lead. . . . And if
a woman in a higher position encounters a problem, [employers] equate that
to the fact that she was a woman.

A black male executive noted that, while women in general are often
stereotyped as poor administrators, black women are also judged in
terms of their racial characteristics: "I mean, the stereotype, women are
not managers and that type of attitude. Being black is compounding the
problem." Here again we see the character of the double jeopardy black
women face everyday in U.S. workplaces.

It follows that, probably more so than for white women, black women
are often not accepted as authority figures, as this female manager noted:

I've had to be responsible for having a white male working under my direction, and that did not work. White men do not want to take direction from
black women.

Having been exposed to negative images of black women, white women
also tend to have difficulty accepting the authority of black women:

A white woman who's scheduled to come into our program and . . . has a doctorate also . . . has told me that her concern is that she would have a problem
taking directions from me.

Reflecting on the dovetailing of present workplace experiences with
the racialized past of African-Americans, another respondent cut to the
bottom line:

It's a problem. It's a problem that white folk have not come to grips with.
They still have the plantation mentality, the plantation mentality is alive and
well.

Characterizations of black women as proficient professionals whose talents, knowledge, and leadership are worthy of praise are incompatible
with this plantation mentality and with black female inferiorization.

Excessive Demands. Despite deeply rooted notions of incompetence, black women are frequently subjected to unreasonable expectations. If black women are "naturally" incompetent but their presence in the workplace confers advantages on white employers, one might expect their performance to be rated on the basis of a separate set of standards below that used to evaluate white coworkers. To the contrary, black women are usually held to higher expectations, as one woman put it: "[As a black woman] you have to be better than anybody else just to get half as much; twice as good to get half as much." The incongruous relationship between greater expectations and reminders of professional incompetence suggests the intent of the white demands is to create a stressful situation where failure or low achievements may match the white images of black incapacity. Black women are compelled to perform, as one interviewee put it, "three or four times better just to show that they're competent for the position."

As a rule, and in every major industry, the standard is the white male in corporate America:

> In the corporate world . . . you have to show that you're tough enough, and you know more than . . . a white man in that situation.

Having to show they "know more than a white man," black women, who face discriminatory barriers and lesser resources, must be super-achievers even to stay in the corporate game.

Problems of Training and Unfair Dismissals. One black female respondent explained how she was ignored and denied training at her workplace:

> So, I'm sitting in here six months with my hands folded trying to figure out—what am I supposed to be learning. These other [white] women are being placed in the right area, getting the right kind of training.

Then she noted a common complaint of women employees everywhere:

> And we wind up a lot of times having to train our bosses. They come in unqualified. . . . When we train them, the first thing they do is make a move to get rid of us, because we're a threat.

There are ample opportunities to "get rid" of black women if an employer desires to do so. Another respondent who worked at a country club revealed how she was abruptly terminated upon returning to work from leave:

> I tried to get pregnant for five years, and finally I was successful. Let my employer know the day after I found out . . . which was probably twenty-one days along. [We] both had signed a written agreement three months prior to my going on maternity leave, which stated when I would leave, when I would return, the position I would return to, what I would be paid while I was gone. Everything was in order. . . . When I returned to my job, I was told that I had been laid off due to budgetary reasons. I was unhappy about that, but I understood . . . with the exception of the part that the reason the budget had to be cut was they were going to remodel the golf course. What could I do? I was laid off.

In contrast, she further noted: "Two white females within a three-month period of time after that went on maternity leave and returned to their jobs." The work needs of these coworkers' situations were treated differently, suggesting the interaction of gender and racial factors in the decision-maker's mind. Despite a clear breach of contract and the woman's sense of being cheated, she did not challenge the dismissal, but quietly endured. This understandable reaction in the face of power nonetheless strengthens images of black women as likely to acquiesce to the discriminatory decisions of employers regarding their careers. Oppression breeds more oppression.

Exclusion from Cliques. Work cliques and other informal networks among male employees can be important sources of information, yet they are routinely off-limits to women, and especially to women of color:

> The . . . thing about men that they do have in their advantage is they have at least more opportunities to access the good old boy network than we women do. . . . There's the interest in sports, there's the locker room talk, there's the bathroom talk. There's a lot of wheeling and dealing that goes on in what I call those corridors of power, that women are just not privy to. . . . And so it is because of that I'm thinking more and more that women are at the bottom of the totem pole. And it's tough for us.

Backstage is where important information is shared and where, drawing on experience, male managers often mold certain male workers into promotable protégés. It is where mentoring takes place and where skills are honed. The selection of participants for these critical sessions usually entails "affirmative action" for white men. It should therefore be expected that black women who are excluded from such circles and thus from key advice and mentorship (see MacLachlan 1993) will likely perform less successfully within an already hostile workplace culture.

Neglect and Harassment. In many workplaces that have long been dominated by white men, certain traditional issues facing black women are ignored. The old problem of child care provides one illustration: "They don't give a damn about child care . . . until it's affecting white America." Lack of attention to the child care issue is consistent with a hypothesis of the inferiorization of women, particularly for women of color, who are more likely to need child care. Adequate child care might free black women to where, having more time and energy to devote to their careers, they might become more defiant in their demands for better jobs. With good child care there might be little room for the type of control evident in the statement previously made to a black female manager: "We did not give you a certain position because we knew you had a child." Adequate child care might make working women less controllable and exploitable. The provision of adequate child care or any other program that threatens the security of the male-dominated hierarchy, or does not reproduce the historical patterns of inferiorization, is unlikely.

Black women, who are unlikely to report sexual harassment (Fullwood 1991), may become targets of advances not only from coworkers but even their coworkers' spouses. Seen as Jezebels who are "free of social constraints [and who] legitimize . . . the wanton behavior of white men" (Fox-Genovese 1988, p. 292), black women are often seen as available targets. One successful black female entrepreneur related her experience with unwelcome familiarity:

> My husband worked with this . . . Anglo guy, and he called one night, and he was drunk, and my husband was not at home. . . . And I said, you really need to go home, because you seem like you need to get off the streets. . . . He

made a pass at me. "Hey, don't put your hands on me, I don't want your white hands on me. Don't touch me." No, I'll never forget.

Undue familiarity can progress to more serious harassment. The willingness to cooperate in sexual ways with the boss may be a prerequisite for promotion:

> A lot of times you hear it all the time about being hard for a black woman or a woman to get ahead. Sometimes the boss may want her to do little favors and so forth. . . . I've heard of sexual favors in some instances, from friends.

One respondent observed that "It doesn't seem like [black women] get the respect from everybody that they deserve." The following comment by a Ph.D.-trained counsellor on a college campus is a good illustration of this point:

> I kind of get that sort of subtle harassment that comes . . . in the forms of sexual innuendos about black women in general, those kinds of myths. I've also had white male students, one student in the same session, called me a "nigger" and asked me out at the same time.

Here a racial affront is comfortably mixed with a request for a date! The comment shows that in the mind of its originator "nigger" is more than just a racial slur. This incident reveals double jeopardy, the inferiorization of black women in terms of both race and gender. It shows the white image of black women as sexual players, as impure, as "whore" or "cultural prostitutes" (Staples 1979, p. 31). The white man's imagination justifies black women's oppression in variegated forms.

Stigma and Affirmative Action. The barriers to productivity for black women are not the only problems faced in the workplace. Even affirmative action, which most whites see as a successful program for African-Americans (or as "reverse discrimination"), can make the lives of black women and men more difficult. For instance, black women may be counted twice in corporate affirmative action accounting, yielding returns to white employers that black men cannot match:

> Number one, they can put a black woman in a job and knock two stones out
> with every bird—you've got a woman and you've got a minority.

Indeed, the word "twofer" has been used to denote the quota advantage
allegedly produced by black women (see Gaiter 1994):

> There was a time, late '60s or early '70s . . . where the term "twofer" came up,
> two for one. . . . People were hiring black women over black men every-
> where.

However, while white employers derive added benefits from the workers brought in by affirmative action, including the "public relations
value" (Gaiter 1994), black women are disadvantaged in the process.
Being perceived as a double-statistical revenue may mean that black
women are expected to produce accordingly. One female respondent
noted this:

> We [black women] may have more of a chance. . . . But . . . not only do you
> have to work twice as hard as others, as the men, other black men, other
> white men, and other white females, I mean, you've got to compete with all
> of them, on top of everything else. . . . That double-minority has helped you
> to maybe get in just a little bit easier, but it's not gonna necessarily help you
> stay in.

Other consequences of affirmative action entail its stigma and cost
to black women in terms of their self-esteem:

> If I'm chosen because of a quota, that doesn't make me feel really good. . . .
> Now, even though that might be an administrative job or that might be a
> high-salary job, I don't see how you can feel too good about that. I don't
> think people should be hired based on a quota system, that you're black or
> a lady. I think you ought to be hired based on your qualifications and your
> job performance and the expertise that you can bring to the job.

Yet, in general affirmative action is meritorious, because it is based on
the recognition that deeply rooted injustices in this intolerant society
need serious redressing:

It's unfortunate in this country that we have to have a quota system in order for people to even be considered for certain jobs. If we didn't have the quota system, I doubt if some blacks or women would be in the positions they're in today.

Affirmative action began as a federal program pressuring employers with federal contracts to take positive action "to have a racially representative workplace" (Hacker 1992, p. 119). Effective affirmative action programs force employers to recognize the talents of people who do not fit the white middle-class male model. It aims to deter white male decision-makers from structuring the workplace in the image of the dominant group. In theory if not always in practice, affirmative action helps reduce workplace homogeneity.

However, in a successful distortion of the original intent, some white male employers utilize affirmative action programs to their own benefit—to replace black men with black women, thereby demanding that the latter produce proportionally to their assumed quota value. Moreover, there are constant reminders to these women that they are in their positions primarily for racial or gender balancing, transforming the workplace into an intolerable milieu where occupational gains may symbolize incompetence and enhance the sense of inferiorization that decreases self-esteem.

Of course, many of these gender issues are relevant to the situations of nonblack women (see MacLachlan 1993). However, for African-American women, so often draped in the Euro-American symbolism of the color black—the "sapphires" who are the "epitome of female evil and sinfulness" (hooks 1981, p. 85)—the problems of gender take a different twist and are thereby intensified. These are not only women; they are also black, and therefore *bad* or *deviant* women.

Black women embody a double jeopardy, and thus have problems that are related to neither gender alone nor race alone. Their problems sometimes parallel those of either black men or white women. But their problems are often different as well. Unflattering images, excessive or odd work demands, "jungle fever" harassment, and many other gendered-racist barriers, all anchored in a patriarchal and white-supremacist past, shape black women's lives, transforming them into one of the most brutalized and inferiorized of all racial-gender groups.

The Meaning of Gendered Racism

The gendered racism faced by black women today has deep meanings because of its relation to a past of similar suffering. This past is indelibly imprinted in individual, family, and community memories. Maurice Halbwachs has written about two aspects of human memory:

> On the one hand a memory . . . a framework made out of notions that serve as landmarks for us and that refer exclusively to the past; on the other hand a rational activity that takes its point of departure in the conditions in which the society at the moment finds itself, in other words, in the present. (1992, p. 183)

Understandings of the present and of the past are intimately intertwined, and the present is often historicized. Streams of experience vary over time, but past experiences generally set persisting landmarks for present understandings: "We may never step into the same river, but it still has persistent characteristics, qualities that are not shared by any other river" (Halbwachs 1992, pp. 28–29).

Collective memories help transform individuals into real communities:

> Communities have a history, they are constituted by their past and for this reason we can speak of a real community as a "community of memory," one that does not forget its past. (Bellah et al. 1985, pp. 152–5).

Yet, as we have seen, individual and collective recollections are not just about successes. They also incorporate adversities:

> Remembering heritage involves accepting origins, including painful memories of prejudice and discrimination that . . . earlier efforts at "Americanization" had attempted to deny. (Bellah et al.

> 1985, p. 157).

Memories of group oppression create strong communities of memory, and the shared suffering creates "deeper identities than [shared] success" (Bellah et al. 1985, p. 153). In the African-American case, discriminatory actions—and the contending responses to that oppression—become inscribed in collective memory. This can strengthen the struggles of later generations against oppression.

Periodically, our respondents refer to the long "struggle between black America and white America" and how historically black men have "been put down." They note the significance of offering work opportunities to black women before black men and the effects associated with the reality of double jeopardy. Moving from individual memory of particular incidents to group memories of prior incidents or of hostile racial climates, their narratives link contemporary workplace realities to the long heritage of racial suffering and societal consensus to destroy black men and women. It is not our intention to connect each particular instance of discrimination with a historical past remembered by our respondents. Rather, we show how these black Americans use their collective remembrances of racism and their understanding of the racist structure of the United States to make sense of their racist present.

The racist past, as we have seen, constantly intrudes. In an interview one respondent laughed and said:

I think there's a conspiracy. . . . I think white America is deliberately trying to keep down black men.

This thesis is found in other interviews, and there is much historical evidence for it:

In the early days, black women had a greater opportunity and were treated better than black males. That was because the white male wanted to, so-called, psychologically castrate the black male. So black women could get things that black males couldn't get. But even today the whole goal is to do away with the black male, really. Black women have more education. I'm not saying that one has it better than the other, but I'm saying that the black female, even today, does have a great opportunity to do certain things that a black man would be punished, would be sent to jail for. . . . Right now, they've been given jobs before black males, because the whole effort to destroy the black male is still there.

Social science researchers such as Dollard (1957, p. 289) have made similar points. Under slavery it was white men who controlled black women. Gains for black women in terms of employment are the continuation of this fundamental condition, often involving a calculated move to humiliate black men. As one respondent stated:

> In the work world [the black man has] always been put down. . . . So, he's never been able to fulfill his manhood. . . . In today's society, the white man uses the [black] woman as a substitute for the black man.

Replacing black men with black women in the workplace has repercussions for the private sphere of black families. As major breadwinners, black women frequently provide stability and economic security for the black family. Where traditional gender roles change and black men become more economically dependent on black women, the blow to masculinity—masculinity as defined by the larger patriarchal society—can translate into tensions in the home, in the present as in the past. One black male respondent argued for this link between the position of the black man and the state of the black family:

> The black man or . . . any male, period—is usually the breadwinner of the family and probably brings in most of the finances. Therefore, if we can keep the black male down we can keep the black family down. So I think there's a lot more attention given to destroying the black male mentally, physically.

Other outcomes of nontraditional gender roles may include a rise in marital separations as well as difficulties in the socialization of children.

If a black woman wishes to be primarily a wife and mother, to work only at home and rear her children, she will likely be deterred not only by economic and other practical considerations but also by certain historical uses of black females, "whose womanhood was negated in slavery" (Fox-Genovese 1988, p. 301). One female clerical worker was blunt on this issue:

> I feel that [black women] are being used as a tool to keep the black family

apart.... Just the mere fact that the black woman has been elevated and
given ... positions to achieve head of household.... It's causing more
divorces. The black men aren't loving black women like they were.... And
I think it's intentional.... You have more white males that are able to have
their white females at home, whereas ... it's going to ... be a rare occasion
that you are going to [see a] black woman ... at home raising the kids.

In other words, most black women lack the choices available to many
white women. As in the past when they were "exploited ... to the limits of physical endurance and sometimes beyond" (Fox-Genovese
1988, p. 302), their role as primary workers often has to supersede that
of parent or spouse.

Despite contemporary changes, black women's lives resemble their
slave ancestors in remarkable ways:

> The struggle between black America and white America is the family. And
> the thing that white America ... saw in black America was strong family
> roots.... In the slave mentality, the thing was that you castrated the male
> out of the family and made the woman strong.... It separated the family.

The conspicuous presence of black women in the workplace often
serves to support white exclusion of black men. What at times appear
as gains for women are no more than hidden forms of inferiorization
that impact the whole black community—a domino effect. To the
extent that such practices contribute to societal reproduction, it makes
sense that, as one respondent put it, "if anybody's going to be a manager it is likely to be the black female."

Another respondent, a young college-educated male, underscored the
complexity of the issue of patriarchalism in regard to the black family:

> Black males live in a sexist society, a sexist culture, that doesn't let black
> males express themselves, or play the role of the sexist in the society. I'm not
> trying to argue that sexism is right, because it's not. But ... there's a role that
> society sets forth, and the man ... cannot play that role, I think that can be
> often times damaging.

The argument of the last few respondents is basically that black men are not allowed to play the valued male-dominant role in a society that is currently patriarchal. Of course, it would be much better and more humane for black men and black and white women if this patriarchal society did not exist. Yet so long as it does persist, the black man is not allowed to hold the most respected male role.

The domino effects from the black woman's treatment flow uncontrollably into the lives of black men. Thus, discussions of whether black men suffer more from white bigotry than black women are misdirected. As one respondent put it, "We've both suffered." The lives of black men and women are intertwined, with the experiences of one group necessarily affecting the other:

> If one [group] experiences difficulty, the other [group] necessarily experiences the same difficulty because black men marry black women, black women marry black men. And if black men can't find jobs, then half of one household is not going to work, and vice versa.

Even as they underscore the vulnerability of men and women to intolerance, they also recognize that "the black woman does suffer, terribly":

> Being a woman, trying to prove [she] can do as good as a man, and then trying to prove that [she] can do as any white person, a white man in particular. So, that's a lot for a woman to overcome.

We have noted previously that black women suffer not only from gender oppression but also from multiple doses of direct and cumulative racial discrimination. Racial discrimination is a notable factor in black women's lives:

> The bottom line is you're discriminated against because you're black. Institutional racism identifies you as being black. . . . You ultimately have to realize that the initiation of this culture was white male oriented. . . . And this is reinforced every day in our society.

In a white-racist society, black women never escape their blackness. If racism is gendered, and forms and intensities that racial exclusion takes do vary from men to women, then one group is as likely as the other to be savaged and hurt. This underscores the importance of focusing centrally on racial factors in a double-jeopardy analysis. A young male college student noted the problem of combatting multiple oppressions:

> Black feminists shall differ with me, but I say we ought not lose sight of the fact that blacks (or black women for that matter) cannot effectively fight a two-front battle (racism and sexism) at the same time. They must pick their battles one at a time, and I suggest that racism be tackled first.

There seems to be a consensus among many of our respondents that the experiences of black women and men ought not to be fragmented, but should instead be evaluated in combination:

> I think there are more similarities in the plight of black women and black men than there are differences. I get some newer, younger-generation individuals trying to draw a distinction or difference between their own plight as a woman and being black.... I don't.... The obstacles of racism are the same, they're not different.

Implied in the statement are generational differences in perceptions of how race and gender (or double jeopardy) affect black women. While older cohorts may underscore the influence of racial factors, younger African-Americans may place equal stress on both forms of oppression.

Some respondents urge black men and women to consolidate efforts in working for racial equality:

> I think as a people ... we're running into a serious problem and getting caught up in racism versus sexism ... and which is worse. When you're a black female, you're going to get it from many different angles. And if you're a black male, you're going to get hit from many different angles.... I need you fighting with me, and I certainly can't afford you fighting against me.

Examining the present in light of the past reveals a meaningful, continuing connection between the situations of black men and women. From this perspective, ungendered and antiracist strategies need to be devised to combat the double jeopardy of sexism and racism in the contemporary U.S. workplace.

Conclusion

In this analysis, we have attempted to understand better the experiences of black women with racial/gender bigotry and discrimination in the workplace, to look for evidence of the domino effects of discrimination, and to listen for cues linking black women's current experiences to the collective past of gendered racism.

Emerging from the data are the following themes:

(1) The high visibility of black women in traditionally white workplaces benefits their employers but is often detrimental to black women since, once hired, the women are objectified or commodified. Their achievements are slowed by multiple barriers.

(2) It is seldom possible to separate racism from sexism. While the sexism that black women experience resembles that experienced by white women, most of the time that sexism is intensified by racism.

(3) There are great similarities in the experiences of black women and black men with racial exclusion. However, the racism that black women experience is often different in subtle or obvious ways. The racism they face is mediated by factors unique to their gender.

(4) The experiences of black women with discrimination usually have a domino effect on the black men in their lives and on black families generally. As many of our respondents see it, the abuses of black women in the workplace are rooted in long-standing white machinations going back to slavery, that is, in attempts to weaken the father/mother, husband/wife roles within the black family.

(5) There is a striking resemblance between the lived experiences of black women today and those of their female ancestors. Despite contemporary twists, these experiences are linked by respondents through reflections to a long heritage of family and community suffering, a history that must first be understood before the full meaning of the present experiences can be ascertained.

Acknowledgments

We would like to thank Melvin Sikes, James Iddings, Barbara Brents, Barbara A. Zsembik, Carol Ronai, and Julius Rivera for helpful comments on this paper.

References

Bellah, Robert N., Richard Madsen, William M. Sullivan, Ann Swidler, and Steven M. Tipton. 1985. *Habits of the Heart: Individualism and Commitment in American Life.* New York: Harper & Row.

Bernstein, Jared. 1995. *Where's the Payoff?* Washington DC: Economic Policy Institute.

Bobo, Lawrence and Susan A. Suh. 1995. "Surveying Racial Discrimination: Analyses from a Multiethnic Labor Market." Unpublished research report, Department of Sociology, University of California, Los Angeles, August 1.

Dollard, John. 1957. *Caste and Class in a Southern Town.* Garden City, NY: Anchor.

Essed, Philomena. 1991. *Understanding Everyday Racism.* Newbury Park: Sage.

Feagin, Joe R. 1996. "Fighting White Racism: The Future of Equal Rights in the United States," in *Civil Rights and Race Relations in the Post Reagan-Bush Era,* ed. S.L. Myers, Jr. (Greenwood Press, forthcoming).

Feagin, Joe R. and Melvin P. Sikes. 1994. *Living With Racism: The Black Middle-Class Experience.* Boston: Beacon.

Fox-Genovese, Elizabeth. 1988. *Within the Plantation Household.* Chapel Hill: University of North Carolina Press.

Fullwood, Sam, III. 1991. "Black Women Seen as Reluctant to Claim Harassment." *Los Angeles Times,* October 10, p. A8.

Gaiter, Dorothy J. 1994. "The Gender Divide: Black Women's Gains in Corporate America Outstrip Black Men's." *Wall Street Journal,* March 8, p. A1.

Hacker, Andrew. 1992. *Two Nations: Black and White, Separate, Hostile, Unequal.* New York: Ballantine.

Halbwachs, Maurice. 1992. *On Collective Memory.* Chicago: University of Chicago Press.

hooks, bell. 1981. *Ain't I a Woman: Black Women and Feminism.* Boston: South End Press.

MacLachlan, Suzanne L. 1993. "African-American Women Chip Away at 'Concrete' Ceiling." *Christian Science Monitor,* October 22, p. 8.

Malson, Michelene Ridley. 1983. "Black Women's Sex Roles: The Social Context for a New Ideology." *Journal of Social Issues* 39: 101–113.

Roberts, Sam. 1994. "Black Women Graduates Outpace Male Counterparts: Income Disparity Seen as Marriage Threat." *New York Times,* October 31, p. A12.

Staples, Robert. 1979. "Social Inequality and Black Sexual Pathology: The Essential Relationship." *Black Scholar* 21: 29–37.

Turner, Margery Austin; Michael Fix, and Raymond J. Struyk 1991. *Opportunities Denied: Discrimination in Hiring.* Washington, DC, Urban Institute Report 91–9, August.

U.S. Department of Labor. 1994. *Employment and Earnings.* Washington, DC: Government Printing Office.

11

Higher Education as Gendered Space

Asian-American Women and Everyday Inequities

SHIRLEY HUNE

They saw
I was Asian
and offered to revise the program.

So I could read
my poetry
first.

I wouldn't want to follow
HIM

He is very articulate.

(Mirikitani 1987)

Introduction

Every day, Asian-American women are increasing their participation
on American campuses as students and faculty, and every day they face
challenges as described in the above poem to develop personally and
professionally in fulfillment of the American Dream of success, mobility, and happiness. Schooling in the U.S. can be viewed as either an
instrument of social control or one of social change. As the former,
educational institutions are seen as political, economic, and cultural
power structures within a capitalist system. They maintain hierarchies
and reproduce inequities along sex, race, and class lines. As the latter,
educational institutions provide opportunities for social mobility

through their credentialing powers. They can enable members of marginalized groups to alter their status, class position, and earnings potential (Carnoy and Levin 1985; Nasaw 1979; Tokarczyk and Fay 1993).

The tension between education as hegemonic and education as emancipatory is a long-standing one. Educational institutions are contested spaces between those who seek to preserve the dominant order and those who seek to subvert it, or at the least, to make it minimally more accommodating to historic outsiders. They are also workplaces where women and men are socialized.

Following the GI Bill, which lowered class barriers to universities and colleges after World War II, and school desegregation of the 1950s, the doors of higher education were opened further by student protest movements of the 1960s and 1970s, and more women and men from working-class and racial-ethnic communities have been gaining access to the "master's house" (Hune 1989, 1995; Lavin, Alba, and Silberstein, 1981). Since the 1980s, the dominant order has challenged continuing efforts to ungender, deracialize, and declass American universities. The rising costs of higher education and the campus wars over curriculum, speech, and standards for student admissions characterize a movement to reassert hegemony, while proponents of the movement continue to speak of the value of diversity (Altbach and Lomotey 1991; Arthur and Shapiro 1995).

A current contradiction in higher education is the gap between the promise and the reality of a diverse faculty. Female and racial-ethnic faculty serve as a supportive environment for diverse students, develop and teach the kind of multicultural curriculum demanded by students, provide new theoretical perspectives, methodologies, and research areas that are often at the cutting edge of scholarship, and enhance links between campus and society. Women of color, in particular, have great demands placed upon them. To develop a diverse faculty, higher education must adopt a "pipeline approach," whereby qualified students are admitted, mentored through doctoral programs, hired as faculty, and tenured and promoted. To have sufficient numbers in the pipeline, it is recommended that intervention begin in the junior high school years (Justus, Freitag and Parker 1987, pp. 56–59).

Have Asian-American[1] women found opportunities or barriers in higher education? The university is a different place for women now from some twenty-five years ago, when I entered its doors. As a third-generation Chinese-American and the first of my family to attend college, I did not envision an academic career. I was not taught by a single woman or person of color during my undergraduate years. I was more fortunate in my graduate years and I had the guidance of two African-American scholars, one a woman. Over the years, I have seen the number of women faculty increase, but diversification of higher education is far more complex than simply counting bodies. We must also give attention to the academic quality of life of women as students and faculty.

Spaces of Difference and Everyday Inequities

The end of legal discrimination and the introduction of affirmative action (now under siege) would suggest that sexism is no longer an issue in higher education. Nonetheless, the dominant order maintains spaces of difference to ensure a divide between its members and "others" deemed inferior (Soja and Hooper 1993). Feminist scholars (Patricia Hill Collins 1991; Sandra Harding 1991; bell hooks 1984; Dorothy Smith 1987; Daphne Spain 1992) contend that gender is an organizing principle of hierarchy in education. It is embedded in epistemology, the knowledge base, theorizing, language, spatial arrangements, research methodologies, standpoint, and other aspects. "Hegemonic masculinity" is the gendered space of the academy (Thornton 1989). For women of color, race also matters.

Scholars have begun to address the role of everyday interactions in the creation and maintenance of spaces of difference. Informal practices are significant "mediums for the demarcation of boundaries of difference" (Laguerre 1996). Dominant group members employ these mechanisms to maintain their hegemony and the formal system of control. Subordinates undertake informal practices to adapt to or resist domination, but must do so within spaces of difference created by the dominant order.

Gender is a space of difference and is socially constructed. It is "a powerful ideological device, which produces, reproduces, and legitimates the choices and limits that are predicated on sex category" (West and Zimmerman 1987, p. 147). "Doing gender," West and Zimmerman argue, is embedded in the everyday interactions of individuals in social situations whereby girls and boys and women and men are treated differently. Doing gender properly means adhering to the hierarchy of men as dominant and women as subordinates. In other words, formal laws and policies are not required to subjugate the other, limit outsiders, or constrict the outsiders within when informal practices—everyday sexism and everyday racism—will do.

This article examines the progress and experiences of Asian-American women in higher education. It does not deal with issues of cultural identity and socialization in Asian-American communities. The focus is on the dynamics of educational institutions and the significance of informal practices in gendered space. Using Asian-American women as a case study, I examine the intersection of gender and race in higher education and locate my analysis within discourses on doing gender and maintaining spaces of difference that preserve existing hierarchies and inequities. I identify the challenges and some barriers, notably in everyday interactions, that confront academic women. What follows is an Asian-American feminist gaze at the situation of Asian-American women as students and faculty. But first, what do we know about Asian-American women in education?

Race, Gender, and the "Model Minority" Construct

The literature on Asian-American women in education is sparce. Studies on Asian-American education, including those of critical theorists (Chan and Wang 1991; Lee 1994; Osajima 1991), generally utilize race as the major category of analysis. Furthermore, what we do know about Asian-American women is subsumed in the racial discourse on the "model minority," a so-called "positive" stereotype of Asian-Americans that originated in the late 1960s and is regularly reinforced by the media. Once viewed by the dominant order as the "yellow peril," Asian-Americans are now seen as having overcome past discrimination and present obstacles, if any, to achieve significant educational and economic gains. Asian cultural values for education, family, and respect for authority are also used to explain Asian-American advancement and are presented as a model for other racial-ethnic groups to emulate. Studies that address disparities among Asian-Americans and their communities have yet to override this dominant image of "success" (Chan and Hune 1995; Osajima 1988). The "model minority" construct plays a primary role in discounting Asian-Americans and often renders them invisible. In contextualizing them as a "success story," higher education diminishes the racial barriers and other difficulties faced by Asian-Americans. Race alone, however, does not tell the full story for minority women. Asian-American women endure spaces of difference that are gendered and racialized. What follows is an analysis of their experiences at different points in the educational pipeline.

Asian-American Women at the Undergraduate Level

Women are more than one-half of the U.S. population. In 1981, women reached parity with men in bachelor's degrees earned. They now receive the majority of such degrees, which was 54 percent in 1992. Asian-Americans increased their percentage of bachelor's degrees from 2.8 percent in 1982 to 4.8 percent in 1992.[2] To put this in context, they were 2.9 percent of the U.S. population in 1990. Asian-American women, however, lagged behind women of all racial-ethnic groups and did not reach parity with Asian-American men in bachelor's degrees until 1991 (Carter and Wilson 1995, p. 73).

College degrees have not provided Asian-American women with career mobility or income equity. Those with four or more years of college are occupationally segregated, overrepresented in clerical work, and selectively employed in entry-level "professional-managerial" positions with little or no authority. The bachelor's degree has served primarily as a "hedge" against employment in service and operative sectors, where foreign-born Asian-American women who lack English fluency are heavily concentrated (Woo 1989).

Asian-American Women at the Graduate Level

Master's Degrees. Women have earned more than half the master's degrees for each year since 1981. Asian-Americans earned 3.6 percent of all such degrees in 1992. While more Asian-American women are engaged in graduate studies, they lag behind their male counterparts, and were 44 percent of all Asian-American master's degrees (numbering 5,596) in 1992, a gain of 5 percent from 1981 (Carter and Wilson 1995, p. 74). Studies are needed to determine whether the master's degree is a terminal degree for Asian-American women and their new "hedge" to secure professional and white-collar jobs, or whether it is a stepping-stone to other studies.

Doctoral Degrees. Women are changing doctoral studies. They earned 45 percent of all U.S. doctoral degrees in 1993, a 28.8 percent gain from 1983 (increasing in numbers from 9,239 to 11,902). While men showed a loss of 4.2 percent in this same period (decreasing from 15,120 to 14,484), they continued to earn more doctorates than women. White men and women continue to hold the vast majority of doctorates (88 percent in 1993).

Asian-Americans were 2 percent of all U.S. doctorates in 1983 and 3.4 percent by 1993, which approximates their representation in the population. In absolute numbers, the doctorate pool is very small. In 1993, Asian-American women earned 337 doctorates and Asian-American men 554 out of a total number of 26,386 U.S. doctorates. In the intersection of gender and race, Asian-American women are startlingly disadvantaged. At 38 percent of all Asian-American doctorates, Asian-American women had the lowest percentage for women of all racial-ethnic groups in 1993 and the smallest percentage gain for all groups since 1983. In contrast, women comprised 45 percent of doctorates earned by whites, 60 percent of African-American doctorates, 50 percent of American Indian doctorates and 49 percent of Hispanic doctorates in 1993 (Carter and Wilson 1995, p. 86). Numbers and percentages, however, provide an incomplete picture. An analysis of the campus climate for Asian-American women and all women is critical for understanding their experiences as doctoral students.

Doing Gender in the Doctoral Process

How do we account for the small representation of Asian-American women in doctoral programs? One major obstacle is the doctoral process itself and its exclusivity. Academic careers are traditionally apprenticeships (some refer to this as "the old boys' network") where doctoral students are selected and "groomed" as the next generation of scholars by mentors bent on replicating themselves. As white males are the vast majority of the professorate, they predominate as potential mentors. Mentors build faculty by "placing" their graduates in each other's institutions. Prominent senior faculty, generally white males, wield power and influence in departments and disciplines far beyond their own universities, and can be of assistance for jobs, research funds, and publication opportunities throughout one's career (Justus, Freitag, and Parker 1987, pp. 6, 22–24, 53–55).

Same-sex identification is an important influence on mentoring. Men have long acknowledged the support of male advisors and female academics point to the vital role of other women in their career development. Similarly, faculty of color have been mentoring racial-ethnic students (Justus, Freitag, and Parker 1987, pp. 53–55; Sandler and Hall 1986, p. 16). Asian-American women must compete for faculty attention within gendered and racialized spaces of difference, and there are few Asian-American women faculty on American campuses (see below) to serve as advocates. Asian-American women, therefore, are too often rendered invisible, discounted, or ignored, and are not being identified for and guided through doctoral programs and academic careers.

Once in doctoral programs, able and highly motivated women often lose their confidence. Studies on the "chilly climate" in higher education (Hall and Sandler 1982, 1984; Sandler and Hall 1986) support West and Zimmerman's (1987) theoretical conception of how gender is done. Through everyday interactions, doing gender means women are valued less than men and are treated differently in the classroom, in meetings with advisors, and in consideration for research, teaching, publication, and other opportunities. The academic classroom style is normalized as "masculine," and women must adapt to survive. Women's scholarly abilities and commitments are more likely to be questioned than those of men. As women advance in their studies the "male" academic climate increases as they interact with fewer women as classmates and faculty. Typically, women students work in isolation and are given less encouragement. In a gendered campus climate, women contend with a wide range of nonacademic issues, including questions about their personal lives (will you finish your doctorate if you get married) and sexual harassment.

Asian-American women are doubly silenced in interactions with faculty and classmates. They are silenced in their gendered experiences and as Asian-Americans, through the power of cultural colonialism as well as the "model minority" myth (Chan and Hune 1995; Osajima 1991). Geraldine Kosasa-Terry (1994) views American academic discourse as a historical and ongoing process of U.S. colonialism whereby non-Western peoples and cultures are disparaged and silenced. She calls for Asian-Americans to break the silence and contest the educational power structure through a strategy of "talking back." Women's studies and ethnic studies are spaces for "talking back" and locations for empowering students. Most everyday interactions of Asian-American women, however, take place in spaces of difference and disempowerment.

Doctoral students with interests in women's studies and ethnic studies can still experience difficult apprenticeships. Finding sympathetic faculty who will understand and promote the research interests and standpoints of women students, especially minority women, is critical to their intellectual development. On campuses weak in such programs, Asian-American women are likely to find faculty still unfamiliar with and, in some cases, hostile to the new scholarship. Hence, effective mentoring for Asian-American women is frequently lacking (Justus, Freitag, and Parker 1987, p. 6; Thompson and Tyagi 1993, pp. 87–90).

Financial support for graduate students is vital to their survival and advancement and it, too, is gendered. Men are more likely to be given research assistantships connected with their interests, enabling them to spend more time on their own work, while women are more likely to be assigned teaching assistantships, which generally involve work separate from their research. These types of institutional privileges, along with personal ones (women are less likely than male counterparts to have employed spouses who can contribute to household support, and women still bear the larger share of household and child care responsibilities), enable more men than women to finish their doctoral studies before assuming full-time faculty positions (Sandler and Hall 1986, p. 16).

Doctoral students are generally advised to finish their degrees before assuming full-time academic positions, because writing the dissertation is full-time work in itself. Women in all racial-ethnic groups, but notably Asian-American women, are twice as likely as their male counterparts to begin a full-time faculty position while concurrently completing their doctoral degree. Once again, women are disadvantaged. An all-but-dissertation (ABD) situation encumbers faculty in their first professional years, as they struggle within a designated time period to conclude the Ph.D. degree and the research and scholarly work beyond the dissertation that are necessary for re-appointment and tenure (Carter and O'Brien 1993, pp. 10–11). Given the small number of Asian-American women doctorates, each one who chooses the academy is a valuable resource to be nurtured and retained.

Asian-American Women as Faculty

Women are also changing the professorate, but their presence is not commensurate with their representation as doctorates. The advancement of women of color is especially challenging and slow. Women are more likely than their male counterparts to hold non-tenure-track positions and to teach part-time while awaiting a full-time position. This gendered and racialized hiring pattern contributes to Asian-American women leaving the academy. In 1991, women were 31.8 percent of all full-time faculty, a gain of 5 percent from 1981. In 1991, Asian-Americans, excluding foreign-born Asians, were 2.9 percent of all faculty. Asian-American women were approximately one third of all Asian-American faculty (Carter and O'Brien 1993).

Spaces of difference are evident in tenure, a critical point in the pipeline when faculty are given some security of employment. Fewer women receive tenure than men, and racial-ethnic faculty have lower tenure rates than whites. In 1991, the tenure rate was 70 percent for all faculty and 58 percent for all women. At the intersection of gender and race, Asian-American women and American Indian women were both tenured at a rate of 49 percent in 1991, the lowest for all groups (Carter and Wilson 1995, p. 91). There is little evidence of a "model minority" here. How do we explain the low representation of Asian-American women faculty and their dismal tenure rate?

Doing Gender and the "Revolving Door"

The number of women and minorities leaving higher education altogether for alternative employment has been described as a "revolving door." Less likely to be tenured, they are replaced with others, and the cycle repeats itself. Some leave prior to tenure, worn down by the inhospitable climate, and others are no longer willing to put their professional lives on hold with part-time and non-tenure-track positions. Discrimination is the major explanation. Dominant group members view subordinates as "deficient" and lacking in abilities for an academic career and treat them differently (Carter and O'Brien 1993, pp. 9–11; Justus, Freitag, and Parker 1987, pp. 24–26; Sandler and Hall 1986; Swoboda 1990, pp. 1–10).

The "chilly climate," which serves to maintain hierarchy and spaces of difference in the doctoral process, is also experienced by Asian-American women as faculty. Doing gender and doing race are subtle as well as overt, and embedded in academic practices. Differences, and hence inequities, are expressed in how faculty are recruited (if this candidate doesn't work out, we'll get another); the way research is valued (gender and ethnic studies are seen as advocacy and not scholarly); teaching loads (women and minorities do more by teaching overloads to accommodate student interests and in designing new courses); advisement loads (in addition to regular advisees, women and minorities mentor diverse students in their own departments and other areas); and service assignments (subordinate faculty have a disproportionate amount of committee work for which they receive little credit). Being a woman, especially a woman of color, means having your time and energies, which could be put to scholarly endeavors, consumed by the dominant order. Most importantly, with maleness as the norm, the research, publications, and theoretical perspectives of women faculty, like women graduate students, are often challenged by men and seen as trivial, even when equal or superior to that of male colleagues. This discrepancy is especially harmful during tenure and promotion review (Carter and O'Brien 1993; Justus, Freitag, and Parker 1987; Sandler and Hall 1986; Swoboda 1990). In short, while more women faculty are working in "the master's house," it is not yet their home. Nor are women's "tools" appreciated (Hune 1995).

In everyday interactions, women find little support and mentoring from their departments and a lack of respect for issues of importance to them. Asian-American women are consulted on diversity matters, but rarely as colleagues with academic expertise. Frequently "solo" in their department, they are often seen as tokens. On those occasions when their expertise and skills are sought, Asian-American women are expected to be "superstars." Sexual and racial incidents can be part of their daily environment (Carter and O'Brien 1993; Sandler and Hall 1986; Swoboda 1990).

Student interactions also contribute to the "chilly climate." Students are more likely to challenge the authority and expertise of subordinate faculty in the classroom than that of dominant group members. They have higher expectations of female faculty and are demanding of their time and consultation. Male students, in particular, are hypercritical of female faculty. Sexist and racist statements on student evaluations of faculty are not uncommon (Sandler and Hall 1986, pp. 6–10). The following was received by a third-generation Asian-American woman teaching an advanced managerial cost accounting course:

> Pretty boring but what do you expect from a fat dumb little nip. She should go back to Japan and let some interesting, deserving American teach. While my fathers were building this country her fathers were trying to destroy it. What right does she have taking my money? (Cited in Swoboda 1990, p. 5)

Adding to the spaces of difference is a generation gap between how work and family were combined in the past and current realities. Today's faculty are often dual-career households. Yet traditional faculty continue to view the professional and family responsibilities of women and men differently, and this is manifested in academic practices. Asian-American women can receive mixed messages from colleagues, as well as from family, with regard to their academic and personal goals and ambitions. A few institutions are revising standard academic practices, such as the timeline to tenure, by providing additional years for women (in rare cases, for men too) to combine reproduction with scholarly production prior to tenure review. Asian-American women face similar and added tensions in meeting professional demands and contributing to their ethnic communities at the same time (Sandler and Hall 1986, pp. 5–6; Swoboda 1990, pp. 14–16).

Finally, it should be of no surprise that faculty rank and salary are gendered. Women, especially women of color, are found primarily in the lower ranks. Women and minority men also average lower salaries than white men in all faculty ranks. Nor are Asian-American women visible as administrators. In 1991, when women held 40 percent of the full-time administrative positions, mostly in two-year and four-year institutions, Asian-American women were 2 percent of all female administrators or .05 percent in total (Ottinger and Sikula 1993, pp. 8–9).

The underrepresentation of Asian-American women as full-time, tenure-track and tenured faculty, and as administrators has gained the attention of the American Council on Education. The council has called for research on why so few Asian-American women, compared with their male counterparts, earn doctorates and become faculty. It has also called for higher education institutions to examine their policies and practices toward Asian-Americans (Escueta and O'Brien 1991, p. 9). Increasing the presence of Asian-American women on college campuses and redressing the quality of their experiences, however, will require attention to informal practices as well as formal policies.

Conclusion

Higher education is providing increased access to women and minorities. At the same time, it continues to reproduce inequities. The dominant order maintains spaces of difference between its members and subordinates to ensure hierarchies and hegemony.

Women are changing higher education, but they do so within gendered space. Feminist theorists have identified gender as an organizing hierarchical principle. It is a space of difference that devalues women, their viewpoints, and their work. Dominant group members do gender by treating women and men differently. These practices contribute to the reduction of women in the pipeline as doctoral students and as faculty compared with their majority participation as recipients of bachelor's and master's degrees.

Race is also a space of difference for women of color. Asian-Americans encounter cultural colonialism, which subordinates non-Western peoples and their standpoints. In addition, they are seen as a problem-free "model minority." Higher education thus renders a visible minority invisible.

Asian-American women experience both opportunities and barriers in higher education. Far from being a "success story," they exist in both gendered and racialized spaces of difference as articulated by Mirikitani in her poem that opened this essay. These boundaries contribute to their diminished presence in the pipeline when compared to male counterparts and to all women. Asian-American women are underrepresented in doctoral programs, as full-time, tenure-track and tenured faculty, and as administrators. They experience isolation and alienation, and their views and interests are often discounted. They need to be included in policies and programs to diversify universities, and guided and supported for the length of the educational pipeline. Studies on the specific experiences of women in each of the many Asian- and Pacific-American communities are also in need.

In challenging the "hegemonic masculinity" of the university, Asian-American women and all women experience everyday inequities that undermine policies to increase diversity. Numerous programs have been identified toward building a diverse faculty and we must continue to pursue and to implement policies that ensure access. But formal structures and edicts alone are incapable of changing the hierarchy of higher education and replacing a "chilly climate" and a "revolving door" for women with a climate of inclusion and advancement. In our efforts to increase the presence of women, we cannot ignore the quality of their experiences and the climate of higher education as learning and working environments. Attention must also be given to the power of informal practices—the everyday interactions of sexism and racism—that preserve the dominant order. Emancipatory education includes transforming academic culture, dissolving spaces of difference, creating spaces of empowerment, acknowledging and appreciating different world-views and intellectual interests, and sharing decision-making powers.

Acknowledgments

The author wishes to thank Kenyon S. Chan, Ellen Benkin, and the editors of this volume for their insightful comments and assistance on earlier drafts.

Notes

1. Asian-Americans are persons who call the United States their homeland and who trace their ancestry to countries from the Asian continent, such as China, Japan, Korea, India, Vietnam, Cambodia, Laos, and Thailand, and to those of the Pacific Basin, such as the Philippines, Samoa, and Micronesia. Hawaiians, native to the United States, are also included within this broad category.
2. Educational data on Asian-Americans often combines U.S. citizens and permanent residents with international students and nonresident aliens from Asia, most of whom enter American educational

institutions as graduate students and subsequently return home. Such data distort analyses of access and mobility for racial-ethnic groups in the U.S. In this article, I utilize data on Asian-Americans (includes Pacific Islanders) referring only to U.S. citizens in an effort to more accurately portray the educational advancement of persons of Asian descent born and raised in the U.S.

References

Altbach, Philip G. and Kofi Lomotey, eds. 1991. *The Racial Crisis in American Higher Education.* Albany: State University of New York Press.

Arthur, John and Amy Shapiro, eds. 1995. *Campus Wars: Multi-Culturalism and the Politics of Difference.* Boulder: Westview Press.

Carnoy, Martin and Henry M. Levin. 1985. *Schooling and Work in the Democratic State.* Stanford: Stanford University Press.

Carter, Deborah J. and Eileen M. O'Brien. 1993. "Employment and Hiring Patterns for Faculty of Color." *Research Briefs* 4: 6. Washington, DC: American Council on Education.

Carter, Deborah J. and Reginald Wilson. 1995. *Thirteenth Annual Status Report on Minorities in Higher Education 1994.* Washington, DC: American Council on Education.

Chan, Kenyon S. and Shirley Hune. 1995. "Racialization and Panethnicity: From Asians in America to Asian-Americans," in *Toward a Common Destiny,* eds. Willis D. Hawley and Anthony W. Jackson. San Francisco: Jossey-Bass Publishers, pp. 205–233.

Chan, Sucheng and Ling-Chi Wang. 1991. "Racism and the Model Minority: Asian-Americans in Higher Education," in *The Racial Crisis in American Higher Education,* eds. Philip G. Altbach and Kofi Lomotey. Albany: State University of New York, pp. 43–67.

Collins, Patricia Hill. 1991. *Black Feminist Thought.* New York: Routledge.

Escueta, Eugenia and Eileen O'Brien. 1991. "Asian-Americans in Higher Education: Trends and Issues." *Research Briefs* 2: 4. Washington, DC: American Council on Education.

Hall, Roberta M. and Bernice R. Sandler. 1982. *The Classroom Climate: A Chilly One for Women?* Washington, DC: Project on the Status and Education of Women, Association of American Colleges.

Hall, Roberta M. and Bernice R. Sandler. 1984. *Out of the Classroom: A Chilly Campus Climate for Women?* Washington, DC: Project on the Status and Education of Women, Association of American Colleges.

Harding, Sandra. 1991. *Whose Science? Whose Knowledge?* Ithaca: Cornell University Press.

hooks, bell. 1984. *Feminist Theory: From Margin to Center.* Boston: South End Press.

Hune, Shirley. 1989. "Opening the American Mind and Body: The Role of Asian-American Studies." *Change* (November/December): 56–63.

———. 1995. "Pragmatism, Liberal Education, and Multiculturalism: Utilizing the 'Master's Tools' to Restructure the 'Master's House' for Diversity," in *The Condition of American Liberal Education: Pragmatism and a Changing Tradition,* ed. Robert Orrill. New York: The College Board.

Justus, Joyce Bennett, Sandra B. Freitag, and L. Leann Parker. 1987. *The University of California in the Twenty-First Century: Successful Approaches to Faculty Diversity.* Berkeley: Office of the President, University of California System.

Kosasa-Terry, Geraldine E. 1994. "Localizing Discourse," in *New Visions in Asian-American Studies,* eds. Franklin Ng, Judy Yung, Stephen S. Fugita, and Elaine H. Kim. Pullman: Washington State University Press, pp. 211–221.

Laguerre, Michel. 1996. "The Informal City: The Implosion of Urban America." Paper presented at the Social Science Research Council Conference on International Migration to the United States, "Becoming American/America Becoming." Sanibel Island, Florida, January 18–21.

Lavin, David E., Richard D. Alba, and Richard A. Silberstein. 1981. *Right Versus Privilege: The Open Admissions Experiment at The City University of New York.* New York: The Free Press.

Lee, Stacey J. 1994. "Behind the Model-Minority Stereotype: Voices of High- and Low-Achieving Asian-American Students." *Anthropology & Education Quarterly* 25 (4): 413–429.

Mirikitani, Janice. 1987. *Shedding Silence.* Berkeley: Celestial Arts.

Nasaw, David. 1979. *Schooled to Order.* New York: Oxford University Press.

Osajima, Keith. 1988. "Asian-Americans as the Model Minority: An Analysis of the Popular Press Image in the 1960s and 1980s," in *Reflections on Shattered Windows,* eds. G. Okihiro, S. Hune, A. Hansen, and J. Liu. Pullman: Washington State University Press, pp. 165–174.

———. 1991. "Breaking the Silence: Race and the Educational Experiences of Asian-American College Students," in *Readings on Equal Education,* ed. Michele Foster. New York: AMS Press, 115–134.

Ottinger, Cecilia and Robin Sikula. 1993. "Women in Higher Education: Where Do We Stand?" *Research Briefs* 4: 2. Washington, DC: American Council on Education.

Sandler, Bernice R. and Roberta M. Hall. 1986. *The Campus Climate Revisited: Chilly for Women Faculty, Administrators, and Graduate Students.* Washington, DC: Project on the Status and Education of Women, Association of American Colleges.

Smith, Dorothy E. 1987. *The Everyday World as Problematic.* Boston: Northeastern University Press.

Soja, Edward and Barbara Hooper. 1993. "The Spaces that Difference Makes," in *Place and the Politics of Identity*, eds. Michael Keith and Steve Pile. London: Routledge.

Spain, Daphne. 1992. *Gendered Spaces.* Chapel Hill: University of North Carolina Press.

Swoboda, Marian J., ed. 1990. *Retaining and Promoting Women and Minority Faculty Members: Problems and Possibilities.* Madison: The University of Wisconsin System.

Thompson, Becky W. and Sangeeta Tyagi. 1993. "The Politics of Inclusion: Reskilling the Academy," in *Beyond a Dream Deferred*, eds. Becky W. Thompson and Sangeeta Tyagi. Minneapolis: University of Minnesota Press, pp. 83–99.

Thornton, Margaret. 1989. "Hegemonic Masculinity and the Academy." *International Journal of the Sociology of Law* 17: 115–130.

Tokarczyk, Michelle M. and Elizabeth A. Fay. 1993. "Introduction," in *Working-Class Women in the Academy*, eds. Michelle M. Tokarcyzk and Elizabeth A. Fay. Amherst: The University of Massachusetts Press, pp. 3–24.

West, Candace and Don H. Zimmerman. 1987. "Doing Gender." *Gender & Society* 1 (June): 125–151.

Woo, Deborah. 1989. "The Gap Between Striving and Achieving: The Case of Asian-American Women," in *Making Waves*, ed. Asian Women United of California. Boston: Beacon Press, pp. 185–194.

12

The Gendered Spaces
in Ethnopolitical Life

Social Identities and
Political Activism among Chicanos

BARBARA A. ZSEMBIK

Chicanas are vital, active agents in the public spaces of political life in communities and workplaces, but they act in a historically situated context of sexism, racism, and classism. Indeed the public discourse on the social action movements of the 1960s and 1970s has been demarcated by Chicano men or Anglo, middle-class feminists. Chicanas have been routinely excluded from analyses of the political process, based on assumptions that they reflect ethnic and class interests identical to those of Chicano men or Anglo women.

The purpose of this study is to explore the gendered nature of ethnopolitical activism among Chicanos, locating it in the historical context of strengthening cultural nationalism and women's movements in the 1970s. Interpreted within a theoretical framework of gendered space, I examine the National Chicano Survey to see if simultaneous isolation as Chicanos from mainstream political action by non-Latinos and exclusion as women from the Chicano cultural nationalism movement by men's leadership restrained women's commitment to political action. Specifically, I contend that their growing gender, ethnic, and class consciousness and identity, in the context of the social action of the 1970s, constitute different social locations for women and men in relation to political action. Not only did Chicana women and Chicano men both participate in collective social action in communities and workplaces, albeit with different strategies, they based these gendered strategies in women's and men's separate gender, ethnic, and class identities, private locations within the self.

The Gendered Nature of Ethnic Identity

Chicanas are believed to be uninterested or poorly suited for participation in political life (Blea 1992; Cantu 1990), an assumption that conceals their contributions to social change (Valadez 1994); yet analyses of ethnic political action infrequently explore the role of women (Zsembik 1995). Their political disinterest is attributed to Chicanas' weak ethnic identity, yet it was everyday sexism in the political landscape that marginalized Chicanas from the public domains of political life. Marginalization did not dampen the political ardor of Chicanas.

Ethnic identity among Chicanos translates into an ethnic-based political consciousness and plays a decisive role in generating and sustaining political action (Gomez-Quinones 1990; Valadez 1994; Zsembik and Beeghley 1996). The Chicano movement intended to secure Chicanos' integration into public places, while preserving their cultural autonomy (Gutierrez 1993) and expressing virtually no concern about integration of communities, social associations and organizations, friendship networks, and families and households. Indeed, preservation of ethnic culture rested primarily on maintaining the strict sexual division of labor of family life. Chicanas sat at the margins in the contemporary cultural nationalism movement, an experience similar to that of African-American and Asian-American women, although women shared in the deepening, rediscovery, and redefining of ethnic identity (Chow 1987; Garcia 1989; hooks 1984). Men's patriarchal control over the agenda of the movement effectively eliminated concerns defined as "women's issues" and constrained women's participation to stereotypic tasks (Garcia 1989; Orozco 1990; Segura and Pesquera 1992). When Chicanas did press for women's issues within the ethnic struggle, their ethnic identity, femininity, or sexual orientation was questioned (Gutierrez 1993). The political identity dilemma—one's primary identity is either gender or ethnic—translated into the liberation dilemma—one's primary goal is either ethnic or gender equality.

The Gendered Nature of Class Identity

Chicanos' cultural nationalism movement grew out of land and labor organizing (for example Cesar Chavez's National Farmworkers of America and Reies Lopez Tijerina's land ownership claims in New Mexico), in contrast to the other civil rights efforts (Fernandez 1994). Therefore, the Chicano movement concerned itself with national ethnic identity, but one solidly and primarily based on class identity. Scholars traditionally have assumed that women derive their class consciousness and identity from men, usually husbands and fathers (Deutsch 1994). More recent research, however, shows that women and men encounter class differently. Working-class women and men, for example, experience class through the gendered workplace, intimately linking labor and class issues with ethnicity and political activism. Chicanas' seeming invisibility in the workplace has facilitated the omission of women's contribution to ethnic- and class-based social movements. Historical revision currently works to pull women's long presence in the workplace from the shadows (Deutsch 1994; Rose 1995; Zavella 1987). In fact, reclaiming their historical presence shows how actively Chicana women have been in labor organizing (Rose 1995; Ruiz 1987; Weber 1989).

But middle-class Chicanas rarely focus on the workplace as a locus of social action and social change, the social interstices primarily of working-class women. They concentrate instead on the patriarchal character of the cultural nationalism movement and the role of women in the family and household. The gendered nature of ethnicity and political activism contains women's struggle to resist within the sexism of the Chicano movement and the racism of the feminist movement. Alma Garcia (1989) names the sexist dynamics of the Chicano movement as the origins of Chicana feminism, especially its interest in preserving the patriarchal nature of ethnic family life. Other researchers focus on women's strengthening of ethnic consciousness and identity as they recognize their marginalization within the Anglo-dominated feminist movement (Segura and Pesquera 1992). Clearly, middle-class women hold a stronger gender awareness than working-class women, although gender and class mutually define a woman's own experience.

The multiple literature streams are blended in this research to offer a more coherent framework for understanding and observing the gendered nature of ethnopolitical life among Chicano women and men. I begin with two assumptions. First, Chicano women hold class and ethnic identities that are distinct from men's, not vicarious representations of men's identities. Second, perceptions of women's roles vary by social class, encouraging less traditional gender ideologies among the middle class than the working class. These assumptions shape the research expectations for this analysis: political activism in public spaces is different among women and men, partially informed by the gendered nature of private spaces, their social identities, and partially shaped by the particular type of political activity.

Data and Methods

I examine these questions with data from the 1979 Chicano Survey (NCS), a household survey of persons representative of nearly 90 percent of the Mexican-ancestry population in the United States as of 1979. This is the only survey data available for analyses of social identities and political activism in the 1970s. The late 1960s and early 1970s were a critical time for social action groups, the changing economic fortunes of Chicanos, and the changing social climate governing women's experiences, thereby positioning these data at a useful historical juncture for understanding gender, ethnic, and class identity, and political activism among Mexican-Americans. Data on support for political activism and social identities of the women and men in this survey are provided in Table 1. Gender differences in a set of control variables are also provided in Table 1.

The public domain of political activism is defined by seven questions that ask whether engaging in a particular action was a good thing for persons of Mexican descent who want to increase their influence or "get something done":

(1) to pressure employers to hire more people of Mexican descent;
(2) to go to a demonstration to get a law changed or protest an unfair policy;
(3) to get a group of people of Mexican descent to vote for a candidate they support;
(4) to express your opinion individually by voting;
(5) to shop at stores owned by people of Mexican descent;

Table 1. Characteristics of the Chicanas and Chicanos in the Survey

	Chicanas	Chicanos
Political Activism		
Pressure employers to hire Chicanos	83%	76%
Attend demonstrations or protests	76%	80%
Lobby Chicanos to support a candidate	88%	88%
Express opinion by voting	95%	94%
Shop in minority stores	76%	75%
Boycott companies	49%	55%
Support bilingual education	91%	96%
Social Identities		
Ethnic identity score	18	21
Class identity score	29	33
Gender role ideology score	28	26
Control Variables		
Education (in years)	8	9
Income (in categories)	$9–10,000	$9–10,000
Age	40	40
Mexican-born	33%	46%

(6) to avoid buying goods produced by companies that Mexican-American organizations oppose; and

(7) to support bilingual education or bring pressure to get it in your local schools.

Women and men are roughly equivalent in their support of a variety of political activities to increase Chicano political power, ranging from moderate support of company boycotts to strong support of individual voting behavior and bilingual education programs. More than 75 percent of the Chicanos support multiple political activities, except boycotting companies. Chicanas are only slightly less supportive than men of demonstrating and endorsing bilingual education. Boycotting received the least support, but showed the widest gender difference; Chicanas are proportionately more supportive than men of boycotting businesses. In contrast, women are proportionately supportive than Chicano men of pressuring employers to hire persons of Mexican origin.

Social Identities

The ethnic identity scale rates how strongly (50) or weakly (10) a person identifies with a series of ethnopolitical labels: *pocho/pocha,* Indian, *cholo/chola,* Chicano/Chicana, *mestizo/mestiza,* and *la Raza.* These designations carry strong political connotations that directly emerge from the Chicano movement of the 1960s. Class consciousness is composed of four identities (middle-class, Hispanic, Latino/a, working-class) and ranges from 10 (weak class identification) to 50 (strong class identification). Gender role ideology represents the recognition of women's separate interests in cultural nationalism. The gender role ideology index is created from four Likert-scaled attitudinal items about women's social roles, and ranges from 10 (traditional gender role attitudes) to 40 (less traditional). Chicanas hold weaker ethnic and class identities, and less traditional gender role ideologies, compared to men, although the whole sample indicates a moderate salience of ethnic and class identities and moderately less traditional gender attitudes.

Level of education and family income reflect a Chicano's objective socioeconomic status, social class. The level of education among this sample is low, but women have slightly less education than Chicano men. Family income, including all salaries, pensions and other income sources, ranges across thirteen categories from "less than $2,000" to "$30,000 or more." The average Chicano woman or man in this sample has a family income that ranges between $10,000 and $10,999 and is approximately 40 years old. Women are disproportionately born in the U.S. compared to men.

Method of Analysis

Political activism is estimated with logistic regression procedures, using weighted data for each of the seven political actions. Each social identity is treated as a separate influence on political activism for ease of statistical interpretation, whereas they are complexly intertwined in everyday life. The odds ratio for gender is provided in the row beneath the logistic regression coefficient for gender. The odds ratio presents the relative odds that women, compared to men, would support a particular political action. Odds ratios higher than one indicate a higher proportion of support that women offer over men. An odds ratio of less than one, however, shows a lower proportionate support by women, relative to men, for that action.

Results

The indicators of the public domain of political activism are shown in Table 2. There are clear gender differences in support for particular political strategies, therefore indicating the gendered nature of political action. Women are more likely than men to advocate pressuring employers to act affirmatively, voting, and shopping in ethnic-owned stores. Specifically, women are 13 percent more likely than Chicano men to support making purchases from minority business owners, and 35 percent more likely than their male counterparts to support employer pressure. Also Chicanas are 61 percent more likely than men to agree that voting is a useful political strategy. Women are less sup-

Table 2.   **Chicanas and Chicanos and Political Activism**
(Logistic Regression Coefficients)

	Pressure Employers to Hire Chicanos	Attend Demon- strations or Protests	Lobby Chicanos to Support a Candidate	Express Opinions by Voting	Shop at Ethnic Stores	Boycott Companies	Support Bilingual Education
Gender							
Women	.303*	−.110*	−.013	.475*	.119*	−.148*	−.598*
(Odds ratio)	1.35	0.90	0.99	1.61	1.13	0.86	0.55
Social identities							
Ethnic identity	.048*	.026*	.013*	.025*	.019*	.011*	−.016*
Class identity	−.002	.007*	−.005	.021*	.010*	.007*	.018*
Gender role	−.005*	−.002*	.003*	.003*	−.003*	.001	−.001
Socioeconomic status							
Education	−.096*	−.067*	−.036*	−.041*	−.041*	−.039*	−.116*
Income	−.080*	−.033*	.013	.154*	−.068*	.019*	−.067*
Demographic factors							
Age	−.001	−.011*	.005	.027*	.016*	.001	.012*
Mexican-born	.113	.692*	−.045	−.361*	.398*	−.018	.644*
Intercept	3.4	2.2	1.0	−.9	1.4	1.2	4.5
Model chi-square	1019*	624*	71*	361*	664*	115*	416*
N	861	866	867	868	864	852	867

Note: **Model or coefficient significant at p < .05*

portive than men of political demonstrations, company boycotts, or advocacy of bilingual education programs. In fact, women are 45 percent less supportive of bilingual education than Chicano men. Women and men equally advocate the utility of campaigning for politicians in elections to further the political interests of Chicanos.

In nearly every type of political activity, a stronger ethnic identity promotes political activism. Curiously, a stronger ethnic identity is associated with diminished support for bilingual education, perhaps more reflective of a stigmatized, poor-quality program than of ideological opposition. Class identity less consistently affects support for activism. Chicano women and men who report a salient class identity, whether working-class or middle-class, favor the following political strategies: demonstrations, voting, frequenting minority-owned businesses, company boycotts, and bilingual education programs. Persons who hold less traditional gender role attitudes tend to believe that campaigning and voting are useful political strategies. In contrast, more gender-traditional women and men favor pressuring employers to act affirmatively, demonstrating, and shopping at Chicano-owned stores.

Among the control variables, the socioeconomic factors carry more weight than the demographic characteristics in estimating support for political activism. In most instances, Chicano women and men in the middle classes are less supportive of political activism than Chicanos in the lower classes. When age or nativity serves as an indicator of support for political activism, in approximately half of the types of political activities, older Chicanos and persons born in Mexico more strongly advocate political action.

Conclusions

Chicanas are political actors, in contrast to the assumption and stereotype of their interest as equivalent to that of men. Also contrary to assumption, the level of support given by women and men depends on the particular political strategy. The results document the gendered nature of political life, activities that occur in public spaces. The collective variability of the effects of gender and social identities observed across multiple political strategies provides further evidence for the interweaving influence of gender, ethnicity, and social class, and for the role of the private spaces of social identity in the public spaces of political action.

This research effectively demonstrates that Chicanas' struggles occur across multiple situations in everyday life, and as women they are especially predisposed to express their political opinion by pressuring employers to act affirmatively, voting, and frequenting Chicano-owned businesses. Men, however, more strongly advocate than women the use of demonstrations, bilingual education, and company boycotts as effective political strategies. Political activism is a gendered public domain, perhaps because of an interaction of gender and ethnic identity.

This analysis of the relations among gender, social identities, and political activism among Chicanos bears implications for the gendered nature of current political life among Chicanos. Their exclusion from mainstream political life by Anglos and Anglo women and from the cultural nationalism movement has supported women's organization of the Chicana movement and Chicana feminism (Chabram Dernersesian 1993; Pesquera and de la Torre 1993). Yet increasing ethnic group solidarity will depend on women's inclusion at all levels of political organizations. Regardless of men's leadership, the lessons of the earlier Chicana movement, women's increased labor force participation, and expanding gender role ideologies will encourage women to press for further political involvement. The current political climate forecasts Chicanas' success in electoral and nonelectoral political action (MacManus, Bullock, and Grothe 1986; Pachon et al. 1994).

Acknowledgments

I would like to thank Joe R. Feagin and Carol Ronai for helpful comments on this paper. An earlier version was presented at the annual meeting of the Southern Sociological Society, April 6–9, 1995, Atlanta, GA.

References

Arce, C. 1979. *Mexican Origin People in the United States: The 1979 Chicano Survey.* (Machine-readable data file.) Principal investigator, Carlos H. Arce. Ann Arbor, MI: ICPSR.

Blea, I.I. 1988. *Toward a Chicano Social Science.* New York: Praeger.

———. 1992. *La Chicana and the Intersection of Race, Class, and Gender.* New York: Praeger.

Cantu, N. 1990. "Women, Then and Now: An Analysis of the Adelita Image Versus the Chicana as Political Writer and Philosopher," in *Chicana Voices: Intersections of Class, Race, and Gender,* eds. T. Cordova, N. Cantu, G. Cardenas, J. Garcia, and C.M. Sierra. Colorado Springs, CO: The National Association for Chicano Studies.

Chabram Dernersesian, A. 1993. "And, yes … The Earth Did Part: On the Splitting of Chicana/o Subjectivity," in *Building with Our Hands: New Directions in Chicana Studies,* eds. A. de la Torre and B.M. Pesquera. Berkeley: University of California Press.

Chow, E. N. 1987. "The Development of Feminist Consciousness among Asian American Women." *Gender & Society* 1: 284–299.

de la Torre, Adela and Beatriz M. Pesquera, eds. 1993. *Buiding With Our Hands: New Directions in Chicana Studies.* Berkeley, CA: University of California Press.

Deutsch, S. 1994. "Gender, Labor History, and Chican/a Ethnic Identity." *Frontiers* 14: 1–22.

Fernandez, R. 1994. "Abriendo Caminos in the Brotherland: Chicana Writers Respond to the Ideology of Literary Nationalism." *Frontiers* 14: 23–50.

Garcia, A.M. 1989. "The Development of Chicana Feminist Discourse, 1970–1980." *Gender & Society* 3: 217–238.

Gomez-Quinones, J. 1990. *Chicano Politics: Reality and Promise, 1940–1990.* Albuquerque: University of New Mexico Press.

Gutierrez, R.A. 1993. "Community, Patriarchy and Individualism: The Politics of Chicano History and the Dream of Equality." *American Quarterly* 45:44–72.

hooks, b. 1984. *Feminist Theory: From Margin to Center.* Boston: South End Press.

MacManus, S.A., C.S. Bullock III, and B.P. Grothe. 1986. "A Longitudinal Examination of Political Participation Rates of Mexican American Females." *Social Science Quarterly* 67: 604–612.

Orozco, C. 1990. "Sexism in Chicano Studies and the Community," in *Chicana Voices: Intersections of Class, Race, and Gender,* ed. T. Cordova, N. Cantu, G. Cardenas, J. Garcia, and C.M. Sierra. Colorado Springs, CO: The National Association for Chicano Studies.

Pachon, H., L. Arguelles, and R. Gonzalez. 1994. "Grass-Roots Politics in an

East Los Angeles Barrio: A Political Ethnography of the 1990 General Election," in *Barrio Ballots: Latino Politics in the 1990 Elections*, eds. R. de la Garza, M. Menchaca, and L. DeSipio. Boulder, CO: Westview.

Rose, M. 1995. "'Woman Power Will Stop Those Grapes': Chicana Organizers' Middle-Class Female Supporters in the Farm Workers' Grape Boycott in Philadelphia, 1969–1970." *Journal of Women's History* 7: 6–36.

Ruiz, V.L. 1987. *Cannery Women/Cannery Lives: Mexican Women, Unionization, and the California Food Processing Industry, 1930–1950*. Albuquerque: University of New Mexico Press.

Segura, D.A. and B.M. Pesquera. 1992. "Beyond Indifference and Antipathy: The Chicana Movement and Chicana Feminist Discourse." *Aztlan* 19: 69–92.

Valadez, J. 1994. "Latino Politics in Chicago: Pilsen in the 1990 General Election," in *Barrio Ballots: Latino Politics in the 1990 Elections*, eds. R. de la Garza, M. Menchaca, and L. DeSipio. Boulder, CO: Westview.

Weber, D.A. 1989. "Raiz fuerto: Oral History and Mexicana Farm Workers." *Oral History Review* 17: 47–62.

Zsembik, B.A. 1995. "Racial and Ethnic Conflict: Perspectives From Women." *Annual Review of Conflict Knowledge and Conflict Resolution* 4.

Zsembik, B.A. and L. Beeghley. 1996. "Determinants of Ethnic Group Solidarity Among Mexican Americans: A Research Note." *Hispanic Journal of Behavioral Sciences*. 18: 51–62.

13

Which "We" Are We?

The Politics of Identity in Women's Narratives

BARBARA ELLEN SMITH

Which "we" are we? Within the trio of key social inequalities, which provides the firmest ground for a sense of self? Class? Gender? Race? How do those who are multiply oppressed by these relationships make choices regarding their social allegiances? Which evokes their most fervent political commitment?

The perspective that race, class, and gender are inseparable, interactive, equally significant features of the stratification system in the United States has become commonplace (albeit not unanimously endorsed) among social scientists (Andersen and Collins 1995; Cyrus 1993; Rothenberg 1995; Rothman 1993). These identities are inseparable in part because they are omnipresent elements of individual biography; we are all multiply positioned by and define ourselves through our race, gender, and class. More subtly, they cannot be separated because they interact in ways that are mutually transformative: so, for example, the meaning and experience of gender are different for a black middle-class woman and a white working-class woman. At a structural level, race, class, and gender are equally significant because they are all constituted in and determinant of key features of the social system: power relations, life chances, historical possibilities.

The broadening of stratification scholarship to encompass race and gender, in addition to its traditional focus on class, was occasioned by the great social upheavals of the 1960s, particularly the civil rights and women's movements. Ironically, however, these movements did not define race, class, and gender as inseparable and equally significant, but as discrete and hierarchical. Each movement tended to focus on a singular aspect of social inequality and identity, race, *or* gender. To this day, African-American women and, more generally, women of color, are faced with an impossible choice between loyalty to their race and to their gender. (Does one support the Million Man March? Anita Hill? The NOW?) Although it has received less contemporary attention, white working-class women face an analogous political dilemma: Does one support class-based organizations that seem intransigently sexist, for instance trade unions, or pursue feminist demands that might weaken such organizations when they are already embattled?

Therein lies the contradiction that this article seeks to explore: race, class, and gender are inseparable, but they are also "incommensurable" (Calhoun 1994). They intertwine in the heart of individuals' social identity, yet—for those who are oppressed, not privileged, by these relationships—they split apart in mutually exclusive allegiances. How do women, particularly those who are working class and/or of color, construct a coherent sense of self out of such fragmentation? How do politically active women make choices of which battles to fight?

This article examines these questions in the life stories of three women, each of whom has been active in community-based organizations in the Southeastern United States for at least the past fifteen years. Cynthia Brown is African-American, Connie White and Chris Weiss are of European descent. All are between the ages of 35 and 55. They self-identify as working class in origin, and have been involved as staff or leaders in organizations with primarily working-class constituencies. Following the protocols of oral history, the identity of each woman, by her own choice, is not disguised. Each has read this article and, with only minor changes, approved its representation of her life.

The interviews with these women are part of a larger study of contemporary women's activism in the South (Smith 1995). To date, ten interviews with seven women have been conducted and transcribed. (Cynthia Brown was interviewed in three separate sessions and Chris Weiss in two.) The interviews combine the formats of life history and oral history: they begin with open-ended questions designed to elicit a biographical narrative with minimal intervention from the interviewer; then they move to more focused questions about political motivations, commitments, and priorities. The resulting narratives reflect in part my intentions and presuppositions as a researcher interested in the connection between social experience and political sensibility, individual biography, and collective action.

In the three interviews selected for examination in this article, each woman grounds her social identity in and directs her politics to a singular inequality: race (Cynthia), class (Connie), or gender (Chris). This enables us to disentangle and compare the distinct ways that each form of oppression impinges on and is constituted through each woman's life story. Most striking is the contrast between the community solidarity born of race and class in the stories of Cynthia and Connie, respectively, and the tale of gendered exile told by Chris. Their narratives suggest that, although race, class, and gender may be equivalent in ultimate theoretical or political significance, they are certainly not identical. Differences in their structural articulation are manifested in and shaped by these three women's social experiences and political resistance.

Solidarities of Race and Class

Cynthia Brown, like several recent analysts of race, turns earlier historiography on its head by depicting the segregated South as a golden age, a time and place where African-Americans could enjoy the social cohesion and material resources of stable, intact communities. She grew up in a small town in North Carolina, where strong familial and community ties wove together in a dense web of support and accountability:

> To me, it was significant that all of us were in school together. All your relatives are there in the same school with you, and they provide you the kind of support you needed, emotional or otherwise.... I remember that all of my teachers were black. All of the people who were in leadership roles in the school were people that I went to church with, too. They were people who knew my family, and they would look out for you.

Connie White describes her rural, white working-class community in east Tennessee in familial terms that are similar to Cynthia's:

> Right where I grew up, my grandmother and grandfather lived next door; and I had an aunt and cousins lived up on the hill from them and then another aunt and uncle and cousins lived down the hill from them. And my

great-aunt and great-uncle lived on down the creek a little ways and so, mostly just kin right there where I grew up.

Race implicitly dovetails with class and kin to reinforce the bonds of commonality within this rural community. Connie's images are of homogeneity and social equality among people who make their livings from small farms and working-class jobs in local factories and utilities. Her connectedness to this community is not articulated in the language of class solidarity, with its undertones of exploitation, division, and antagonism, but in metaphors of seamless unity with the land:

> It feels like a way to be connected with everything that's gone before you; your people have been right there on that spot, on that piece of dirt, for so long. . . . [Y]ou grow up walking in those same woods. . . . It's just sort of like things that are forever and stay the same, and you just feel—I feel real connected to the land, and feel like it's a very great privilege to live right there in that spot.

In Cynthia's community, by contrast, class distinctions complicate relationships within her extended family and preclude an undifferentiated solidarity based on race. Cynthia's own class disadvantage alienates her, especially from the more privileged members of her family:

> All these folk [her mother's siblings] graduated from college, all these folk had a certain standing in the community, all these folk owned their homes, . . . and all of them had jobs that they dressed up to go to. Whereas *my* mother worked in a plant. We had real relaxed kinds of standards. We weren't real proper about a whole lot of things.

Class divisions notwithstanding, Cynthia locates her self and her childhood in the supportive bonds of a racial collectivity. Similarly, Connie narrates a life story of continuous personal and familial rootedness in a specific social and physical place. For both women, individual identity emerges in the crucible of a primary collectivity that continues to orient them as adults. Their stories of community cohesion and nurture contrast dramatically with the tale of estrangement and ostracism told by Chris.

Gender and Exile

Chris Weiss unifies her entire narrative, her childhood and adulthood, her episodes of political activism, and her periods of more conventional activity as a mother and wife, around the theme of gender. She recounts her life as a series of confrontations with adversaries who seek to dominate and confine her. They are invariably male and their motives are at least partially sexist. For example, Chris centers her accounts of childhood on the dynamics of power within her immediate family, which is dominated by her patriarchal father:

> My family was very hierarchical. My father was very domineering; my mother was also very feisty and still is very much her own person. We witnessed through all the years of their 53-year marriage lots of struggle. My mother's insistence on keeping herself as a person and my father's domination—it was a very rocky and volatile marriage.

Chris describes a showdown between herself and her father as a "turning point" in her life. During her first year of college he wanted her to join a sorority and she refused:

> So we had this enormous horrible discussion and it was, you know, "You either do as I say or I'm not paying for your dormitory any more." And the way I solved that problem was to get pregnant and get married.

The tension between conventional expectations of upwardly mobile white women and her own rebellious behavior from childhood informs the structure of Chris's narrative, which breaks into three pieces: childhood, which ends with the confrontation with her father and subsequent marriage; the interregnum of her first marriage, which ends in divorce; and her present adulthood, which begins with her second marriage and subsequent feminist activism. Each period is framed by her changing relationship with a man. The first two are subverted by her drive to define herself more autonomously, that is, *not* in relationship to a man, but accomplishing this requires her to separate from her family of origin and, later, from her first husband.

In Cynthia's and Connie's narratives, by contrast, gender exists as a largely unrecognized but influential subtext. Neither woman spontaneously and explicitly mentions gender in her stories of childhood; neither presents herself as a *girl*, but as a child of a specific race (Cynthia) or place (Connie). When asked directly about gender at the end of their interviews, both women argue that egalitarian treatment rendered sexism and gender consciousness insignificant in their early lives.

For example, Connie asserts:

> I never felt like that less was expected of me, from my father, because I was a girl. Now, I did feel that way from my mother some. But my father always talked to all of us about being able to be independent, to be financially independent, to be able to support ourselves. And talked to me and my sister just as hard about that as he did my brother. . . . And he never let me out of stuff because I was a girl either. We all worked the tobacco, we all fed the cows.

Similarly, when Cynthia was asked about sexism in her childhood during a follow-up interview, she responded:

> See, the thing about it is—it may have, but I don't, I can't say that I can like put a finger on it. Because there have been so many other things that made up who I was, that may have had a greater impression.

She went on to attribute the relative insignificance of sexism to the role models of her mother and grandmother, and to the exigencies of race and class oppression, which required women to earn wages and men to take on domestic responsibilities.

> My mother was a single mother. She did what she had to do, you know what I'm saying? . . . You know, my mother turned over the washing machine and fixed it. My mother would take the light switch down and work on the wires and stuff, scared me to death. . . .
>
> All the women in my family worked. . . . There was never that influence of a man who sat down at the table and waited for somebody to wait on him. That was just never the case. My grandfather combed heads, my grandfather worked three jobs outside of the home and came home and helped clean house.

Despite these disavowals, gender marks each woman's narrative in distinct but indirect ways. Connie, for example, deploys gendered symbols of domestic ordinariness to convey her modest self-assessment, her lack of entitlement or responsibility "to say my opinion somewhere beyond the supper table." However, she attributes this self-effacement primarily to class: "work ... is just physical work; you can't conceive that you'd be valued for intellectual contribution."

In a similarly paradoxical manner, Cynthia uses her mother's example to demonstrate the irrelevance of sexism, yet her mother's downward mobility, precarious financial circumstances, and responsibility for all domestic tasks had much to do with gendered inequality. As a working-class black woman, her earning power was at the time (1960s and 1970s) far lower than that of black men, and her gendered responsibilities for children far greater. In other words, the childhood poverty that Cynthia attributes to class disadvantage also derived from gender (and, of course, race). That gender is not labeled as such may be due to the factors Cynthia identifies: the absence of sexist proscriptions on her activities and aspirations, and the flexible division of labor between women and men in her extended family. It may also be due, in her case as well as Connie's, to the unfortunate hegemony of middle-class white women's experiences as definitive of sexism.

In Chris's narrative, by contrast, stories of race and class turn back to and cannot be separated from gender. So, for example, the showdown with her father over joining a sorority (cited above) is the climax to a story that starts out on the subject of class differences. Similarly, a story about racial awareness turns back to her father and his insistence that she break off a relationship with a Latino boyfriend: " ... [A]t that moment I really understood in a very clear way that there were boundaries for me as a white woman that I could not, should not, go beyond."

Each of these three women, then, coheres her life story around a primary inequality and subordinates others to that central source of identity. Their childhood stories of racial and class collectivities (Cynthia and Connie) and patriarchal punishments (Chris) function as explanatory anchors for their later political involvements. At the same time, each woman's experience with multiple forms of inequality—however much her narrative mutes or submerges their recognition—ultimately leads her to reject identity politics in favor of a more universal political sensibility.

Social Experience and Political Resistance

Political activism, focused on the collectivity with which she most identifies, is central to each woman's adult life. Cynthia Brown works with a predominantly African-American constituency as the director of a Southern economic justice organization. Connie White works with a grassroots, working-class environmental organization in east Tennessee. Chris Weiss is the founder of a statewide women's organization in West Virginia.

The stories they tell of the evolution of their activism diverge, but remain consistent with their overall self-representations. Cynthia Brown, for example, relates her own coming of age as a story of increased exposure and resistance to white racism. She suggests that her youthful activism derives from the potent blend of race and class oppression, a familial tradition of union and community organizing, and her own sense of responsibility as the oldest child in her family. She embodies these contributing factors in her mother, with whom she immediately aligns herself at the beginning of the interview: "I was born in New York. But before that, let me say a little bit about my mother. My mother is the oldest of six children. . . . And I'm the oldest of six children in my family." In this revealing opening, Cynthia conveys familial, biological, and political continuity by posing her mother as the initial subject of Cynthia's own history, speaking of her mother in the present tense (she is deceased), and aligning herself with her mother through the comparison in birth order. Cynthia further suggests her mother's influence in her own activism by telling or alluding on three occasions to a pivotal story about her mother's defiant interaction with the white principal of Cynthia's grade school, who was reputed to be a member of the Ku Klax Klan. Consequently, she relates parallel stories of her own activism in high school.

In Connie White's stable nest of kin and community, by contrast, there is no legacy of political activism or class antagonism. As an adult, professionally trained for social service work, she aligns herself with poor and working-class people not so much out of political conviction as from a sense of identity and belonging:

> The first real job I had out of school was at the Department of Human Services. . . . But I never felt like I fit there because I felt like I fit more with the

people I was working with. . . . I guess I've always felt like I fit with people
who were just sort of what I would think of as ordinary: . . . people that
didn't talk proper, had voices sounding like yours, didn't pay that much
attention to grammar, didn't live in fancy houses. . . .

Although this identity with "ordinary" people functions to cohere
her entire life story and justify her politics, Connie relates the beginning of her activism as a conversion experience that divides the ongoing narrative of her life:

When I moved to Morgan County, strip mining was all around. . . . And so
I went to a SOCM [Save Our Cumberland Mountains] meeting because a
friend asked me to go, and it was a really good, wonderful experience. Even
though I didn't know anything, they made me feel like I did have something
to contribute. . . . And so there's just been this whole wonderful lifetime, this
twenty years of learning, and these experiences that have just totally
changed my life, and changed my idea of what I could do and of what I have
to contribute.

Chris's story of the evolution of her activism combines elements of
the other two. Despite her self-presentation as a fighter from an early
age, and despite a history of involvement in the civil rights, antiwar,
and feminist movements, she dates her mature political activism from
1979. In Charleston, West Virginia, where she had moved with her second husband in 1972, another group of powerful male adversaries—
local politicians and officials in the building trades union—conspired
to defund a nontraditional jobs for women program that she directed.
Her story of the epiphany that ensued displays the same thematic contrasts between the pliant and uppity woman, conventionality and
rebellion, that unify her entire life history. On this occasion, however,
she inverts the imagery to suggest that, even when playing by the rules,
she can not insulate herself from the depredations of sexism:

I just remembered going home and for about three weeks, just crying and
crying and crying. And then I just got really angry. How can they do this to
us? And understanding in some sort of a gut way, some very basic things
about oppression. This was just little Chris Weiss, this nice, by this time

middle-class, white woman with kids, who was just trying to do good. They could do that to me, too.

Despite these differences in the evolution and focus of each woman's activism, their current political philosophies are remarkably similar. In all three cases, class awareness functions to undercut a unilateral politics of identity. So, for example, class appears in Cynthia's narrative and sounds a note of dissonance in her otherwise harmonious community. This theme of division appears repeatedly through comments about political differences, skin color discrimination, and the disparity between those who resist versus those who capitulate to racism—all distinctions that she associates in part with class. She observes that race "will get you killed faster and make you more worthless" than any other inequality, and believes that nationalism has been an important and effective strategy in certain contexts; however, for herself, no single identity ultimately suffices as the source of political orientation. The confluence of racial and class oppression radicalizes and universalizes her outlook, leading her to a politics that seeks to transcend all unjust hierarchies: "I identify with folk who are not valued, who are not respected, who are not empowered, who are not given the tools they need to do for themselves. I identify with that place."

Connie constructs links between the egalitarian class structure and ethos of the community in which she grew up and her populist, democratic, political sensibility. As noted previously, she utilizes gendered domestic imagery to convey the modesty and "ordinariness" of her life. She then deploys similar symbols to legitimate egalitarian political participation, even leadership, by all: "leadership . . . is just like taking your turn; just like you wash the dishes at home, you take your turn."

Chris Weiss dryly suggests that the heavily working-class context of the coalfields where she lives influences her politics. Equality with men, the seemingly self-evident goal of the more mainstream, middle-class wing of the women's movement, is not the point. "One of the things that I think we instinctively knew here in the mountains is that to be equal to an unemployed coal miner was just no big deal. We could do better than that." When pressed to elaborate what "better than that" means, Chris commented:

I guess that means safer jobs, well-paid jobs, stable communities. We could have communities which we controlled, in which we, men and women, could control our own destiny and not be reliant on a coal company, a mega-employer, who would basically call the shots.

Despite these similarities in their current political philosophies, the context and consequences of their individual resistance to oppression diverge in ways that suggest important distinctions in the social construction of race, class, and gender. For Chris, challenging the constraints of gender required her to separate herself from her father, her family of origin, and the community in which she came of age—to go "into exile" as she put it. Her resistance is a story of estrangement, divorce. Feminist activism eventually brought her into a network of allies, friends, and mentors, but set her apart from the rural community in which she settled with her second husband. Cynthia's and Connie's resistance, by contrast, are stories of solidarity with and affirmation of the living collectivities into which they were born.

This link to a people, an ethnos, and through it to collective memory and myth, undergirds the final, profound contrast in the course of each woman's political resistance. Although Chris refers to numerous contemporary women who have influenced and supported her, they do not form a collective memory or tradition in her narrative. Their history is too young and their ties to earlier women's movements (suffragism, for example) too distant and abstract. Historical sensibility is not absent from her narrative, however: she implicitly positions herself at the beginning of a new era, as a founder of new traditions. This is evident, for example, in her references to working-class women who endured the risks and insults of nontraditional, blue-collar work as "pioneers."

Connie, by contrast, echoes her earlier references to the continuity of rural place when positioning herself in a larger populist tradition:

It's a real treasure and a gift to feel like you've done something that might live on past you somehow, that you've made a difference somehow, so that it mattered that you lived. And I really feel like being a member of a democratic, long-term, citizens' group gives people an opportunity to do that.

For Cynthia, race provides a storehouse of rich cultural traditions involving identity, collective memory, and a mythic, inspirational view of the past. It is a past that judges and calls the present to accountability. Note that her account is about gender as well as race: it implicitly recalls her opening statement of alignment with her mother, but expands the relationship to all African-American women who ensure both biological survival and historical continuity.

> I heard this woman talking about the bones that scatter the Atlantic Ocean, bones of people that none of us knows. And I starting thinking about what was required for people to survive.... They talk about mothers being sold from their children, when children were left on plantations, mothers who had like their own breast milk for their own children, sharing their breast milk with other children, so that they could survive. And you just think about that kind of commitment to help you *be* here. And it's like—that's about *something,* and you cannot ignore that. If you do, you have to pay for it. And I ain't never been one to pay for shit I didn't have to (laughs).

Conclusion: The Construction of Race, Gender, and Class

Each of these women constructs a life story that derives coherence from a primary collectivity that grounds her identity and explains her politics. These collectivities are not identical, however, in their lived experience nor the story that is told of that experience. Especially striking in these narratives is the contrast between, on the one hand, race and class as narrated by Cynthia and Connie, and, on the other hand, gender as narrated by Chris.

Race and class, in these accounts, involve deeply felt, horizontal relationships of community and kin. Resisting the injustices of race and class oppression involves taking a stand on the firm ground of a collective history, ethos, group life. At a structural level, this collectivity may be explained by historical patterns of land ownership, racial segregation, and the proscriptions against certain social relationships, especially interracial marriage; these and other factors continue to generate relatively homogeneous, race- or class-defined communities and cultures in some locations. The depth and persistence of such ties stand as a caution to those who would render social identity entirely fluid and situational.

Obviously, gender is not constituted or resisted in the same manner. The emphasis on intimate heterosexual relationships within race-class groups lends gender less homogeneity and cultural determinance. The *embeddedness* of gender within race and class may partly explain the implicit (embedded) presence of gender in Cynthia and Connie's narratives. The rules and dynamics of gender relations are among the most significant features of group life; they become naturalized, inextricable from the meaning and identity of the group itself.

To transgress or to challenge gender means to risk, as did Chris, exile from the larger group. Her experience suggests that the individualism so often associated with mainstream feminism may not be due simply to the cultural ethos and upward mobility of its largely white, middle-class constituency. For women of all races and classes, challenging sexism may result in being forced out of the group (however defined), required to live as an isolated individual or to form an intentional community with others similarly ostracized. Some feminists have, of course, done precisely that.

Even as each woman grounds her identity in a different collectivity, however, her politics do not reflect a singular, exclusionary affirmation of that group. The "politics of identity," today so often associated with a strident claim to the legitimacy and significance of a specific group experience, does not adequately describe their activism (Gitlin 1995). Rather, Cynthia, Connie, and Chris all ultimately refer to a complex configuration of gender, class, and race to explain and justify their political activities and beliefs. It is the *intersection* of these oppressions that becomes central: Cynthia cannot exclusively embrace nationalism because her class experience complicates and transcends her apprehension of race; similarly, Chris can not be satisfied with the limited goals of mainstream feminism. Precisely because their social experience of oppression is multiply defined, no single identity suffices as the basis of their politics. The larger "we" that their multiple identities ultimately require is a human collectivity that their politics seeks to construct.

References

Andersen, Margaret and P. Collins. 1995. *Race, Class, and Gender: An Anthology.* Belmont, CA: Wadsworth Publishing Company.

Calhoun, Craig. 1994. "Social Theory and the Politics of Identity," in *Social*

Theory and the Politics of Identity, ed. Craig Calhoun. Cambridge, MA: Blackwell Publishers.

Cyrus, Virginia. 1993. *Experiencing Race, Class, and Gender in the United States.* Mountain View, CA: Mayfield Publishing Company.

Gitlin, Todd. 1995. *The Twilight of Common Dreams: Why American is Wracked by Culture Wars.* New York: Henry Holt and Company.

Rothenberg, Paula S. 1995. *Experiencing Race, Class, and Gender in the United States: An Integrated Study.* New York: St. Martin's Press.

Rothman, Robert A. 1993. *Inequality and Stratification: Class, Color, and Gender.* Englewood Cliffs, NJ: Prentice Hall.

Smith, Barbara Ellen. 1995. "Crossing the Great Divides: Race, Class and Gender in Southern Women's Organizing, 1979–1991." *Gender and Society* (9) 6: 680–696.

14

Sexual Harassment Protection for Whom?

The Case of Women in Part-Time, Temporary, and
Independent Contractor Employment

DULA J. ESPINOSA

Women have long been subjected to sexual harassment at work. Indeed, the subjugation of women to unwelcome touch, solicitation, and outright intimidation for sexual favors has historically been a well-known and common condition of female employment. This type of sex discrimination exists as a form of everyday sexism for all kinds of women employed in all realms of work. Sexually harassed women span the range from Chicanas employed as maids in private homes in El Paso, Texas (Romero 1992), to highly paid assistants and secretaries at Del Laboratories (Jacobs 1995).

Yet foreshadowing the continual sexual harassment of female workers are changes in the economy that are literally altering the occupational structure. The result is a shift of women workers from full-time permanent positions to "contingent" positions. The change has been so great that the contingent workforce now accounts for 25 to 30 percent of the entire U.S. civilian labor force, with women constituting the majority of these workers (reported in Appelbaum 1992). Indeed, women account for just under two-thirds of all part-time workers (U.S. Department of Labor 1994a, p. 222) and three-fifths of all temporary workers (U.S. Department of Labor 1994b, p. 144). Also rising is the number of self-employed women. Their numbers more than doubled from 1975 to 1990 (Devine 1994, Table 3, p. 22).

This change in employment status is literally altering a woman's ability to be protected from sexual harassment. The problem stems from a loophole in federal sexual harassment law, which allows gendered spaces in many worksites to remain uncovered. As Chapter 1 of this volume points out, "gendered spaces are social arenas in which a person's gender shapes interpersonal dynamics and generates differential interaction practices." For contingent workers, these uncovered gendered spaces have the net effect of leaving a large and growing number of female workers unprotected from sexual harassment. In essence, the movement of women from fully protected positions to nonprotected positions is inappropriately turning public spaces into private spaces. Women employed in "contingent positions" are left unprotected from sexual harassment as a result of economic shifts. Ironically, these unprotected women are among the most economically vulnerable and, therefore, the most exploitable, of all female workers.

Wendy Breen and the Law

Illustrative of the fact that federal sexual harassment law does not apply to all employed women is the case of Wendy Breen. As Silverman recently reported (1993), Wendy Breen was fired two days after her employer tried to rape her at an office party. Wendy Breen turned to a federal agency for help. Even though the agency concluded that she had been "subjected to continual sexual harassment," the agency could do nothing to help her (Silverman 1993, p. E5). The problem concerned her employment as a real estate agent. As Wendy Breen discovered, real estate agents are considered under federal law to be independent contractors, who are, by definition, self-employed (Silverman 1993). The fact that Wendy Breen was sexually harassed by a man who acted like her employer by hiring her, paying her, and, later, firing her, was of no relevance whatsoever.

What Wendy Breen had tried to do was to file a sexual harassment case in federal court. The ability of any woman to file such a charge is based on the Civil Rights Act of 1964. Although the 1964 Act does not specifically mention sexual harassment, Title VII of the act bans employer discrimination based on sex discrimination. Sexual harassment is, instead, defined in guidelines issued by the Equal Employment Opportunity Office (EEOC), the federal agency charged with enforcing Title VII provisions.

Although the types of behavior actionable as sexual harassment are explained in the guidelines, the question of who qualifies for protection is more open. Title VII defines as protected "an individual employed by an employer," with political appointees exempted (U.S. Code of Federal Regulations 1995, sec. 2000e.f). Women must fit within this definition in order to qualify for federal protection from sexual harassment. In other words, a woman must prove that she is a "true" employee of the person being charged in order for a sexual harassment suit to go forward in federal court.

As expected, the question of who qualifies as a Title VII employee has already reached the federal courts. Two tests have been developed by the courts. The first test concerns stability of employment, with stable jobs receiving Title VII protection. Under this doctrine, the courts have granted Title VII rights to part-time workers in permanent positions. The crucial decision to extend Title VII coverage to part-timers occurred in the 1983 case, *Thurber v. Jack Reilly's Inc.* (717 F.2d, 633–635).

The courts have also developed a second test. The "control" test is used to determine if temporary workers qualify for Title VII coverage. While temporary agency employers may not sexually harass temporary agency workers under the employee rule of Title VII, the question is less clear when the temporary worker is contracted out. The question is complicated because the temporary worker is typically paid by the temporary agency, even though the work is performed for and on the premises of the external contractor. In this circumstance, the temporary worker is protected under federal law only if she can prove that the external contractor had some degree of control over her work and working conditions. If there is no control, as in the case of a secretary sent for a one-day period to answer phones as a "Kelly girl," there can be no employee-employer relationship and no actionable behavior under Title VII. This test was first developed in the 1984 case, *Amarnare v. Merrill Lynch, Pierce, Fenner & Smith* (611 F.Supp., 344–351), and later applied to a 1992 case, *Magnuson v. Peak Technical Services, Inc.* (808 F. Supp., 500–516).

Less complicated is federal sexual harassment law as it applies to self-employed women, as in the case of Wendy Breen. In this circumstance, the question is not one of control, but rather one of independence. In 1990, a federal court determined that unsupervised workers paid by commission only were independent contractors and, therefore, ineligible for Title VII protection (*Knight v. United Farm Bureau Mutual Insurance Company,* 742 F.Supp., 518–524). The same conclusion was reached three years later in another case involving an independent contractor, even though the issue of control was before the court. In the case, *Barnes v. Colonial Life and Accident Insurance Co.,* a federal court ruled that the control test did not apply to independent contractors (818 F.Supp., 978–982).

To review, Wendy Breen would have been able to file a sexual harassment suit in federal court had she been a permanent full-time or part-time employee. She would also have been protected as a temporary employee if she could have proved that the real estate manager had some control over her work and work environment. As a self-employed worker, however, Wendy Breen could not claim access to the same rights as other workers. Her independent contractor status denied her the "right" to be federally protected from sexual harassment. The fact that her boss may have had some say in her work and working conditions did not alter her unprotected status.

These decisions are, of course, in flux. Although the courts now apply Title VII to part-timers and some temporary workers, the issue of Title VII qualification in terms of contingent workers has not come before the U.S. Supreme Court. Until then, any one of these decisions is subject to review. Reversals are, however, highly unlikely, as the Supreme Court has cited these lower court decisions in several of its rulings.

Implications

The implications of what happened to Wendy Breen are enormous. One implication concerns her level of awareness. Wendy Breen appeared unaware of her status as a contingent worker and was certainly unaware that she did not have sexual harassment protection. This plight is likely to be shared by increasing numbers of women as employers turn to contingent labor, especially to independent contractors, to cut labor and benefit costs. Indeed, the use of independent contractors cuts costs because most of them work for one company with no benefits and "no guarantee of work" (Carré 1992, p. 68). As Carré notes, these workers are overlooked largely because there are no government statistics tracking their employment (1992, p. 68). What is clear is that independent contractors are self-employed, and that the number of self-employed workers is growing and becoming increasingly female.

A second and equally disturbing implication concerns the stripping of legal rights by shifting employment statuses. As Piore first pointed out in 1975, most organizations have two types of jobs: (1) jobs within the "primary sector," in which promotion, working conditions, and stability are greatest; and (2) jobs within the "secondary sector," in which these benefits are worse (Piore 1975, p. 126). In this sense, the shift to contingent work may represent a return of women to a lesser employment status than men. Indeed, the lack of protection accorded to women may be interpreted as a clear reminder that they are little more than their stereotypes—beings who are sexually exploitable and willing to work for lower wages and lesser employment opportunities. From this perspective, it would appear that all women are becoming vulnerable, since the stripping of rights through employment status changes reinforces the notion that it is, indeed, a man's world.

In a more direct sense, federal sexual harassment law is creating a two-tier system of employment. It is now possible for two individuals, performing the same work in the same worksite for the same employer, to be entitled to different levels of federal sexual harassment protection. Protected are full-time and part-time female employees and temporary workers who are able to demonstrate that their work is in some way controlled by the employer (or the employer's agent) sexually harassing them. All other workers are left unprotected, especially those employed as independent contractors.

Conclusion

This paper has used the Wendy Breen case to illustrate that women are being shifted into contingent positions, putting them at greater risk of sexual harassment. The source of the change is employers, who are searching to reduce labor costs. The result is increased female vulnerability to low-paying, low-benefit jobs in which protection from sexual harassment at the federal level is often nonexistent.

The situation is not entirely bleak, however, as there is reason to believe that contingent employment may soon improve. Novack (1994) recently reported that the U.S. Labor Department is exploring the

extension of labor laws to part-time, temporary, and independent contractor workers. This decision comes on the heels of earlier congressional bills. One bill proposed by Representative Pat Schroeder in 1992
would have provided part-time and temporary workers with health and
pension benefits (Carré 1992, p. 82). Although Schroeder's bill failed,
Senator Edward Kennedy has recently proposed another bill that would
require health care coverage for part-time workers (Kosterlitz 1994).

Whatever the outcome of the proposed legislation and U.S. Department of Labor investigation, the message is clear—women in contingent positions need greatèr protection from sexual harassment as well
as from other forms of sexism that keep their pay and employment
opportunities low. Just as Title VII has helped to make public the once-
private gendered spaces in which women were routinely subjected to
sexual harassment, the law must now be changed to protect all
employed women. Although altering federal law is unlikely to stop the
widespread flow of sexual harassment at work, it will give women
employed in the most marginalized positions in the workplace access
to federal law—an important tool in battling everyday sexism.

References

Amarnare v. Merrill Lynch, Pierce, Fenner & Smith. 1984. *Federal Supplement*
611: 344–351.

Appelbaum, Eileen. 1992. "Structural Change and the Growth of Part-time
and Temporary Employment," in *New Policies for the Part-time and Contingent Workforce*, ed. V. duRivage. Armonk, NY: M.E. Sharpe, pp. 1–14.

Barnes v. Colonial Life and Accident Insurance Co. 1993. *Federal Supplement*
818: 978–982.

Carré, Françoise J. 1992. "Temporary Employment in the Eighties," in *New
Policies for the Part-Time and Contingent Workforce*, ed. V. duRivage.
Armonk, NY: M.E. Sharpe, pp. 45–87.

Devine, Theresa J. 1994. "Characteristics of Employed Women in the United
States." *Monthly Labor Review* 117 (3): 20–34.

Jacobs, Margaret A. 1995. "Del Laboratories Agrees to Record Sum for Settling
Sexual Harassment Lawsuit." *Wall Street Journal,* August 4, B7, column 3.

Knight v. United Farm Bureau Mutual Insurance Company. 1990. *Federal Supplement* 742: 518–524.

Kosterlitz, Julie. 1994. "A 50 Per Cent Solution?" *National Journal* 26 (30): 1748.

Magnuson v. Peak Technical Services, Inc. 1992. *Federal Supplement* 808: 500–516.

Novack, Janet. 1994. "Is Lean, Mean? Labor Department Examines Benefits for Contingency Workers." *Forbes* 154 (4): 33–90.

Piore, Michael J. 1975. "Notes for a Theory of Labor Market Stratification," in *Labor Market Segmentation,* eds. Edwards, Reich, and Gordon. Lexington, MA: D.C. Heath and Company, pp. 125–150.

Romero, Mary. 1992. *Maid in the U.S.A.* New York: Routledge.

Silverman, Stuart. 1993. "Gap in the Safety Net: Independent Workers Lose Legal, Economic Help." Byline *Los Angeles Times. Arizona Republic,* February 22, E5.

Thurber v. Jack Reilly's, Inc. 1983. *Federal Supplement* (second edition) 717: 633–635.

U.S. Bureau of the Census. 1994. *Statistical Abstract of the United States: 1994.* 114th Edition. Washington, DC: U.S. Government Printing Office.

U.S. Code of Federal Regulations. 1995. *Title 42: Containing the General and Permanent Codes of the United States.* 1994 Edition. Washington, DC: U.S. Government Printing Office.

U.S. Department of Labor. 1994a. *Employment and Earnings.* Bureau of Labor Statistics. January 1994. Washington, DC: U.S. Government Printing Office.

U.S. Department of Labor. 1994b. *1993 Handbook on Women Workers: Trends and Issues.* Women's Bureau. Washington, DC: U.S. Government Printing Office.

Contributors

Edith Wen-Chu Chen is a Ph.D. candidate in the Department of Sociology at the University of California, Los Angeles. Her dissertation focuses on the formation of pan-Asian-American and feminist identity in Asian-American sororities and fraternities.

Andreana Clay is a graduate student in the Department of Sociology at the University of Memphis. Her research interests include social issues concerning biracial women, women of color and feminism, and women of color and abortion.

Kimberly J. Cook is an Assistant Professor in the Criminology Department at the University of Southern Maine. She earned a Ph.D. in Sociology from the University of New Hampshire in 1994. She is currently writing a book examining abortion and death penalty opinions in the United States. She is continuing research on gender and the Internet, shelters for battered women in the Deep South, and domestic violence in rural areas. She is cofounder, with J.R. Bjerklie, of Sociologists Against Sexual Harassment.

Dula J. Espinosa is Assistant Professor of Sociology at Arizona State University. Her research explores the consequences of public policy in terms of stratification and discrimination. Forthcoming is her book, *Affirmative Action: The Truth Behind the Rhetoric*, which documents the historical, legal, and political development of the most controversial civil rights policy of our time.

Joe R. Feagin is the Graduate Research Professor in Sociology at the University of Florida. For thirty years he has done extensive research on discrimination issues, which can be seen in such recent books as *Modern Sexism: Blatant, Subtle and Covert Discrimination* (Prentice Hall, 1995); *Living with Racism: The Black Middle Class Experience* (Beacon, 1994); and *The Agony of Education: Black Students at White Colleges and Universities* (Routledge, 1996). He has served as Scholar-in-Residence at the U.S. Commission on Civil Rights.

Shirley Hune is Professor of Urban Planning in the School of Public Policy and Social Research and Associate Dean for Graduate Programs in the Graduate Division at the University of California, Los Angeles. She received her Ph.D. in American Studies, is a past President of the Association for Asian American Studies and conducts research on immigration policy and human rights as well as gender and race. Her recent publications include "Rethinking Race: Paradigms and Policy Formation," in *Amerasia Journal* (1995); *Bearing Dreams, Shaping Visions: Asian Pacific American Perspectives* (Washington State University Press, 1993), which she coedited; and *Women's Realities, Women's Choices: An Introduction to Women's Studies*, 2nd ed., (Oxford University Press, 1995), a collaborative work of the Hunter College Women's Studies Collective.

Melissa J. Monson is a graduate student in Sociology at the University of Nevada, Las Vegas. Her research interests include sexual harassment and domestic violence, with an emphasis on interlocking systems of oppression.

Christine Michele Robinson is a doctoral student in the Department of Sociology at the University of Kansas in Lawrence. Her research interests include the social construction of race, class, gender and sexuality, social inequality, and multicultural feminist theories. She is currently studying a Midwestern lesbian and bisexual women's community, specifically attending to social control, sexuality, age, and social class.

tammy ko Robinson is working towards her M.A./Ph.D. in sociology at the University of California, Santa Cruz. Her current interests include postcolonial feminism, cultural studies, diaspora studies, migratory movements, and writing ethnography. Presently she is working on a research project on international adoption.

Carol Rambo Ronai received her Ph.D. from the University of Florida in 1993 and is currently an Assistant Professor of Sociology at the University of Memphis in Memphis, Tennessee. Ronai's areas of specialization include interpretive theory and qualitative methods. Her current interests focus on the various ways narrative can be utilized as a resource in research.

Yanick St. Jean is Assistant Professor of Sociology at the University of Nevada, Las Vegas. She received her Ph.D. from the University of Texas at Austin in 1992. Recent publications include "The Family Costs of White Racism: The Case of African Americans," in the *Journal of Comparative Family Studies*, forthcoming, and "Racial Masques: Black Women and Subtle Gendered Racism," in *Subtle Sexism: Current Practices and Prospects for Change*, edited by Nijole V. Benokraitis, forthcoming. She is currently conducting focus groups with African-American women in Las Vegas and analyzing national interview data for a book on black women and their families.

Barbara Ellen Smith has been an activist and writer on labor and women's issues in the South for the past twenty-five years. Her works include *Digging Our Own Graves: Coal Miners and the Struggle over Black Lung Disease* (Temple, 1987) and, with coeditors John Gaventa and Alex Willingham, *Communities in Economic Crisis: Appalachia and the South* (Temple, 1990). She is currently an Associate Professor of Sociology at the Center for Research on Women at the University of Memphis.

Dorothy E. Smith is a feminist sociologist and the author of *The Everyday World as Problematic: A Feminist Sociology* (1987), *The Conceptual Practices of Power: A Feminist Sociology of Knowledge* (1990) (both published by Northeastern University Press), and *Text, Facts, and Femininity: Exploring the Relations of Ruling* (Routledge 1990). She is currently Professor in the Department of Sociology in Education at the Ontario

Institute for Studies in Education (Toronto, Canada) and Adjunct Professor at the Department of Sociology, University of Victoria (Victoria, Canada).

Phoebe M. Stambaugh is an Assistant Professor in the Department of Criminal Justice and an affiliate of the Women's Studies Program at Northern Arizona University. She earned a Ph.D. in Justice Studies at Arizona State University in 1995. She teaches undergraduate and graduate courses on the law, social science research methods, and women in the criminal justice system. Her areas of research include gender and conflict on the Internet and women and litigation.

Barbara A. Zsembik is an Associate Professor of Sociology at the University of Florida, where she teaches courses on race and ethnic relations, population studies, and research methods. Her current research interests are the lives and experiences of older Latinos, and Latina women and work.

Index